REVISING WILDE

SOCIETY AND SUBVERSION
IN THE PLAYS OF
OSCAR WILDE

SOS ELTIS

CLARENDON PRESS · OXFORD
1996

Oxford University Press, Walton Street, Oxford OX2 6DP
Oxford New York
Athens Auckland Bangkok Bombay
Calcutta Cape Town Dar es Salaam Delhi
Florence Hong Kong Istanbul Karachi
Kuala Lumpur Madras Madrid Melbourne
Mexico City Nairobi Paris Singapore
Taipei Tokyo Toronto
and associated companies in
Berlin Ibadan

Oxford is a trade mark of Oxford University Press

Published in the United States
by Oxford University Press Inc., New York

British Library Cataloguing in Publication Data
Data available

Library of Congress Cataloging in Publication Data
Data available

ISBN–0–19–812183–0

1 3 5 7 9 10 8 6 4 2

Typeset by Graphicraft Typesetters Ltd, Hong Kong
Printed in Great Britain
on acid-free paper by
Biddles Ltd,
Guildford and King's Lynn

Acknowledgements

I am hugely indebted to a large number of people for their help and encouragement, without which this book would either never have been written or would have taken a very different form. Most importantly, I am enormously grateful for the meticulous, patient, and invaluable help and the unceasing encouragement of my supervisor, Dr Nicholas Shrimpton. I would also especially like to thank the following for supporting me financially while I completed this work: St John's College and St Hilda's College, Oxford; and Mrs Hilary Walton, who funded the Barbara Pym Junior Research Fellowship in memory of her sister. Particular thanks are also due to Christopher Butler for the original germ from which the thesis grew, and, more recently, for great encouragement and incisive criticism; to Dr John Kelly for initiating me into postgraduate work and giving me friendly support ever since; to Professor Kerry Powell for generous and selfless encouragement; to Russell Jackson and Ian Small for organizing the Oscar Wilde conference in 1993, and for much helpful advice. Special thanks are due to Merlin Holland for much help and encouragement and, most importantly, for permission to quote from his grandfather's unpublished manuscripts.

I am eternally grateful to the following friends for helping to make this work not only possible, but enjoyable: to Richard Rowland for vital support and many pints; to Mary Bly for teaching me what footnotes were and how to use them; to Kirsten Shepherd for numerous inspiring discussions; to Tammy Dodd for keeping me sane and away from my work; and to my family for their unstinting love and support. Above all, my eternal love and thanks to Mark Haddon, for unlimited faith, superb editing, great cooking and always being there, especially when my computer broke down.

I am extremely grateful to the following libraries for permission to quote from manuscript material in their collections: the British Library; the Arents Collections, New York Public Library, Astor, Lennox, and Tilden Foundations; the Beinecke Rare Books and Manuscript Library at Yale; the Harvard Theatre

Collection; Magdalen College Archive Library; the Herbert Beerbohm Tree Collection at the Bristol University Drama Library. I owe a major debt to many of the staff members at those libraries, and at the Bodleian Library and the Ellen Terry Museum.

S.E.

Contents

Abbreviations

Add. MS	additional manuscript
Aut. MS	autograph manuscript
BL	British Library
LCP	Lord Chamberlain's Plays
Letters	*The Letters of Oscar Wilde*, ed. Rupert Hart-Davis (London: Hart-Davis, 1962)
LW	*Lady's World*
More Letters	*More Letters of Oscar Wilde*, ed. Rupert Hart-Davis (London: John Murray, 1985)
Notebooks	*Oscar Wilde's Oxford Notebooks: A Portrait of Mind in the Making*, ed. Michael S. Helfand and Philip E. Smith (Oxford: Oxford University Press, 1989)
PRO	Public Record Office, Chancery Lane, London
Selected Letters	*Selected Letters of Oscar Wilde*, ed. Rupert Hart-Davis (Oxford: Oxford University Press, 1979)
WW	*Woman's World*

Introduction

Surely you do not think that criticism is like the answer
to a sum? The richer the work of art the more diverse are
the true interpretations. There is not one answer only, but
many answers. I pity that book on which critics are agreed.
It must be a very obvious and shallow production.[1]

IN May 1893 Wilde wrote to George Bernard Shaw, thanking
him for a copy of his most recent play, probably *Widowers'
Houses*, in the following terms:

I must thank you very sincerely for Op. 2 of the great Celtic School.
I have read it twice with keen interest. I like your superb confidence
in the dramatic value of the mere facts of life. I admire the horrible
flesh and blood of your creatures, and your preface is a masterpiece—
a real masterpiece of trenchant writing and caustic wit and dramatic
instinct. I look forward to your Op. 4. As for Op. 5, I am lazy, but
am rather itching to be at it.[2]

Shaw's copy of *Lady Windermere's Fan* was inscribed by Wilde
as 'Op. 1 of the Hibernian School, London '93', which made
Op. 2 Shaw's *Widowers' Houses*, Op. 3 *A Woman of No Importance*, Op. 4 Shaw's next play, *The Philanderer*, and Op. 5
Wilde's next play, *An Ideal Husband*.[3] Wilde's coupling of his
own well-received, commercially successful dramas with the
unperformed and relatively unknown drama of Shaw was both
generous and unexpected. Wilde detected a close kinship between his own work and the radically challenging, socially
concerned plays of his fellow Irishman. Yet critics of Wilde's
plays have most frequently grouped him with the more conventional popular playwrights who dominated the London stage
with their reassuringly orthodox 'well-made' plays—plays which
Shaw despised and whose hold on the theatre his own plays
and those of his hero Ibsen were designed to break.[4] In 1912

---

[1] To W. E. Henley (?Dec. 1888), *Letters*, 234.

[2] To Bernard Shaw (postmark 9 May 1893), *Letters*, 339.

[3] This is Hesketh Pearson's ingenious interpretation of the numbers in Wilde's
letter, as reproduced in *Letters*, 339 n.

[4] See e.g. 'The Technical Novelty in Ibsen's Plays', in George Bernard Shaw, *The
Quintessence of Ibsenism: Now Completed to the Death of Ibsen*, rev. edn. (London: Constable, 1913), 187–90.

the playwright St John Hankin criticized Wilde for having squandered his talents on writing popular plays which conformed to the fashions of the time:

He looked around him at the kind of stuff which other playwrights were making money by, examined it with contemptuous acumen, saw how it was done—and went and did likewise . . . The result was that in the age of Ibsen and of Hauptmann, of Strindberg and Brieux, he was content to construct like Sardou and think like Dumas fils.[5]

Subsequent decades have served to qualify, but not to reject, this judgement. In a recent study, Norbert Kohl set firm limits to Wilde's originality, and offered the following conclusion:

The beginnings of the problem play, which dominated the English theatre from Shaw through to the First World War, are to be found in the work of T. W. Robertson, H. A. Jones and A. W. Pinero . . . This was a tradition, however, that did not suit Wilde at all, for it ran quite contrary to his anti-realistic concept of art, and in any case he was not really interested in social problems. He lacked the involvement necessary to plead for social reform. As a conservatively liberal aesthete, it suited him both politically and artistically to adopt the lofty detachment of the observer poking fun at the weaknesses and deficiencies of social man and his institutions, ridiculing the rigidity of social conventions without ever actually departing from them . . .

It is as if Wilde took one step towards reality, but then stopped because he lacked the courage to commit himself. Illusion remains preferable to reality. This extraordinary mixture of Victorian orthodoxy and anti-Victorian provocation, theatrical cliché and verbal originality, is typical of an author who in his writings as in his life remained consistently a conformist rebel.[6]

Wilde is most commonly grouped with the more commercial and less experimental nineteenth-century playwrights: with French playwrights like Sardou and Dumas *fils*, for example, or with the crowd-pleasing British dramatist, Sydney Grundy.

Even where modern critics admit Wilde's intention to be satiric, it is argued that the means he adopted undermined his end. Regenia Gagnier, for example, interprets his dramas as a

---

[5] 'Wilde as Dramatist', from *The Dramatic Works of St John Hankin*, iii (London, 1912), 185–201, repr. in Richard Ellmann (ed.), *Oscar Wilde: A Collection of Critical Essays* (Englewood Cliffs, NJ: Prentice Hall, 1969), 70–1.

[6] Norbert Kohl, *Oscar Wilde: The Works of a Conformist Rebel* (Cambridge: Cambridge University Press, 1989), 251–4.

critique of society's superficiality, and of the fetishizing of commodity, but adds that by mirroring the luxury of society Wilde was simultaneously flattering his audience. The sentimental melodrama of the society plays, Gagnier argues, offered the audience an easy escape from their more uncomfortable implications, just as the farcical comedy of *The Importance of Being Earnest* enabled the audience to dismiss the satire as deliberate nonsense.[7]

Similarly, in his recent study, *Oscar Wilde and the Theatre of the 1890s*,[8] Kerry Powell allows that Wilde struggled against established theatrical conventions, but argues that his work was ultimately compromised by his desire to succeed in the popular theatre. Powell places Wilde's plays in their contemporary theatrical context, demonstrating how each play was written to fit a distinct popular genre, and listing the numerous plays which bear significant resemblances to Wilde's own. He finally concludes that Wilde failed to escape fully from the influence of his predecessors, too often sacrificing originality to dramatic convention.

Katharine Worth, on the other hand, emphasizes the radical aspects of Wilde's drama. In her study, *Oscar Wilde*, she comments that 'His first play was about a revolutionary movement and his later plays of fashionable life can all be seen as thoroughly undermining the Victorian hierarchy'.[9] Professor Worth recognizes that Wilde's radical sympathies found expression in his drama through his portrayal of women and their position in society. Even she, however, suggests that Wilde allotted to women the essentially passive role of victim:

In the treatment of women by the patriarchal society of his day Wilde found an ideal subject, both for his ideas on self-fulfilment and for his revolutionary social sentiments. Women are shown as victims in various ways, most obviously as 'women with a past' who have become social outcasts but also as the 'good women' who in effect policed society on behalf of the male Establishment.[10]

---

[7] Regenia Gagnier, *Idylls of the Marketplace: Oscar Wilde and the Victorian Public* (Aldershot: Scolar Press, 1987), ch. 3.
[8] Cambridge: Cambridge University Press, 1990, see esp. pp. 4–13.
[9] London: Macmillan, 1983, 11.   [10] Ibid. 14.

Some degree of social and technical radicalism has thus been recognized in Wilde's plays, but the recognition has always been accompanied by severe qualifications.[11]

This study will attempt to justify Wilde's own estimate of his plays as genuinely innovative, challenging rather than reproducing the conventions of the popular nineteenth-century dramas on which they were modelled. It will endeavour to link the radical Wilde who attacked Victorian society in 'The Soul of Man Under Socialism', mocked moral seriousness in 'The Decay of Lying', and outraged conventional sexual and social codes in *The Picture of Dorian Gray*, with Wilde the playwright, the reputedly careless craftsman.

Contrary to the impression that Wilde sought to create that his plays were effortlessly thrown off—he complained that one scene in *The Importance of Being Earnest* had taken him 'fully five minutes to write'—the plays were in fact the result of a painstaking process of correction and revision.[12] The numerous manuscript versions are evidence of Wilde's careful redrafting. Distinct patterns emerge from these successive drafts; Wilde's revisions carefully drew his texts away from their conventional origins, transforming them from derivative imitations of the plays on which they were modelled into far more subtle and subversive works.

Consequently this book involves both an analysis of Wilde's method of composition, and a study of the French and English plays from which he borrowed. In arguing that Wilde was a

---

[11] For other modern critical analyses of Wilde's work, according it different—but always limited—degrees of radicalism, see e.g. Alan Bird, *The Plays of Oscar Wilde* (London: Vision Press, 1977); Philip Cohen, *The Moral Vision of Oscar Wilde* (London: Associated University Press, 1978); Christopher Nassaar, *Into the Demon Universe: A Literary Exploration of Oscar Wilde* (New Haven, Conn.: Yale University Press, 1974); Peter Raby, *Oscar Wilde* (Cambridge: Cambridge University Press, 1988); Epifanio San Juan, *The Art of Oscar Wilde* (Princeton, NJ: Princeton University Press, 1967); Rodney Shewan, *Oscar Wilde: Art and Egotism* (London: Macmillan, 1977); George Woodcock, *The Paradox of Oscar Wilde* (London: Boardman, 1949).

[12] Quoted in H. Montgomery Hyde, *Oscar Wilde* (London: Mandarin, 1976), 222. The multiple drafts of each play are catalogued in the following editions, to which I am greatly indebted: *Lady Windermere's Fan: A Play About a Good Woman*, ed. Ian Small (London: Benn, 1980); *Two Society Comedies: 'A Woman of No Importance' and 'An Ideal Husband'*, ed. Russell Jackson and Ian Small (London: A. & C. Black, 1983); *The Importance of Being Earnest*, ed. Russell Jackson (London: Benn, 1980); *Oscar Wilde's 'Vera; or, The Nihilist'*, ed. Frances Miriam Reed (Lewiston: Edwin Mellen, 1989).

political radical, a harsh critic of his society and its moral and
sexual laws, this analysis will attempt to place his plays in the
context not only of the contemporary theatre but also of late
nineteenth-century society, demonstrating how the plays enter
into contemporary debates on sexual roles and the position of
women, on individual duty and morality, and on the dangers
of social revolution and unrest.

In concentrating on certain aspects of Wilde's radicalism—in
particular his anarchist, feminist, and socialist sympathies—I
have inevitably neglected other topics, most importantly his
homosexuality and its influence on his work, a topic on which
much excellent research has recently been done.[13] Nor does this
book encompass the entire body of Wilde's dramatic work—
The Duchess of Padua and *Salome* are notable omissions—for,
sadly, limited space dictated that I focus exclusively on the
plays set in and specifically criticizing nineteenth-century society.

In 1892 John Barlas, a poet, revolutionary socialist and self-
declared anarchist, wrote in praise of Oscar Wilde in *The Novel
Review*. Barlas defined Wilde as 'a revolutionist' and explained
his methods thus:

He does not use dynamite but the dagger—a dagger whose hilt is
crusted with flaming jewels, whose point drips with the poison of the
Borgias. That dagger is the paradox. No weapon could be more
terrible . . . With a sudden flash of wit he exposes to our startled eyes
the sheer cliff-like wall of the rift that has opened out, as if by a silent
earthquake, between our moral belief and the belief of our fathers.
That fissure is the intellectual revolution.[14]

It is this revolutionary Oscar Wilde that I wish to recover: the
Wilde who challenged social, sexual, and moral conventions,
satirizing and subverting the orthodox values on which Victorian society was based.

---

[13] See e.g. Ed Cohen, 'Writing Gone Wilde: Homoerotic Desire in the Closet of
Representation', *Publications of the Modern Language Association*, 102/5 (1987),
801–13; id., *Talk on the Wilde Side: Toward a Genealogy of a Discourse on Male
Sexualities* (New York: Routledge, 1993); Jonathan Dollimore, 'Different Desires:
Subjectivity and Transgression in Wilde and Gide', *Textual Practice*, 1/1 (1987),
48–67; Richard Dellamora, 'Traversing the Feminine in Oscar Wilde's *Salome*', in
Thaïs Morgan (ed.), *Victorian Sages and Cultural Discourse: Renegotiating Gender
and Power* (New Brunswick, NJ: Rutgers University Press, 1990).
[14] John E. Barlas, *Oscar Wilde: A Study* (Edinburgh: Tragara, 1978), 11, repr.
from *The Novel Review* (Apr. 1892).

Oscar Wilde: Anarchist, Socialist, and Feminist

DISOBEDIENCE, rebellion, and resistance to the decrees of authority were the central tenets of Wilde's personal philosophy. In a commonplace book he kept while he was a student at Oxford, Wilde noted that: 'To Dissenters we owe in England Robinson Crusoe: Pilgrims Progress: Milton: Matthew Arnold is unjust to them because "not to conform to what is established" is merely a synonym for progress.'[1]

The young Wilde viewed rebellion against authority as essential to human advancement and social development. As he observed a few pages later: '<u>Progress</u> is simply the instinct of self-preservation in humanity, the desire to affirm one's own essence.'[2] Wilde's belief in the overriding importance of disobedience, self-assertion, and dissent endured throughout his life and formed the basis of his individual code. His interest in radical politics, his sympathy with women's struggle to assert their individual rights in opposition to the strictures of Victorian convention, his distrust of all forms of government, influence, and control, can all be seen as logical consequences of his belief that 'Progress in thought is the assertion of individualism against authority'.[3]

Wilde has often been dismissed as an idle aesthete, an uncommitted poseur, a mere dandy. Yet, as Regenia Gagnier has observed, this apparent detachment was itself a challenge to orthodox Victorian values: 'The history of dandyism is inseparable from that of aestheticism. Aestheticism was a protest against Victorian utility, rationality, and realism, or the reduction of human relations to utility and the market and the

---

[1] Wilde's Commonplace Book, 2, repr. in *Notebooks*, 108. According to Smith and Helfand this commonplace book could have been begun as early as 1874, but was certainly kept during 1878–9.

[2] Commonplace Book, 14, repr. in *Notebooks*, 110.

[3] Commonplace Book, 69, repr. in *Notebooks*, 121.

representation of this in bourgeois literature.'[4] Wilde's life was an affront to the Victorian establishment and the Victorian public: his refusal to conform on questions of dress and manners, his deliberate exhibitionism and the flaunting of his carefully cultivated difference, were taken as direct insults by the Victorian masses.

Wilde's feminism is one of the least commonly recognized aspects of his progressive politics.[5] Wilde was, however, a consistent champion of women's rights both in his life and his work, supporting all the primary demands of late nineteenth-century feminism.[6] There was no one set of beliefs which unified all those involved in or sympathetic to the struggle to improve women's position in society, and many individuals approved of some reforms while rejecting others. There was, none the less, agreement about the main areas in which women were fighting for better rights and opportunities: higher education for women; entry to a wider range of professions, especially medicine; improved legal rights, especially with regard to matrimonial law; and a stronger role in politics, including the right to vote in general elections and to take a seat on county councils. In his personal life, in his writing, and through his editorship of the *Woman's World* Wilde displayed his progressive views on these issues.

Wilde's opinions on the position of women may well have owed something to his admiration for his mother, Lady Jane Wilde, a formidable woman who wrote verse and campaigned for Irish Home Rule under the pen-name 'Speranza'. Constance

[4] Introduction, to Gagnier (ed.), *Critical Essays on Oscar Wilde* (New York: Twayne, 1991), 3.

[5] See e.g. Patricia Flanagan Behrendt, *Oscar Wilde: Eros and Aesthetics* (London: Macmillan, 1991), in which she argues that Wilde's championing of homosexual as against heterosexual relationships results in a distinctly misogynist view of women; see also Norbert Kohl's assertion that, in Wilde's plays, 'the basic distinction between good women and those with a past undoubtedly corresponds to the two extremes of the historical Victorian view of woman: virgin and whore, mother and *demi-mondaine*, idealised domestic angel and despised fallen woman' (*Oscar Wilde*, 221).

[6] The use of the term 'feminist' is, of course, somewhat problematic, as it was not coined until the end of the 19th c., and entered into common usage only just before the start of the First World War. See Karen Offen, 'Defining Feminism: A Comparative Historical Approach', *Signs*, 14 (1988), 119–57.

Lloyd, the woman whom Wilde chose as his wife, though by
no means as strong a character as her mother-in-law, was also
an active and intelligent woman. She published two children's
books, edited the *Gazette* of the Rational Dress Society during
1888 and 1889, and in April 1888 addressed a conference
sponsored by the Women's Committee of the International Arbi-
tration and Peace Association. She was also a good friend of
Lady Sandhurst, and helped campaign for her election to the
London County Council; Lady Sandhurst gained a majority
but was disqualified from taking her seat on the grounds of
being a woman.[7]

Before he accepted the position of editor of the *Lady's World*,
Wilde wrote to Wemyss Reid, general manager of Cassell's
publishing company, to offer his opinion of the magazine as it
stood. Having studied copies of the magazine, he judged that
'it is too feminine, and not sufficiently womanly', concluding
that it should 'deal not merely with what women wear, but
with what they think, and what they feel'.[8] Wilde's intentions
were clearly signalled in this letter: he listed among the numerous women he hoped would contribute to the magazine Olive
Schreiner, author of the highly controversial novel, *The Story
of an African Farm*, Mrs Julia Ward Howe, the American author
and reformer, and Mrs Fawcett, a leader of the campaign for
female suffrage. What Wilde planned, and achieved, was a complete transformation of the magazine under his editorship.

The *Lady's World* before Wilde took it in hand was, as he
observed, 'a very vulgar, trivial, and stupid production, with its
silly gossip about silly people, and its social inanities'.[9] Regular
monthly features were 'Fashionable Marriages', 'Society Pleas-
ures', 'With Needle and Thread: The Work of To-day', 'Five
O'Clock Tea' (an account of the latest fashionable tea-parties
and receptions), and 'Pastimes for Ladies', of which typical
examples were shell- and pebble-painting, mirror-painting, or,
for the more adventurous, sleighing. A feature on the fashions
for the month was the only section that, considerably curtailed,

---

[7] Richard Ellmann, *Oscar Wilde* (London: Hamish Hamilton, 1987), 267–8;
Anne Clark Amor, *Mrs Oscar Wilde* (London: Sidgwick & Jackson, 1983), 72–9.
[8] To Wemyss Reid (Apr. 1887), *Letters*, 194.
[9] To Mrs Hamilton King (?Sept. 1887), *Letters*, 205.

Wilde retained. The original 1886 prospectus for *The Lady's World, A Magazine of Fashion and Society* had promised that 'Ladies' work in the World of Education, Art, Literature, Science and Medicine will be manifested and thoroughly appreciated in their most extended sphere.'[10] Articles on these topics were, however, rare and their tone uniformly patronizing. Drama reviews were principally concerned with the actresses' costumes. In the only article to deal with books, literary comment had to be adapted to the delicate female mind, and so took the form of a 'Letter from Aunt Agatha to her Country Nieces'. The loving aunt recommends a new novel, *Sir James Appleby, Bart*, with the assurance that: 'You will be certain to fall in love with the Rev. Jacob Seymour, and I only hope that when you get married you will model your wifely devotion on that of the affectionate but sensible Lucy.'[11] The one acknowledgement of women's educational advances was, if possible, even more condescending in tone. The article 'A Day at Girton College' began by asserting that 'Some girls are constitutionally too delicate to apply themselves to anything like a course of study', but then reassured the anxious reader that the students of Girton were reasonably healthy, decorated their rooms prettily, and had regular meals. The writer concluded this searching account by declaring: 'The great aim of the College course is not to exalt the ideas of the students, or raise them above their proper sphere, as women, by thus competing with men, which would only make them unwomanly.'[12]

Wilde clearly had no such reservations about the intellectual abilities of women and, rather than seeking to tailor the magazine to their supposedly limited understanding, he turned to women of his acquaintance to supply the more demanding material he sought. In a letter requesting Helena Sickert to write an article for him on political economy, Wilde explained that: 'The magazine will try to be representative of the thought and culture of the women of this century, and I am very anxious that those who have had university training, like yourself, should

---

[10] Simon Nowell-Smith, *The House of Cassell, 1848–1958* (London: Cassell, 1958), 147–8.

[11] 'A Chat about Books—A Letter from Aunt Agatha to her Country Nieces', *LW* (Jan. 1887), 100.

[12] M. F. Donaldson, 'A Day at Girton College', *LW* (Feb. 1887), 142–3.

have an organ through which they can express their views on life and things.'[13]

Wilde started with the name of the magazine, whose original title, the *Lady's World*, he observed to Wemyss Reid, had 'a certain taint of vulgarity about it. . . . It is quite acceptable to the magazine in its present state; it will not be applicable to a magazine that aims at being the organ of women of intellect, culture, and position.'[14] The first issue of the newly titled *Woman's World* duly appeared in November 1887, and bore little resemblance to its predecessor. Along with a sonnet by Violet Fane, a story by Amy Levy, and a description of the Swiss Alps by Mrs Bancroft, were an article on urban poverty by Mrs Francis Jeune, and a long analysis of 'The Position of Woman' by the Countess of Portsmouth, which greeted with approval the recent reforms of the marriage laws, and supported women's claims to higher education and access to the medical profession. An article on 'The Oxford Ladies' Colleges, by A Member of One of Them', also provided a striking contrast to the previous tone of the magazine. The author reported on the students' lectures, debates, pastimes, and studies, and concluded with the provocatively forthright comment:

It is by no means true that all the girls at Somerville Hall and Lady Margaret Hall are exceptionally clever—the fact is almost too obvious to be worth stating; nor does the atmosphere of Oxford, as my lady-friend seemed to suppose, necessarily produce this result; a short acquaintance with the performances of the average pass-man would be quite enough to dispel that illusion for ever.[15]

Wilde's own 'Literary and Other Notes' gave the finishing touch to the first edition; the new editor accompanied his detailed reviews of recent publications with a direct statement of his own sympathies with the women's movement:

[13] To Helena Sickert (27 May 1887), *Letters*, 197–8. Helena Sickert was a writer, lecturer, advocate of women's rights, and a prominent suffragist.

[14] To Wemyss Reid (5 Sept. 1887), *Letters*, 203. Cf. e.g. a cartoon in *Punch* where, in a sketch of a wedding, a shop-girl bride, late of Remnant & Co.'s Ribbon Department, objects to the liturgical question 'wilt thou take this Woman' with a furious correction: '*Lady!*' *Punch* (28 May 1898), 251.

[15] 'The Oxford Ladies' Colleges, by A Member of One of Them', *WW* (Nov. 1887), 32.

The Apostolic dictum, that women should not be suffered to teach, is no longer applicable to a society such as ours, with its solidarity of interests, its recognition of natural rights, and its universal education. ... Nothing in the United States struck me more than the fact that the remarkable intellectual progress of that country is very largely due to the efforts of American women, who edit many of the most powerful magazines and newspapers, take part in the discussion of every question of public interest, and exercise an important influence upon the growth and tendencies of literature and art.[16]

Subsequent editions of the magazine maintained both the high intellectual content and the radical tone of the first issue. The second instalment included an article entitled 'The Fallacy of the Superiority of Man', and the third had articles on medicine as a profession for women by Dr Mary Marshall, MD, on 'Greek Plays at the Universities by A Graduate of Girton', and an account of 'Alexandra College, Dublin' which again stressed the importance of higher education for women. Wilde did not regard the debate on woman's place as closed, and more conservative voices were occasionally heard in the magazine: Miss Lucy M. J. Garnett took issue with Mrs Charles M'Laren's radical article and replied with 'The Fallacy of the Superiority of Woman' in October 1888, following this up with 'Reasons for Opposing Woman Suffrage' in April 1889. Miss Garnett's forthright tone was characteristic of the magazine's writing, but her views were the exception rather than the rule. On the issue of female suffrage and woman's role in politics, for example, the tenor of the magazine was extremely progressive, including articles on 'Women's Suffrage' by Millicent Garrett Fawcett (November 1888), 'On Woman's Work in Politics' by Margaret Sandhurst (January 1889), and 'Political Women: A Study from the MP's Point of View' (January 1889), all of which strongly advocated female emancipation and a greater share for women in public affairs. The magazine similarly championed the cause of higher education for women, and clearly indicated that women's interests were not to be confined within the walls of their own homes.[17] The magazine developed a

---

[16] The editor, 'Literary and Other Notes', *WW* (Nov. 1887), 39.
[17] See e.g. W. L. Courtney, 'The Women Benefactors of Oxford', and Amy Levy, 'Women and Club Life', both in *WW* (June 1888); Miss J. D. Hunting, 'Vassar', *WW* (Aug. 1888).

social conscience, discussing issues ranging from child poverty to the sweated labour of needlewomen and the situation in London's East End.[18]

All these changes were made not just with Wilde's approval but at his instigation, as is demonstrated by his assistant editor's account of Wilde's editorship:

The keynote of the magazine was the right of woman to equality of treatment with man, with the assertion of her claims by women who had gained high position by virtue of their skill as writers or workers in the world's great field of labour.

Some of the articles on women's work and their position in politics were in advance of the thought of the day, and Sir Wemyss Reid, then general manager of Cassell's, or John Williams, the chief editor, would call in at our room and discuss them with Oscar Wilde, who would always express his entire sympathy with the views of the writers and reveal great liberality of thought with regard to the political aspirations of women.[19]

Circulation figures for the *Woman's World* were never high, which may have been due to the fact that Wilde's editions of the magazine were, as Fish put it, 'in advance of the thought of the day'. At the end of the first year the publishers requested certain retrograde steps, and fashion and beauty were given a more prominent position.[20] Wilde acquiesced in these changes, but he was already losing interest in the magazine. Never the man for regular office discipline, his employment at Cassell's was, as Fish observed, a case of 'Pegasus in harness'.[21] In the second year of his editorship his attendances at the office became increasingly rare and his 'Literary and Other Notes' appeared only intermittently. In November 1889 Wilde resigned his editorship. By September 1890, with a new editor in charge, the *Woman's World* had relapsed into its former state, and attracted the scorn of the *Women's Penny Paper* for precisely the faults which Wilde had first sought to remedy: 'As usual

[18] Mrs Francis Jeune, 'The Children of a Great City', *WW* (Nov. 1887); Clementina Black, 'Something about Needle-Women', *WW* (May 1888); Mrs Harriet Brooke Davies, 'Another Voice from the East End', *WW* (Dec. 1888).
[19] Arthur Fish, 'Memories of Oscar Wilde: Some Hitherto Unpublished Letters', *Cassell's Weekly* (2 May 1923), 215.
[20] Nowell-Smith, *The House of Cassell*, 150–1.
[21] 'Memories of Oscar Wilde', 215.

dress occupies a far larger portion of space in Cassell's beau-tifully illustrated and printed magazine than would seem to be at all necessary. To dress is surely not considered the first nor the only duty of women, even by their greatest enemies.'[22]

Wilde's opinions on female emancipation set him apart from the Victorian establishment, but his Irish birth had already en-sured that he regarded England to some extent from the outside. Wilde retained a certain pride in his native roots, often por-traying himself as an Irish rebel against English authority. In 1893 he wrote to congratulate Shaw for a trenchant attack on the institution of stage censorship, adding: 'England is the land of intellectual fogs but you have done much to clear the air: we are both Celtic, and I like to think that we are friends.'[23] When particularly disaffected with the rules of the establishment, Wilde would proudly dissociate himself from England. So in 1892 he explained to an interviewer that, should *Salome* be banned, 'I will not consent to call myself a citizen of a country that shows such narrowness in artistic judgement. I am not English. I am Irish which is quite another thing.'[24] Wilde followed Matthew Arnold in using the word 'Celtic' to describe the imaginative opposite to narrow-minded English puritanism; supporters of the Prison Reform Bill were 'Celtic to a man'.[25]

Celticism stood for the sympathetic capacity which never ignored the individual for the sake of the general rule. It also stood for rebellion, and Wilde never forgot his native land's struggle for independence from England. In 1876 the battle for Home Rule depended strongly on the return of a Liberal government under Gladstone, and one of the Liberal flagships was the Bulgarian question.[26] In 1877 Wilde composed a sonnet,

[22] 'Reviews: Magazines of the Month', *Women's Penny Paper* (13 Sept. 1890), 557.
[23] To Bernard Shaw (postmark 23 Feb. 1893), *Letters*, 332.
[24] *Pall Mall Budget*, 40 (30 June 1892), 947.
[25] To Georgina Weldon (31 May 1898), *Letters*, 751.
[26] In May 1876 a number of Bulgar nationalists revolted against Turkish rule, and Turkey's brutal suppression of the revolt involved mass murder, rape, and pillaging. Disraeli, whose foreign policy favoured Turkey as a means of resisting Russian expansion, sought to minimize the atrocities. Gladstone, however, sup-ported a pro-nationalist policy for the east, opposed Turkish rule, and wrote a pamphlet, *The Bulgarian Horrors and the Question of the East*, which sold 40,000 copies in four days. See R. C. K. Ensor, *England, 1870–1914* (Oxford: Clarendon Press, 1960), 40–54.

'On the Massacre of the Christians in Bulgaria', a copy of which he sent to Gladstone; within its political context, Wilde's sonnet was not simply a poem on a popular and emotive topic, but a deliberate attempt to further the cause of Home Rule.[27] Wilde's view of Gladstone as a vital crusader in the cause of Home Rule is confirmed by later letters in which he greeted the statesman as one whom, 'I, and all who have Celtic blood in their veins, must ever honour and revere, and to whom our country is so deeply indebted', and as the champion who 'will lead us to the grandest and justest political victory of this age'.[28]

Wilde's patriotism could inspire him to both the depths of sycophancy and the heights of invective. While writing reviews for the *Pall Mall Gazette*, for example, he was driven into a fury by J. P. Mahaffy's book, *Greek Life and Thought*, in which the author used parallels with English rule in Ireland to express his disapproval of the Greek nationalist struggle and the whole ethos of autonomy and democracy. Wilde picked holes in his former tutor's arguments, mocked his conclusions, pinpointed his inconsistencies and emphasized the inspiration that nationalism provided for Greek literature.[29] J. A. Froude's novel, *The Two Chiefs of Dunboy*, set in eighteenth-century Ireland, drove Wilde into an even greater rage. He boldly declared his own allegiances in the opening paragraph of his review:

Blue Books are generally dull reading but Blue Books on Ireland have always been interesting. They form the record of one of the greatest tragedies of modern Europe. In them England has written down her indictment against herself, and has given to the world the history of her shame. If in the last century she tried to govern Ireland with an insolence that was intensified by race-hatred and religious prejudice, she has sought to rule her this century with a stupidity that is aggravated by good intentions.[30]

As Wilde commented with bitter humour, 'There are some who will welcome with delight the idea of solving the Irish question by doing away with the Irish people.'[31]

[27] To W. E. Gladstone (14 May 1877), *Letters*, 37.
[28] To W. E. Gladstone (June 1888 and 2 Nov. 1888), *Letters*, 218 and 231.
[29] 'Mr. Mahaffy's New Book', *Pall Mall Gazette*, 46 (9 Nov. 1887), 3.
[30] 'Mr. Froude's Blue Book', *Pall Mall Gazette*, 49 (13 Apr. 1889), 3.
[31] Ibid.

Wilde's politics were not limited to an enthusiasm for Irish Home Rule and a willingness to support Gladstone's Liberal party for the sake of that cause. Wilde had considerably more radical leanings, as he explained to an interviewer in 1894: 'We are all of us more or less Socialists now-a-days . . . I think I am rather more than a Socialist. I am something of an Anarchist, I believe; but, of course, the dynamite policy is very absurd indeed.'[32] Wilde's definition of himself as an anarchist, in the context of late nineteenth-century British politics, was in itself a daring act. Early socialist and anarchist movements were regarded with distrust, hostility, and often fear by the establishment they criticized. Late nineteenth-century London was an international refuge for radical socialists from Germany, Russia, and France, exiled from their native countries by punitive anti-socialist laws. The British authorities surveyed their activities closely and were quick to inflict harsh penalties if they overstepped the mark. When the German exile, Johann Most, published an article supporting the successful assassination of Tsar Alexander II in 1881, he was sentenced to eighteen months in prison. When Most's anarchist newspaper, *Freiheit*, applauded the assassination by Irish Fenians of Lord Frederick Cavendish in Dublin in 1882, the paper was forcibly closed down.[33] Words without deeds were sufficient grounds for imprisonment, and even to define oneself as an anarchist was dangerous. In 1892 four anarchists in Walsall were convicted of being involved in a supposed bomb plot, though a police *agent provocateur* was heavily involved. The anarchist paper, *Commonweal*, was ready to print revelations about the police's methods in the case, when its editors, Mowbray and Nicoll, were arrested and the type-set of the next issue taken. Nicoll found himself prosecuted not for any supposed crime but simply for being an anarchist.

[32] Percival W. H. Almy, 'New Views of Mr. Oscar Wilde', *Theatre*, 23 (Mar. 1894), 124. Wilde's apparent vagueness in defining himself as either socialist or anarchist was inevitable amidst the confusion and cross-currents of contemporary radical politics. For accounts of the alliances and arguments between socialist and anarchist organizations, see e.g. E. P. Thompson, *William Morris: Romantic to Revolutionary* (New York: Pantheon, 1976); G. D. H. Cole, *Socialist Thought: Marxism and Anarchism, 1850–1890* (London: Macmillan, 1954), 379–424; John Quail, *The Slow-Burning Fuse: The Lost History of the British Anarchists* (London: Granada, 1978).

[33] Quail, *The Slow-Burning Fuse*, ch. 1; Hermia Oliver, *The International Anarchist Movement in Late Victorian London* (London: Croom Helm, 1983).

He defended himself, declaring that an anarchist was not necessarily an incendiarist or an assassin, though 'anyone who has seen as much of the poverty and misery of the East End as we have and not use strong language would be absolutely heartless'.[34]

Yet, in spite of the fear, suspicion, and hostility with which anarchists were generally regarded, Wilde was quite ready to declare publicly his allegiance with their cause. So, for example, in 1886 a peaceful anarchist meeting in Chicago was broken up by police. In the ensuing struggle a bomb was thrown, and a number of policemen were among those killed and wounded. Mass arrests of leading anarchists followed, and four were sentenced to death. At their trial it was never proved that they were in any way involved in the bomb-throwing, but the very fact of their being self-confessed anarchists was taken as sufficient proof of their guilt. In England, Bernard Shaw organized a petition for reprieve of the Chicago anarchists, and was agreeably surprised by Wilde's response, as he recalled in a letter to Frank Harris:

I have forgotten the details of the Chicago business of 1886. At the time I was so much interested in it that I tried to get signatures to a petition for the reprieve of the men. Outside the Socialist League and other circles in which it was signed as a matter of course, the only name I got was that of Oscar Wilde. It was really a very handsome thing of him to do, because all the associations of the thing were vulgar and squalid, and Oscar, as you know, was a snob to the marrow of his bones, having been brought up in Merrion Square, Dublin.[35]

Wilde's sympathy with and interest in the anarchist cause may well have been sustained by personal contact with other radical thinkers. Wilde was a friend of William Morris; he visited his family regularly, sent Henry Irving and Ellen Terry's autographs to Morris's daughter, May, and received inscribed copies of Morris's works, the loss of which he was to mourn in prison.[36] Wilde also numbered among his acquaintances actual

[34] Nicoll, trial, 6 May 1892, quoted in Quail, *The Slow-Burning Fuse*, 132.
[35] Shaw, letter to Frank Harris (7 Oct. 1908), *Bernard Shaw, Collected Letters*, ed. Dan H. Lawrence, 3 vols. (London: Bodley Head, 1965–85), ii. 813.
[36] To May Morris (May–June 1881) and to Lord Alfred Douglas (Jan.–Mar. 1897), *Letters*, 77 and 451. When Morris presented Wilde with a copy of his novel *News from Nowhere*, which envisioned a future socialist utopia, Wilde wrote in

bomb-throwing anarchists. Like Walter Sickert, William Morris, and Shaw, he was a friend of Stepnyak, a Russian revolutionary who assassinated General Mezentsev, chief of the Russian secret police.[37] Wilde paid bail for the young revolutionary John Barlas, who was arrested in December 1891 after firing a pistol outside the Palace of Westminster, declaring 'I am an anarchist. What I have done is to show my contempt for the House of Commons.'[38]

Wilde had strong connections with the anarchist movement in France, where avant-garde literature and politics were closely linked. A large number of the leading figures of the French artistic avant-garde, from Symbolist writers to experimental theatre managers, were also actively involved in anarchist politics. Wilde was friendly with a number of the most prominent figures in these radical movements. Félix Fénéon, for example, was both editor of the *Revue indépendante* and the *Revue blanche* and the perpetrator of the bombing of a fashionable Paris restaurant.[39] Wilde met Fénéon in Paris in the 1880s and the friendship endured throughout Wilde's life: Wilde sent Fénéon a copy of *An Ideal Husband* in 1899, and the Frenchman condemned Wilde's imprisonment and repeatedly invited him to dinner and the theatre during his exile in France.[40] Adolphe Retté, who wrote a number of articles on anarchism and was at one point arrested on anarchist charges, was also numbered among Wilde's friends and helped to correct his French in an early version of *Salome*.[41]

thanks: 'I have loved your work since boyhood: I shall always love it.' To William Morris (?Mar.–Apr. 1891), *Letters*, 290–1.

[37] Ellmann, *Oscar Wilde*, 117.

[38] *More Letters*, 108–9. Wilde also addressed Barlas as 'my dear friend and poet', adding: 'We poets and dreamers are all brothers.' To John Barlas (postmark 19 Jan. 1892), ibid.

[39] Joan Ungersma Halperin, *Félix Fénéon: Aesthete and Anarchist in Fin-de-Siècle Paris* (New Haven, Conn.: Yale University Press, 1988), 8–10, 46, and *passim*. La *Revue blanche* was the most important journal to defend simultaneously the causes of Symbolism, free verse, and anarchy. La *Revue indépendante* had similar concerns, and, according to Halperin (p. 46), Wilde wrote its 'Chronique du mois' in Jan. 1885.

[40] To Robert Ross (late Apr. 1898), *Letters*, 732; and ibid. 805. Wilde and Fénéon's association was sufficiently well known for Toulouse-Lautrec to have painted them shoulder to shoulder watching a dancer perform in the street in *The Moorish Dance* (1895).

[41] Richard Sonn, *Anarchism and Cultural Politics in Fin de Siècle France* (Lincoln, Nebr.: University of Nebraska Press, 1989), 22. The echoes of French

Wilde's interest in practical anarchy was enduring, and he happily reported to Reginald Turner in 1898 that among his new acquaintances was an 'intimate friend of Émile Henry, the young anarchist who was guillotined under Carnot, and has told me wonderful things about him and his life'.[42]

Wilde's artistic and political doctrine made him a natural member of this radical circle, and it was therefore unsurprising that he chose to live in France after his release from Reading Gaol. Certainly the French avant-garde remained loyal to Wilde through his troubles. The anarchist writer Paul Adam contributed an article in his defence to *La Revue blanche* in May 1895, entitled 'L'Assaut malicieux', accompanied by a drawing of Wilde by Toulouse-Lautrec.[43] It was Lugné-Poe's experimental Théâtre de l'Œuvre which offered the greatest gesture of solidarity, presenting a production of Wilde's *Salome* on 11 February 1896. Wilde was well aware of the importance of this gesture, as he wrote to Lord Alfred Douglas: 'The production of *Salome* was the thing that turned the scale in my favour, as far as my treatment in prison by Government was concerned, and I am deeply grateful to all concerned in it.'[44] French radicals were quick to recognize Wilde as one of their own. In 1893 *L'Ermitage* conducted a 'Referendum Artistique et Social', which asked 'What is the best condition of social well-being, a free and spontaneous organisation or a disciplined and methodical one?' In the light of Wilde's answers the magazine confidently listed him amongst the anarchist *littérateurs*.[45]

Wilde's clearest statement of his political beliefs was made in his essay, 'The Soul of Man under Socialism', first printed in the *Fortnightly Review* in February 1891. Written in Wilde's characteristically witty and epigrammatic style, the essay set forth a coherent political and philosophical doctrine, in line with many of the most influential nineteenth-century radical thinkers.

Symbolism and of the experimental theatre of Maeterlinck in Wilde's *Salome* strengthen his links to French avant-garde culture.

[42] To Reginald Turner (postmark 6 Dec. 1898), *Letters*, 768.

[43] Sonn, *Anarchism and Cultural Politics*, 176. Sonn outlines Lautrec's involvement in the anarchist movement. Lautrec also designed the programme for the 1st perf. of *Salome* in 1896.

[44] To Lord Alfred Douglas (?2 June 1897), *Letters*, 588.

[45] 'Referendum Artistique et Social', *L'Ermitage* 4/7 (July 1893), quoted in Sonn, *Anarchism and Cultural Politics*, 187.

The basis of Wilde's essay was a criticism of the gross inequalities which characterized nineteenth-century society. Remarking on the poverty, injustice, and suffering widespread in modern capitalist society, Wilde rejected private charity as merely prolonging the evils it sought to alleviate by sustaining the system which caused those ills. Cavalierly dismissing distinctions between the various revolutionary theories, he turned to the essentials of socialist doctrine as the only cure for the economic maladies he diagnosed:

Socialism, Communism, or whatever one chooses to call it, by converting private property into public wealth, and substituting cooperation for competition, will restore society to its proper condition of a thoroughly healthy organism, and ensure the material well-being of each member of the community.[46]

Observing that the advent of machinery had served not to free mankind but to enrich the few and enslave the many, Wilde advocated the common ownership of the means of production.[47]

Yet Wilde's essay, in line with his later political self-definition, revealed him to be 'something more than a Socialist . . . something of an Anarchist, I believe.'[48] So he outlines the limitations of socialist doctrine: 'I confess that many of the socialist views that I have come across seem to me to be tainted with ideas of authority, if not of actual compulsion. Of course authority and compulsion are out of the question. All association must be quite voluntary.'[49]

Anarchism is by its very nature anti-dogmatic, and it is therefore impossible to point to any one authoritative definition; numerous different models of the ideal anarchist state have been devised by different anarchist thinkers. Yet it is possible to outline the essentials of anarchist doctrine. As one historian has recently noted:

All anarchists reject the legitimacy of external government and of the State, and condemn imposed political authority, hierarchy and domination. They seek to establish the condition of anarchy, that is to say, a decentralized and self-regulating society consisting of a federation of

---

[46] 'The Soul of Man under Socialism', *Fortnightly Review*, 49/290 (Feb. 1891), 293.
[47] Ibid. 303.   [48] Almy, 'New Views of Mr. Oscar Wilde', 124.
[49] Ibid. 296.

voluntary associations of free and equal individuals. The ultimate goal of anarchism is to create a free society which allows all human beings to realize their full potential.[50]

'The Soul of Man' in its essence meets all these criteria, and, though written in Wilde's provocatively playful style, its precepts accord with those set forth by the foremost anarchist philosophers of the day. 'Property is theft', Proudhon had famously declared; 'Property is simply a nuisance', Wilde observed in his turn.[51] In 1868 Bakunin rejected communism, explaining:

I am not a communist because communism concentrates and absorbs all the powers of society into the state; because it necessarily ends in the centralization of property in the hands of the state, while I want the abolition of the state—the radical extirpation of the principle of authority and the tutelage of the state, which, on the pretext of making men moral and civilized, has up to now enslaved, oppressed, exploited and depraved them.[52]

Wilde rejected state socialism and the principle of authority for parallel reasons, though in a more flamboyant style:

It is clear, then, that no Authoritarian Socialism will do. For while under the present system a very large number of people can lead lives of a certain amount of freedom and expression and happiness, under an industrial-barrack system, or a system of economic tyranny, nobody would be able to have any such freedom at all. It is to be regretted that a portion of our community should be practically in slavery, but to propose to solve the problem by enslaving the entire community is childish.[53]

Wilde, like the early anarchist philosopher William Godwin, believed in the innate virtue of mankind, uncontaminated by the pernicious influence of private property and competition. Both deplored the legal system, condemning punishment and imprisonment as a crime far greater than any committed by the

---

[50] Peter Marshall, *Demanding the Impossible: A History of Anarchism* (London: Fontana Press, 1992), 3.

[51] Joseph-Pierre Proudhon, phrase used in pamphlet, *Qu'est-ce que la propriété?* (1840), trans. Benjamin Tucker as *What is Property? An Inquiry into the Principle of Right and Government* (Princeton, Mass.: Benjamin R. Tucker, 1876), 13. 'The Soul of Man', 294.

[52] J. Guillaume, *L'Internationale: Documents souvenirs 1864–1878*, 4 vols. (Paris, 1905–10), I, 74–5, quoted in James Joll, *The Anarchists* (London: Methuen, 1979), 89–90.

[53] 'The Soul of Man', 295–6.

so-called criminals. In Wilde's, as in Godwin's, scheme the gaoler was to be replaced by the doctor: 'When there is no punishment at all, crime will either cease to exist, or, if it occurs, will be treated by physicians as a very distressing form of dementia, to be cured by care and kindness.'[54] Wilde was here expounding a mainstream tenet of anarchist thought. Prince Kropotkin, imprisoned in Russia and France for anarchist activities, and one of the leading anarchist spokesmen in nineteenth-century Britain, expounded precisely this philosophy. In a pamphlet of 1886, 'Law and Authority, An Anarchist Essay', Kropotkin rejected all laws, judgement, punishment, and penalties on the basis of their degrading effect on mankind:

Peoples without political organisation, and therefore less depraved than ourselves, have perfectly understood that the man who is called 'criminal' is simply unfortunate; that the remedy is not to flog him, to chain him up, or to kill him on the scaffold or in prison, but to relieve him by the most brotherly care, by treatment based on equality, by the usages of life amongst honest men.[55]

Wilde's doctrine was in essence that of a utopian anarchist, arguing that, freed from all restraints, mankind would abandon competition for the pursuit of self-development, and that a natural community of independent individuals would result.

'The Soul of Man under Socialism' does not, however, advocate a communal ideal, but on the contrary preaches the doctrine of individualism. Where Proudhon believed that mankind had a natural social sense which led the individual to conform with the wishes of the majority, and Kropotkin believed that unbridled individualism was a modern growth, corrupting mankind's collective and co-operative instincts, Wilde celebrated the inviolable rights of the individual against the masses.[56] Yet

[54] Ibid. 302; cf. William Godwin, *An Enquiry concerning Political Justice, and its Influence on General Virtue and Happiness*, 2 vols. (London, 1793). Wilde again expounded these views in the same interview in which he defined himself as an anarchist: 'To punish a man for wrong-doing, with a view to his reformation, is the most lamentable mistake it is possible to commit. . . . If he has any soul at all, such procedure is calculated to make him ten times worse than he was before.' Almy, 'New Views of Mr. Oscar Wilde', 124.

[55] Pierre Kropotkin, 'Law and Authority: An Anarchist Essay' (London, 1886), 22–3.

[56] See e.g. 'On Justice', in *Selected Writings of Pierre-Joseph Proudhon*, ed. Stewart Edwards, trans. Elizabeth Fraser (London: Macmillan, 1969), 248–53; Pierre Kropotkin, *Mutual Aid* (1902) (Harmondsworth: Pelican, 1939), *passim*.

anarchism and individualism were certainly not mutually exclusive. The German anarchist Max Stirner, for example, anticipated Wilde in his rejection of all allegiance to state or society, advocating instead a 'Union of Egoists'.[57] Similarly, Wilde's essay proposes the abolition of all restraints on the individual in order that each person may develop their own personality and satisfy their own desires without reference to anyone else. Both writers therefore scornfully dismissed the demands of public opinion and the right of the majority to dictate to the few.[58]

Wilde's individualist doctrine also presented many parallels with Taoist philosophy, a philosophy which itself provided one of the earliest bases for anarchist thought.[59] In 1890 Wilde enthusiastically reviewed a translation of the writings of Chuang Tsu, a Taoist disciple of Lao Tsu. Chuang Tsu's philosophy was one of passivity and inactivity, rejecting all forms of government and concluding that, 'Intentional charity and intentional duty to one's neighbour are surely not included in our moral nature. Yet what sorrow these have involved.'[60] Wilde was quick to note the revolutionary potential of such a philosophy, concluding his review with the observation that:

It is clear that Chuang Tsu is a very dangerous writer, and the publication of his book in English, two thousand years after his death, is obviously premature, and may cause a great deal of pain to many thoroughly respectable and industrious persons. It may be true that the ideal of self-culture and self-development, which is the aim of his scheme of life, and the basis of his scheme of philosophy, is an ideal somewhat needed by an age like ours, in which most people are so anxious to educate their neighbours that they have actually no time left in which to educate themselves.[61]

[57] Max Stirner, *The Ego and His Own*, trans. Steven Byington (London: Rebel Press, 1982), 179, 1st pub. 1845.
[58] 'The Soul of Man', 304–14.
[59] 'Anarchism is usually considered a recent, Western phenomenon, but its roots reach deep in the ancient civilizations of the East. The first clear expression of an anarchist sensibility may be traced back to the Taoists in ancient China from about the sixth century BC. Indeed, the principal Taoist work, the *Tao Te Ching*, may be considered one of the greatest anarchist classics.' Marshall, *Demanding the Impossible*, 53.
[60] *Chuang Tzu: Mystic, Moralist and Social Reformer*, trans. from the Chinese by Herbert A. Giles (London: Bernard Quaritch, 1889), 101.
[61] 'A Chinese Sage', review of *Chuang Tzu*, trans. Giles, *Speaker*, 1 (8 Feb. 1890), 146.

The relevance of this doctrine to 'The Soul of Man under Socialism' is clear, and Wilde himself acknowledged the influence of the Taoist sage:

Individualism, then, is what through Socialism we are to attain. As a natural result the State must give up all idea of government. It must give it up because, as a wise man once said many centuries before Christ, there is such a thing as leaving mankind alone; there is no such thing as governing mankind.[62]

The form and structure of Wilde's essay probably owed much to J. S. Mill's *On Liberty* (1859) and to George Bernard Shaw's *The Quintessence of Ibsenism*, which was first published in 1891 but had previously been presented in July 1890 as part of a series of Fabian Society lectures entitled 'Socialism in Contemporary Literature'. Mill's essay, like Wilde's, moved from a concern with the limits to society's legitimate control, to the tyranny of society's demand for conformity, the importance of freedom of expression and personal development, and finally to an impassioned attack on public opinion.[63] Mill, lacking Wilde's anarchist faith in the inherent benevolence of mankind when untrammelled by laws and restraints, admitted the necessity of certain laws to prevent individuals from interfering with or harming each other. When Shaw's *The Quintessence of Ibsenism* was published in 1891, Wilde wrote to his fellow Irishman that 'your little book on Ibsenism and Ibsen is such a delight to me that I constantly take it up, and always find it stimulating and refreshing'.[64] In his essay Shaw emphasized the supreme importance of individual thought, faith, and creation, and rejected the duty owed by the individual to society and public opinion.[65] Both Irishmen used flamboyant wit and paradoxical humour to attack the moral pieties of nineteenth-century society. As Wilde argued in 'The Soul of Man', so Shaw argued in *The Quintessence* that the individual's prime duty is always to him or herself, that charity and self-sacrifice are pernicious and

[62] 'The Soul of Man', 301; cf. also *Chuang Tzu*, trans. Giles, 119.
[63] J. S. Mill, *On Liberty* (London: John W. Parker & Son, 1859). In an article entitled 'To Read or not to Read', Wilde listed under 'Books not to read at all . . . all John Stuart Mill except the essay on *Liberty*'. *Pall Mall Gazette*, 43 (8 Feb. 1886) 11.
[64] To Bernard Shaw, (postmark 23 Feb. 1891), *Letters*, 332.
[65] George Bernard Shaw, *The Quintessence of Ibsenism* (London: Walter Scott, 1891), 15–45.

that, paradoxically, only through selfishness can the individual become truly selfless: 'Only when this sense [of duty to himself] is fully grown, which it hardly is yet, the tyranny of duty is broken; for now the man's God is himself; and he, self-satisfied at last, ceases to be selfish'.[66]

Written as it was in a flamboyantly provocative style, full of paradoxes and epigrams, 'The Soul of Man under Socialism' was not greeted by Wilde's contemporaries as a serious political essay. So, for example, a critic wrote in the *Spectator* that:

All these literary bullets are shot out in defence of the thesis that men should be themselves, in contempt it would seem, not merely of the public, but of all law which restricts their individualism. The article, if serious, would be thoroughly unhealthy, but it leaves on us the impression of being written merely to startle and excite talk.[67]

Yet, in spite of such easy dismissal, 'The Soul of Man under Socialism' was taken seriously by a number of its readers. According to Robert Sherard, millions of copies were sold in central and eastern Europe, and it was read enthusiastically by revolutionaries in Russia, Germany, and Austria.[68] Certainly the essay has achieved a considerable reputation and influence among modern anarchist thinkers. George Woodcock, one of the first critics to study Wilde's works in anything but a bio-graphical light, wrote a number of anarchist pamphlets which

[66] Ibid. 17; cf. 'The Soul of Man', 316: '*Selfishness is not living as one wishes to live, it is asking others to live as one wishes to live.* And unselfishness is letting other people's lives alone, not interfering with them.'

[67] *Spectator*, 67 (7 Feb. 1891), 213. With apparently unconscious irony, this reviewer criticizes the essay as potentially 'unhealthy', a term which Wilde specifi-cally picks out as being misused by the press: 'An unhealthy work of art . . . is a work whose style is obvious, old-fashioned, and common, and whose subject is deliberately chosen, not because the artist has any pleasure in it, but because he thinks that the public will pay him for it. *In fact, the popular novel that the public calls healthy is always a thoroughly unhealthy production; and what the public call an unhealthy novel is always a beautiful and healthy work of art.*' 'The Soul of Man', 308.

[68] Dramatically, Sherard claims virtual canonization for Wilde on the basis of 'The Soul of Man': 'all over Europe amongst the poor, oppressed and outcast, his name is reverenced as that of an apostle of the liberties of man. No writing on the social question, perhaps, has produced a profounder impression than his on the continent, where "The Soul of Man" has been translated into every tongue. Amongst the very poorest·and most forlorn, and most desperate of the helots of Europe, the Jews of Russia and Poland, Oscar Wilde, known to them only as the author of this essay, is regarded in the light of a prophet, a benefactor, a saint.' Robert Harborough Sherard, *The Life of Oscar Wilde* (London: T. Werner Laurie, 1906), 131–2.

read as almost exact reproductions of Wilde's own philosophy.[69] Similarly, Peter Marshall in his recent history of anarchism declares Wilde, on the basis of 'The Soul of Man under Socialism', to be 'the greatest of all libertarians'.[70]

It was entirely characteristic of Wilde to express his serious political convictions in such a deceptively frivolous and witty form as he did in 'The Soul of Man'. A large portion of the essay was devoted to condemning the demands and influence of public opinion, emphasizing the essentially personal nature of true art.[71] In Wilde's view, the masses were to be scorned or humoured, but it was not for their sake that the artist shaped his creations. When Ada Leverson said that Wilde should publish a book '*all* margin', full of beautiful unwritten thoughts, Wilde approved the idea, adding: 'There must be five hundred signed copies for particular friends, six for the general public, and one for America.'[72] Though he was forced to work within the constraints of censorship, and though financial necessity obliged him to pursue commercial success, Wilde wrote for the select few not for the general public.

Wilde's plays can easily be treated as primarily commercial vehicles, filled with all the tricks and clichés of the contemporary popular theatre, clever combinations of sophisticated wit for the circle and extravagant melodrama for the gallery and the pit. Seen in this light, they would be far removed from his more obviously radical works. Certainly, the stereotypical roles, conventional morality, and safely orthodox plots of popular nineteenth-century theatre were strongly at odds with Wilde's feminist and anarchist sympathies. Yet, looking back on his theatrical achievements, Wilde himself declared that his plays were anything but conventional. Writing in Reading Gaol, Wilde emphasized the purely individual nature of his drama, hinting at a hidden layer of meaning beneath its conventional surface:

[69] Woodcock, *The Paradox of Oscar Wilde*; id. 'Anarchism or Chaos?' (London: Freedom, 1944); id. 'Anarchism and Morality' (London: Freedom, 1945); id. 'What is Anarchism?' (London: Freedom, 1945).
[70] *Demanding the Impossible*, 180.   [71] 'The Soul of Man', 304–15.
[72] Ada Leverson, *Letters to the Sphinx from Oscar Wilde and Reminiscences of the Author* (London: Duckworth, 1930), 19–20.

I altered the minds of men and the colours of things: there was nothing I did or said that did not make people wonder: I took the drama, the most objective form known to art, and made it as personal a mode of expression as the lyric or the sonnet.[73]

For Wilde's plays to be a truly personal mode of expression, however, they must surely embrace his strongly held and enduring beliefs in individual freedom, the corrupting influence of authority, and the importance of rebellion. The popular Victorian drama was generally conservative in moral, political, and sexual matters. Yet Wilde claimed to have used the genre to express his own individual views, views which encompassed progressive feminism, anarchist idealism, and the rejection of all forms of authority.

[73] To Lord Alfred Douglas (Jan.–Mar. 1897), *Letters*, 466.

2

Vera; or, The Nihilists

A Russian who lives happily under the present system of government in Russia must either believe that man has no soul, or that, if he has, it is not worth developing. A Nihilist who rejects all authority because he knows all authority to be evil, and welcomes all pain, because through that he realises his personality, is a real Christian.[1]

IN 1880 Oscar Wilde sent a copy of his first play, *Vera; or, The Nihilists*, to the American actor, Hermann Vezin, and wrote ingenuously that 'I have just found out what a difficult craft playwriting is'.[2] Such a statement does not excite any great expectations of merit in the play. *Vera* was Wilde's first dramatic work and has almost universally been condemned as a youthful mistake, an apprentice piece without intrinsic interest or merit. Even Wilde's friend and literary executor, Robbie Ross, dismissed it as 'nothing more than a bibliographical curiosity. . . . It is worthless as literature or drama though interesting as showing how slowly Wilde developed either his literary or dramatic talent'.[3]

Yet *Vera*, though undoubtedly crude and unsophisticated in comparison with Wilde's later plays, does not simply demonstrate how slowly his dramatic talents developed, it demonstrates *how* they developed. It is a conventionally plotted play, generously larded with melodramatic moments and spiced with occasional epigrams and witticisms, but, like Wilde's more respected dramatic works, *Vera* is also a more subtle and cleverly crafted work than it first appears. Wilde found the craft of playwriting more difficult than he first expected, not just because

[1] 'The Soul of Man', 318–19.
[2] To Hermann Vezin (4 Oct. 1880), *Letters*, 71.
[3] Robert Ross, typed and autographed letter (25 May 1910) accompanying the copy of the 1882 edn. of *Vera*, donated by Ross to the BL. This copy of the 1882 edn. includes the author's autograph corrections and served as the text for the uniform edn. of the play (London: Methuen, 1908).

of his lack of experience, but because his dramatic aims were particularly ambitious.

Wilde completed *Vera* in 1880, and immediately set about finding a management willing to produce it. With a youthful combination of hubris and humility, he modestly solicited advice from famous actors and actresses, while simultaneously urging them to perform in or produce his play. He met with success; *Vera* was accepted for production at the Adelphi Theatre, London, with Mrs Bernard Beere in the lead role. On 30 November 1881, however, three weeks before the planned opening, the *World* announced that 'considering the present state of political feeling in England, Mr. Oscar Wilde has decided on postponing, for a time, the production of his drama *Vera*'; the recent assassinations of Tsar Alexander II and of the American President Garfield had forced Wilde to cancel the production.[4] Undeterred, Wilde focused his attention on America, and finally succeeded in persuading Marie Prescott to take on the play and title role. *Vera* opened on 20 August 1883 at the Union Square Theatre, New York, and, though reasonably received by the audience, was panned by most critics. The *New York Sun* proclaimed it a masterpiece, and the *New York Mirror* declared it 'really marvellous', but they were in a small minority.[5] More typically, the *New York Times* summed up *Vera* as 'unreal, long-winded and wearisome', and the *New York Daily Tribune* dismissed it as 'a fanciful, foolish, highly peppered story of love, intrigue and politics, invested with the Russian accessories of fur and dark-lanterns, and overlaid with bantam gabble about freedom and the people'.[6] Since then *Vera* has remained unperformed.[7]

[4] The *World* (30 Nov. 1881), 12.
[5] *New York Mirror* (25 Aug. 1883), repr. in Stuart Mason, *A Bibliography of Oscar Wilde* (London: T. Werner Laurie, 1914), 273.
[6] *New York Times* (21 Aug. 1883), 5; *New York Daily Tribune* (21 Aug. 1883), 5.
[7] Later critics have been equally dismissive: Boris Brasol, for example, labelled it a 'farce', declaring that 'today no one takes *Vera* seriously; the play rather should be regarded as a dramatic failure': *Oscar Wilde: The Man, the Artist, the Martyr* (New York: Williams & Norgate, 1938), 86 and 91; Peter Raby calls it 'somewhat superficial and excessively melodramatic': *Oscar Wilde*, 82; Norbert Kohl condemns it as a '*péché de jeunesse*': *Oscar Wilde*; Katharine Worth is alone among modern critics in greeting the play as 'an interesting stage piece in its own right': *Oscar Wilde*, 38.

The youthful Wilde, however, expressed a high opinion of his precious first play. Though he wrote modestly to Ellen Terry that, 'Perhaps some day I shall be fortunate enough to write something worthy of your playing', his letter to Clara Morris presented his play as equal to her talent: 'the character of the heroine is drawn in all those varying moods and notes of passion which you can so well touch.'[8] While trying to maintain a humble tone in his note to the Examiner of Plays, E. F. S. Piggott, Wilde still betrayed his considerable ambition, explaining that he chose the drama because 'it's *the democratic* art, and I want fame', and informing Piggott that 'the second act is good writing, and the fourth good position'.[9] In his correspondence with Richard D'Oyly Carte and Marie Prescott he exercised no such restraint, and his letters are filled with analyses of *Vera* as an important tragedy and minute comments on how it should best be produced.[10] Wilde took most trouble to emphasize the play's realism. He informed D'Oyly Carte that the title of the first act was to be changed from 'Tomb of the Kings at Moscow' to '99 Rue Tchernavaza, Moscow', and added pointedly that 'the conspirators are to be *modern*, and the room a bare garret, painted crimson. It is to be a realistic not operatic conspiracy.'[11] These letters show that Wilde not only took his first play extremely seriously, but that he regarded *Vera* as anything but the fantastic, extravagant melodrama that critics have declared it to be.

The notice in the *World* announcing that the London production was cancelled for political reasons would also seem to contradict the accepted view of *Vera* as an unrealistic and highly conventional melodrama; the play was sufficiently controversial for its performance to be suspended indefinitely. Admittedly Willie Wilde was on the staff of the *World* at the time the notice was printed, but, whether or not he had a hand in drafting it, the very fact that such a statement could be presented seriously to the public indicates that Oscar was entering a delicate political arena. The assassinations in 1881 of both

---

[8] To Ellen Terry (c.Sept. 1880), *Letters*, 70; to Clara Morris (c.Sept. 1880), *Letters*, 70.
[9] To E. F. S. Piggott (Sept. 1880), *More Letters*, 32.
[10] *Letters*, 104, 142–3, 148–9.
[11] To Richard D'Oyly Carte (Mar. 1882), *Letters*, 104.

Alexander II and President Garfield made any play about political conspiracy dangerously topical, especially one which dared
to extend a hint of tolerance or understanding towards its
assassins. The *New York Times* even suggested that international pressure had been applied, reporting (though not without a touch of scepticism) that their London correspondent
'is credibly informed that the tragedy is not to be done, don't
you know, out of deference to the Russian government, Lord
Granville having received a communication on the subject and
being anxious to do the courteous thing, don't you know, to
the Russian minister'.[12]

All these facts combine to suggest that *Vera* is a more
significant work than the juvenile melodrama it has so long
been labelled. Wilde took considerable care over its composition;
through successive revisions he sharpened the political analysis
which underlies the sensational action. The cancellation of the
London performance attests to the delicacy and importance of
Wilde's chosen topic, and a comparison between *Vera* and other
contemporary plays on similar subjects demonstrates how far
Wilde's treatment of his themes differed from the theatrical
norm.

Wilde's lifelong sympathy with revolutionaries and their ideals
embraced the cause of the Russian nihilists. In 'The Soul of
Man' he condemned as soulless all those who failed to rebel
against the Russian system of government, and six years later
in *De Profundis* he lavishly praised the exiled Russian revolutionary, Prince Peter Kropotkin, describing him as having lived
one of 'the most perfect lives I have come across ... a man
with the soul of that beautiful white Christ that seems coming
out of Russia'.[13]

Yet Wilde's attitude was tinged with ambivalence; he remained
sufficiently idealistic to embrace rebel causes while questioning
their methods. So, for example, when interviewed by an American newspaper reporter about his reaction to the assassination

[12] *New York Times* (26 Dec. 1881), 1.
[13] 'The Soul of Man', 318–19; to Lord Alfred Douglas (Jan.–Mar. 1897), *Letters*, 488. Prince Pierre Kropotkin (1842–1912) joined the International in Switzer-
land in 1872, and returned to Russia to carry on clandestine propaganda. He was
imprisoned and dramatically escaped to western Europe, where he founded and
edited *Le Révolté* until he was imprisoned in France in 1882. Released in 1885,
he went to England.

by Irish terrorists of the Chief Secretary for Ireland, Lord Frederick Cavendish, and the Under-Secretary, T. H. Burke, in Phoenix Park in 1882, Wilde replied: 'When liberty comes with hands dabbled in blood it is hard to shake hands with her.' But he then added: 'We forget how much England is to blame. She is reaping the fruit of seven centuries of injustice.'[14]

This careful hedging is characteristic of Wilde's more youthful statements. By 1891, when he wrote 'The Soul of Man', Wilde had developed the flamboyant style which enabled him to espouse radical causes without embroiling himself in questions of practical application. But in his twenties the young Oscar alternated more cautiously between dangerously revolutionary sentiments and a more safely conservative and moderate position. Wilde's early poems most clearly demonstrate this cultivated ambivalence. Thus in his 'Sonnet to Liberty' Wilde declares that he does not love the common herd of revolutionaries, and could easily accept tyranny were he not fired with an abstract passion for liberty. And yet, he adds, with unintentionally humorous circumspection:

These Christs that die upon the barricades,
    God knows it I am with them, in some things.[15]

This early cautiousness and ambivalence is reflected in *Vera*, where Wilde attempted to present a more complex picture of Russian revolutionary politics than popular opinion allowed, while taking care not to alienate his audience with overtly radical sentiments.

Public opinion in England displayed little of this confusion. In June 1878 the *Illustrated London News* reported with horror the attempted assassination of the emperor–king, William I of Germany and Prussia, by a socialist sympathizer, Dr Nobiling. The article condemned the attempt as an 'infamous and atrocious deed' which 'continues to excite stern indignation throughout the civilised world'.[16] The writer of the article clearly recognized no distinction between differently motivated attempts at assassination, concluding with a list of all attempts on the lives of royal personages and rulers in the previous thirty years, including one attack on Queen Victoria in 1852, and two on

[14] Quoted in Hyde, *Oscar Wilde*, 89.
[15] *Poems* (London: David Bogue, 1881), 3.
[16] 'Nobiling, the Assassin', *Illustrated London News* (15 June 1878), 548.

the tsar in 1866 and 1867.[17] In 1881 Johann Most was successfully prosecuted for writing approvingly of the assassination of
Alexander II, and his paper, *Freiheit*, was forcibly closed down
after it published an article applauding the assassination of
Lord Cavendish.[18] Universal outrage greeted the killing of the
tsar in 1881, and the revolutionaries responsible were treated
with horror and contempt. The *Pall Mall Gazette* characterized
nihilism as a 'murderous conspiracy' and the nihilists as 'a
mere handful of desperate plotters against the principles of
modern society'.[19] *The Times* had even less sympathy for the
rebels, excusing Russian despotism as the inevitable reaction to
anarchist excess, and presenting the attitude of the Russian
people to their tsar as 'the almost idolatrous devotion of millions' offset by 'the bloodthirsty and unscrupulous hatred of a
few'.[20] Even those, like the *Daily Telegraph*, who emphasized
the inhumane cruelty and despotism of the Russian regime
unconditionally condemned the methods of the nihilists: 'No
crimes from above can justify assassination, but the wild despair that especially marks Nihilism has its root in the dreary
and unchecked absolutism of Russian rule.'[21] Even back in
1870s, when the nihilists' methods seemed comparatively harmless, the British press had little sympathy with their cause. In
1878 a commentator in the *Contemporary Review* condemned
those students who risked their lives to disseminate pamphlets
criticizing the government, because 'it is pitiful to see these
youths ruining themselves for a cause without a future, depriving
their country of intellectual and moral powers, which it stands
so much in need of'.[22] One exception to this general antipathy
towards the Russian revolutionaries was the case of Vera
Zassoulich, a young Russian woman whose story aroused international attention. The *Dublin University Magazine*, for example, carried a long and enthusiastic article telling of Vera's
early mistreatment, and how her outrage at the injustice and

[17] 'Nobiling, the Assassin', *Illustrated London News* (15 June 1878), 548.
[18] Donald Thomas, *A Long Time Burning: A History of Literary Censorship in
England* (London: Routledge & Kegan Paul, 1969), 226; Quail, *The Slow-Burning
Fuse*, ch. 1.
[19] *Pall Mall Gazette* (14 Mar. 1881), 2.   [20] *The Times* (14 Mar. 1881), 9.
[21] *Daily Telegraph* (15 Mar. 1881), 4.
[22] T. S. Elizaveta, 'Contemporary Life and Thought in Russia', *Contemporary
Review*, 31 (Feb. 1878), 629.

persecution practised by her government led her, on 24 January 1878, to assassinate General Trepoff, the Chief of Police in St Petersburg.[23] Remarkably the young woman was declared 'not guilty' by a jury, in spite of numerous eye-witnesses and her own confessions of guilt, and, even more remarkably, the British press followed the Russian people in declaring her, as the *Dublin University Magazine* put it, 'the image of an Avenger without a selfish motive'.[24] The shooting of a brutal police chief could be tolerated, the shooting of a king could only be condemned.

Wilde's Vera Sabouroff (named Vera Katinski in the 1880 edition) may owe her name to this popular heroine, both being idealists who embrace assassination as a weapon against injustice and tyranny.[25] There are, however, other possible sources for Vera's name. Another revolutionary figure, Vera Figner, is a likely candidate; she is described by Popov, a minor figure in the movement, as a super-revolutionary, famous for her beauty and elegance, as well as for her remarkable ability to appear with confidence in any society, even the most aristocratic.[26] Nikolai Chernyshevsky's renowned and influential novel, *What Is To Be Done?*, provides another possible source. Its heroine, Vera Pavlovna, is a strong-minded and visionary woman, who falls in love with a medical student and finds her passions temporarily in conflict with her revolutionary ideals.[27] Wilde's Vera shares these women's strength, idealism, courage, and determination.

Other details of *Vera; or, The Nihilists* attest to Wilde's background reading. The conspirators' oaths, for example, imitate passages from the Revolutionary Catechism drafted by S. C.

[23] Article on Vera Zassoulich by Karl Blind, *Dublin University Magazine*, 1 (July 1878), 652–64.

[24] Ibid. 657.

[25] In his early notes for *Vera*, Wilde also names his chief of police 'General Trekoff', echoing Vera Sabouroff's victim. MS notebook, *Vera, or the Nihilists*, containing a fragment of the first draft, twenty-nine fos., Beinecke Library, Yale.

[26] Ronald Hingley, *Nihilists: Russian Radicals and Revolutionaries in the Reign of Alexander II, 1855–81* (London: Weidenfeld & Nicolson, 1967), 109.

[27] *What Is To Be Done?*, trans. Michael R. Katz (Cornell: Cornell University Press, 1989). The novel was first published in the journal *Sovremennik* in 1863, and was available in a French translation in England by 1880. Sir Robert Chiltern unconsciously quotes Chernyshevsky's title in his despairing cry to Lord Goring in *An Ideal Husband* (London, 1899), II. 76.

Nechayev and Mikhail Bakunin in 1869, though the password ritual with which the conspirators introduce themselves has been identified by Richard Ellmann as echoing the masonic rites of the Oxford Rose-Croix, of which Wilde was a member.[28] The use of oaths by the assassins could, however, also have been suggested by more general reading. *Vera*'s nihilists seem to be built on the model of 'Hell', the core of the Russian revolutionary 'Organisation', which was specifically designed for the purposes of political terrorism.[29] The leader of this group, which was broken up in 1866 after an abortive attempt to kill the tsar, laid down that every member must change their name and remain unmarried, keeping no family ties or friends. Wilde's play reveals not only the barbarity but the necessity of such oaths.

In view of the detailed research which went into the play, Wilde's emphasis on its realism, and the cancellation of the first production for political reasons, the basic plot of *Vera* appears surprisingly conventional, melodramatic, and even trite. Vera is first introduced as a young peasant girl. Her natural idealism and sense of justice are outraged when she sees her beloved brother sent to Siberia for daring to challenge the oppressive regime of the Czar. Vera vows revenge and takes the nihilist oath to abandon all ties of love and family until justice and freedom are won. In Moscow, years later, Vera has become a mainstay of the nihilist movement, but falls in love with a fellow nihilist, a young medical student called Alexis. Alexis is revealed to be the Czarevitch in disguise and is denounced as a traitor, but then proves his loyalty by saving the conspirators from detection and death. The second act introduces the Czar and his corrupt councillors, principal among whom is the cynical Prince Paul Maraloffski. Alexis pleads with his father not to introduce martial law, then impulsively declares himself a nihilist and is condemned to death by his father. Before the sentence can be carried out, however, the Czar himself is assassinated by a nihilist. In Act III the conspirators hear that Alexis has accepted the imperial crown and they draw lots to decide who is to execute him. Vera pleads for his life, but, having been reminded of her oath and her dead

[28] Ellmann, *Oscar Wilde*, 117.   [29] Hingley, *Nihilists*, 48.

brother's treatment, she draws her lot and vows to kill her former lover. The final act opens with Alexis in his palace, dreaming of Vera and commencing his reign as an enlightened and reforming czar. Vera enters, bent on her bloody task, but, as Alexis speaks of his love for the people and herself, she renounces her oath and declares her love for Alexis. To rescue Alexis from her nihilist companions, who are outside the window clamouring for his blood, Vera stabs herself with the poisoned dagger, dying in his place. She expires in her lover's arms, declaring 'I have saved Russia!'

This plot is perfectly orthodox. The nihilist conspirators are excessively zealous in their use of terrorist tactics against their oppressors, and they are only thwarted in their bloodthirsty mission by the noble self-sacrifice of Vera. The Czar is not himself evil but has been driven to extreme measures by his fear of the nihilists. The Czarevitch is an enlightened humanist who loves the people and devotes his powers to helping them. Vera, caught between these opposing forces, is a woman whose impulsive nature and powerful passions lead her at first to ally herself with the nihilists, but then, prompted by her love for Alexis, to reject the conspirators and embrace the Czarevitch as the hope of Russia. The overall implication seems to be that the solution to Russia's problems lies in a benevolent constitutional monarchy, perhaps modelled on Britain's own.

Yet, beneath this crudely conventional surface, Wilde was attempting to challenge orthodox attitudes and to present a complex and realistic view of Russian politics. The prologue to *Vera* provides an emotional explanation for Vera's involvement with the nihilists, but it also contradicts the usual portrayal of them as ruthless criminals. When the nihilists first enter, Vera and her father voice the conventional judgement upon them:

PETER. I reckon they're some of those Nihilists the priest warns us against . . .
VERA. I suppose, then, they are all wicked men.[30]

---

[30] *Vera; or, The Nihilists*, prologue. *The Complete Writings of Oscar Wilde* (London: Methuen, 1908), II. 126. Cited hereafter as *Vera* (1908). This edition was based on Wilde's autograph corrections to the 1882 edn., and may therefore be taken to represent the final version of the play as Wilde intended it. Wilde subsequently made further changes for the New York production in 1883 at the request of Marie Prescott. These changes are discussed below.

Vera's next exchange with Colonel Kotemkin immediately challenges this definition, however, when the young woman instinctively allies herself with the nihilist cause:

VERA. Who are our masters?
COLONEL. Young woman, these men are going to the mines for life for asking the same foolish question.
VERA. Then they have been unjustly condemned.[31]

The disclosure that her idealist brother Dmitri is condemned to the salt mines for his revolutionary activities is another challenge to the simple 'nihilist equals guilty' equation. Thus, when the father discovers that his son is among the prisoners, we see him struggling to resist the conclusion that Vera has jumped to:

COLONEL. He is a Nihilist.
PETER. You lie! you lie! He is innocent. [*The soldiers force him back with their guns and shut the door against him. He beats with his fists against it.*] Dmitri! Dmitri! a Nihilist! a Nihilist! [*Falls down on floor.*][32]

The romantic young woman immediately espouses the cause, while even her self-interested and conservative father finds himself bewildered by the contradictions in his beliefs. The audience's prejudices are challenged just as the old man's are.

The politics of *Vera* are not, however, a simple portrait in black and white; neither nihilists nor Czar are straightforwardly innocent or guilty. The crude outline suggested by the bare plot of the play is tempered by the cynical realism of its most original character, Prince Paul Maraloffski. This arch-diplomatist is the only recognizably Wildean figure in the play, and provides an early model for the witty and detached dandy of the later plays. Though cast in the role of evil councillor, Prince Paul also hints at a more complex interpretation of the events portrayed in the play. Coolly undercutting the melodramatic posturing and rhetoric of other characters, he introduces a mocking note of realism and political necessity. The Czarevitch blames his father's cruel autocracy on Prince Paul, remarking bitterly that Prince Paul could not make a chef because, 'you could never have worn your white apron well; you would have soiled it too soon, your hands are not clean enough'. Prince

---

[31] *Vera* (1908), II. 128–9.   [32] Ibid. 136.

Paul's reply—'You forget—or, how could they be: I manage your father's business'—shares the blame between master and servant, suggesting the harsh necessities of power.[33]

It is Prince Paul who first casts doubt on the idealized character of Alexis, the imperial nihilist. The Prime Minister reassures the Czar:

> Your Majesty, there is no need for alarm. The Prince is a very ingenuous young man. He pretends to be devoted to the people, and lives in a palace; preaches socialism, and draws a salary that would support a province. Some day he'll find out that the best cure for Republicism is the Imperial crown, and will cut up the red cap of liberty to make decorations for his Prime Minister.[34]

Prince Paul's prophecy questions the Czarevitch's commitment to the revolutionary cause, and his scepticism is borne out by later events: Alexis accepts the imperial crown and fails to answer the nihilists' summons. Alexis's determination to use his power to good effect does not alter the fact that his professed beliefs have not stood the test. The nihilists remain implacably opposed to all who wear a crown, and Prince Paul himself agrees with their reasoning; as he declares: 'Good kings are the only dangerous enemies that modern democracy has.'[35] For all Alexis's declared allegiance to the democratic cause, there are darker hints of the irresistible effects of power on those who wield it. Newly crowned emperor, Alexis asks himself: 'What subtle potency lies in this gaudy bauble, the crown, that makes one feel like a god when one wears it?'[36] The noble young hero of melodrama reveals his feet of clay; his republican enthusiasms melt away before the superior attractions of power. Constitutional monarchy thus appears a less than ideal solution in view of the corrupting effects of power and the inevitable human failings of even the best-intentioned monarch.

The character of Prince Paul shows Wilde to be more cleverly in control of his material than at first appears. The melodramatic

---

[33] Ibid. II. 175.   [34] Ibid. 195.

[35] Ibid. III. 220. Wilde makes the same point in 'The Soul of Man', where he comments on the corrupting effects of benevolent government, and observes that the worst slave owners were those who perpetuated the system by being kind to their slaves (pp. 292, 301). The same theory is also put forward by George Bernard Shaw in *The Apple Cart* (completed Dec. 1928; 1st pub. in English, 1930).

[36] *Vera* (1908), IV. 249.

rhetoric which fills so much of the play is not simply the result
of heavy-handed amateurish writing; Wilde is already capable
of using it to more subtly self-conscious effect. When Alexis
again declares himself an idealistic revolutionary, Prince Paul
undercuts his rhetoric with a cooler note of realism:

[CZAREVITCH *gives up sword*; PRINCE PAUL *places it on the table.*]
CZAREVITCH. You will find it unstained by blood.
PRINCE PAUL. Foolish boy! you are not made for a conspirator; you
    have not learned to hold your tongue. Heroics are out of place in
    a palace.[37]

The mocking commentary of the older man reveals the verbal
posturing of the Czarevitch as dubious coinage. Prince Paul's ironic
humour deflates Alexis's more extravagant pronouncements:

CZAREVITCH. The star of freedom is risen already, and far off I hear
    the mighty wave Democracy break on these cursed shores.
PRINCE PAUL [*to* PRINCE PETROVITCH]. In that case you and I must
    learn how to swim.[38]

Prince Paul's detached wit hints at a more complex pattern of
motives and results, and cracks the smooth surface of the
melodrama.

    Prince Paul, exiled by the new Czar, joins the nihilists, and
provides a similar ironic commentary on their revolutionary
activities. His sarcastic interpolations mock their solemn catechism, emphasizing the gulf between theory and practice. The
cynical diplomatist echoes Wilde in his distaste for the conspirators' celebration of the dignity of work:

PRINCE PAUL [*reading*]. 'Nature is not a temple, but a workshop: we
    demand the right to labour.' Ah, I shall surrender my own rights
    in that respect.[39]

[37] *Vera* (1908), II. 203.
[38] Ibid. 204. Wilde himself used the same extravagant rhetoric in 1882, when he
wrote in the visitor's book in the hotel at Niagara: 'The roar of these waters is like
the roar when the mighty wave of democracy breaks on shores where kings lie
couched in ease.' He did, however, undercut this extravagance later, when he
commented: 'Every American bride is taken there, and the sight of the stupendous
waterfall must be one of the earliest, if not the keenest, disappointments in American married life.' Quoted in Hyde, *Oscar Wilde*, 80.
[39] *Vera* (1908), III. 215. Cf. 'The Soul of Man', 302–3: 'There is nothing dignified about manual labour at all, and most of it is absolutely degrading...'.

The very fact that Prince Paul is welcomed by the conspirators upsets the simple dichotomy between the government and its opponents which the bare plot of *Vera* seems to assert. Czar and nihilists are drawn together as both find a use for the ruthless and opportunist politician; Prince Paul is a tool that both sides are willing to employ.

Much of the writing of *Vera* may be melodramatic, but the play also contains some delicate touches of humour and irony. The nihilists' long speeches on liberty, which so tired reviewers, are set against self-assuredly extreme statements; their complacency leaves them open to mocking sarcasm. The Professor, for example, declares that the subject of his pamphlet is 'assassination considered as a method of political reform', and thereby brings the entire terrorist philosophy into question in the neat enormity of the phrase.[40] *Vera* does not simply present a straightforward battle of good versus evil, assassination versus reform, tyranny versus democracy. The pattern is more complex, for the dramatic conflicts are underlaid by a more realistic portrayal of the corrupting effects of power and the compromises necessary to secure it. Even Alexis's moment of poetic justice, banishing his father's corrupt advisers and turning their own words against them, is undercut by Baron Raff's observation: 'You remind us wonderfully, Sire, of your Imperial father.'[41]

Interestingly Wilde has Prince Paul voice a political creed which presents a brutal version of his own rather confused views, as expressed in his early poems:

> In these modern days to be vulgar, illiterate, common and vicious, seems to give a man a marvellous infinity of rights that his honest fathers never dreamed of. Believe me, Prince, in good democracy, every man should be an aristocrat.[42]

Vera displays the corrupting influence of power itself, demonstrating the drawbacks of any form of government, whether autocratic or democratic. In this context Prince Paul's creed is not just that of a cardboard villain; a 'democracy of aristocrats' is a fair description of the utopian anarchy advocated in 'The Soul of Man Under Socialism'.

---

[40] *Vera* (1908), I. 144.   [41] Ibid. IV. 246.
[42] Ibid. II. 182. Cf. e.g. 'Sonnet to Liberty' and 'Libertatis Sacra Fames'.

The subject and setting of Wilde's *Vera* were not unusual. Russian plays were common in the 1870s and 1880s, and it was not until 1890 that the fashion waned and a reviewer wrote that 'Plays dealing with Russian life seem, however, somewhat at a discount just now'.[43] Indeed, Marie Prescott ran into trouble in America when an obscure writer, Frank P. Hulette, challenged her right to present Wilde's play, declaring that he himself held the copyright to 'the play "Vera" a Russo-Parisian society drama in five acts' of which he was the author.[44] The plethora of plays set in Russia suggests that Wilde may have selected his subject precisely because of its popularity. Certainly Wilde's play shares a large number of stock elements with other contemporary Russian plays. *The Russian Bride* (1874), *Russia* (1877), *Fédora* (1882), *Mardo, or the Nihilists of St Petersburg* (1883), *The Red Lamp* (1887), *Vera* (1890) and *The Nihilist* (1897) all contain, in different combinations, references to the secret police, nihilists, Siberia and the salt mines, conspiracy and assassination, and to the cruel and arbitrary autocracy of the tsar.[45] Though *Vera; or, The Nihilists* contains all the stock elements of the popular drama, it differs markedly from other 'Russian' plays, presenting similar subject matter in a very different form.

The extremely unsympathetic portrayal of the nihilist movement in other contemporary plays makes clear the need for Wilde's prologue to *Vera*. The meeting of nihilist conspirators with which Wilde opens the first act, for example, was also used to dramatic effect in H. B. Farnie and R. Reece's drama, *Russia*.[46] The hero, a loyal subject of the tsar, is tricked into entering a room where nihilists have gathered. He no sooner

[43] Review of *Vera* by M. Ellis Smith, *St James's Gazette*, 21 (2 July 1890), 7. Beyond the title and references to secret police and Siberia, this play has little in common with Wilde's *Vera*, though it is mistakenly entered in E. H. Mikhail's *Oscar Wilde: An Annotated Bibliography of Criticism* (London: Macmillan, 1978).

[44] Letter to the managers of the Union Square Theatre, New York, from Frank P. Hulette (19 Apr. 1883), repr. in Mason, *Bibliography of Oscar Wilde*, 269.

[45] C. H. Hazlewood, *The Russian Bride* (1874), 1st perf. Britannia Theatre, 9 Mar. 1873 (BL LCP Add. MS 53153E); *Mardo, or the Nihilists of St Petersburg* (1883), 1st perf. Queen's Theatre, Manchester (BL LCP Add. MS 53298G); M. Ellis Smith, *Vera* (1890), 1st perf. Globe Theatre (BL LCP Add. MS 53454). For details of other plays see below.

[46] Farnie and Reece, *Russia* (1877), 1st perf. Queen's Theatre, London, 27 Oct. 1877 (BL LCP Add. MS 53193B).

crosses the threshold and sees the sinister assembly than he cries 'Treason!', in spite of which he is shipped off to Siberia by the secret police who enter moments later. The nihilists are used here simply as a plot device and as an excuse for a dramatic tableau. Their organization is one of dupes, for it is clear from the beginning that the meeting has been convened at the instigation of an *agent provocateur*. After some colourful business with a pack of cards, similar to Wilde's exchange of passwords and oaths, *Russia*'s nihilists are allowed one set speech to profess their beliefs, but the speech is a deliberate collection of contradictions and paradoxes. Their rhetoric reflects the misguided nature of their cause:

> I say, we are not mere conspirators: we claim to be the liberators of sixty millions of souls groaning beneath the yoke of deliberate despotism ... If we conspire, it is to do away with conspiracies; if we are secret, it is to establish frankness; if we are armed, it is to exact that peace which alone can prevail when men are free.[47]

In Tristram Outram's *The Red Lamp* the nihilist conspirators are similarly melodramatic villains.[48] Outram's heroine, Princess Claudia, a sworn enemy of all nihilists, finds that her brother, Alexis, is a member of their circle. The Princess is forced to defend the conspirators from the police in order to save her brother's life. Alexis is allowed a couple of short speeches on the importance of liberty early in the play, but these are offset by the Princess's impassioned defence of the regime and its methods:

> This Nihilism ... on which sentimental foreigners lavish ignorant sympathy, is a sore which neglect has allowed to grow dangerous. It has poisoned Russia to the core, and unless it is mercilessly extirpated with knife and fire, will become the cancer which will one day destroy the Country—if you knew what I know of them you wouldn't pale at the sight of a midnight arrest or speak in terms of pity of a society of assassins.[49]

The Princess's dislike of nihilism is validated when the leader of the nihilist cell, Ivan Zazzulic, betrays his companions for

---

[47] Ibid. I. iii. 14.
[48] *The Red Lamp* (1887), 1st perf. Comedy Theatre, London (BL LCP Add. MS 53377B).
[49] Ibid. I. 18.

money.[50] The climax of the play has Alexis stabbing the evil Ivan and being stabbed by him in turn. The curtain comes down as the Princess destroys the evidence of her brother's guilt and declares that he died for Russia.

The only vaguely sympathetic portrayal of nihilism to be found among these plays is contained in the highly melodramatic play *The Nihilist*, by E. J. Towers.[51] In this play a number of worthy characters declare themselves nihilists in reaction to the dastardly behaviour of Alexander, the Czarevitch. Alexander has married a virtuous, low-born maiden, but regrets his decision and abandons his wife and child. The spurned wife pursues her husband (whose true identity she does not know) accompanied by her ageing father and unrequited childhood sweetheart. Alexander proves his villainy by committing bigamy with a rich princess, and using all his power to dispose of his embarrassing first wife and their young daughter. Having been made tsar, he dispatches them to the salt mines in Siberia, and holds a knife against his daughter's throat in order to force her mother to deny their marriage to his jealous second wife. The second wife, Princess Olga, is presented as a fierce, cruel, and passionate woman, a staunch supporter of the old order, who declares:

> We are aristocrats not philanthropists . . . let all levellers and Nihilists die in their thousands in Siberia. Liberty, Equality and Fraternity can never hold sway in Russia which shall remain to the end of the world a nation of princes and serfs.[52]

The finale proves her prediction sound: the tsar is revealed in all his corruption and is shot; Princess Olga learns the truth and declares the first wife and her companions free; the honest nihilists thereupon abandon their cause. The curtain descends as the former rebels kneel at her feet, declaring themselves 'no longer Nihilists but true and loyal subjects of the Czar'.[53]

---

[50] The kinship between Ivan's name and that of the young assassin, Vera Zassoulich, may indicate that Outram intended his despicable assassin to be a deliberate reply to the popular acclaim which had greeted the female rebel. The numerous different English approximations of Vera's surname included Sassulitch, Zasulich, Zassulic, and Zazzulic.

[51] Towers, *The Nihilist, or Wed Yet No Wife* (1897), 1st perf. Castle Abertillery, 25 Feb. 1897 (BL LCP Add. MS 53624B).

[52] Ibid., Act III.   [53] Ibid., Act IV.

In most of these plays nihilism is synonymous with guilt. Entirely characteristic is the statement of the reformed hero of *The English Nihilist*, who explains that he left their cause because 'assassination was the chief item of the Nihilist creed'.[54] Compared with this stereotypical presentation of nihilism, Wilde's portrayal seems almost revolutionary. The nihilists in *Vera* may appear over-zealous or misguided, but their motives are immaculate despite their questionable methods. The hinted similarities between Alexis and his father, the suggestion that even if he fulfils his promise to become a benevolent dictator then his kindness will only serve to end all hopes of a true democracy, all these combine to validate the nihilists' distrust of all rulers. Wilde's presentation of Russian nihilism certainly failed to appeal to contemporary American reviewers, most of whom dismissed the conspirators' speeches on justice and freedom as tedious ranting. One energetic reviewer devoted several columns to criticizing Wilde for the play's politics, calling nihilists 'merciless despots', and declaring that, 'The Nihilist, as we know him today, is an enemy of social order.'[55]

Wilde not only presented his nihilists as idealistic and courageous people but, even more unusually, made their leader a woman. Great emphasis is laid on the heroism of Vera, when the General narrates how he would once have caught her had she not shot his horse from under him as he pursued her.[56] All the nihilists describe Vera as the guiding light of their movement, and she delivers some of the most stirring speeches on liberty and justice. No other 'Russian' play even includes a woman among its conspirators. The limits of female intrigue are those of Farnie and Reece's *Russia*, where Tatiana, the flighty wife of the hero, explains that a certain Madame Dugarey,

> has constituted herself President of a secret Ladies' Club; at the private meetings of which instruction in the Parisian art of enlivening a ballroom is to be imparted by herself: all the young and pretty women are conspirators, and the object is—the downfall of Russian dullness at dinner parties![57]

[54] G. Daventry, *The English Nihilist*, 1st perf. Variety Theatre, Apr. 1887 (BL LCP Add. MS 53377B).
[55] *New York Times* (21 Aug. 1883), 4. [56] *Vera* (1908), I. 168.
[57] *Russia*, I. i. 2.

In his Russo-Parisian drama, *Fédora*, Victorien Sardou does admit
the existence of female revolutionaries, but their commitment
is presented only as a tantalizing sexual *frisson*; as one character
observes of the widespread nihilist presence at certain parties:

> Ou bien vous valsez avec une adorable jeune fille blonde, vaporeuse,
> exquise. Tandis qu'elle s'abandonne dans vos bras, les yeux au ciel,
> vous pensez: 'A quoi rêve cet ange?' Et c'est à faire sauter un
> train![58]

> [Or indeed, you are waltzing with an adorable young woman—
> blonde, dreamy, delightful. While she abandons herself in your
> arms, her eyes gazing to heaven, you think, 'What is this angel
> dreaming of?' And it's of blowing up a train!]

Wilde's portrayal of a woman as the head of a nihilist cell was
not only radical, it was also realistic. Nikolai Chernyshevsky's
What Is To Be Done? records the vital involvement of women
in the Russian revolutionary movement, and even British newspapers recognized the equal participation of men and women
in the struggle against Russian tyranny.[59]

How seriously Wilde regarded *Vera* is evident from the trouble
he took revising the play. There are three different editions of
Vera: the first, privately printed, 1880 edition; the second, 1882,
edition, with a number of revisions including the addition of a
prologue; and the 1908 edition, based on Wilde's own corrections to the 1882 edition.[60] There also exist an early manuscript
version, a notebook containing a fragment of a first manuscript
draft, and twenty-eight quarto leaves of handmade paper with
writing in Wilde's hand, which appear to be corrections for the
American production.[61] In addition to these a modern scholar,

[58] Victorien Sardou, *Fédora*, 1st perf. Théâtre du Vaudeville, Paris, 12 Dec.
1882. Published in *Théâtre Complet*, i (Paris: Albin Michel, 1934), II. i. 423.
[59] See e.g. 'Contemporary Life and Thought in Russia'.
[60] *Vera; or, The Nihilists. A Drama in Four Acts by Oscar Wilde* (London:
Ranken & Co., 1880). A copy of this edn., which Wilde presented to Ellen Terry,
is housed in the Ellen Terry Museum, Smallhythe Place, Tenterden, Kent (For
Wilde's letter accompanying this copy see *Letters*, 70). *Vera; or, The Nihilists. A
Drama in a Prologue and Four Acts by Oscar Wilde* (USA: privately printed,
1882). These edns. are cited below as *Vera* (1880) and *Vera* (1882) respectively.
Numbers refer to act and page.
[61] The MS version of *Vera* is housed in the William Andrews Clark Memorial
Library, California. For further details see *Oscar Wilde and His Circle: Catalog of*

Frances Miriam Reed, has published *Oscar Wilde's 'Vera; or, The Nihilist'* (1989), a recreation of the play as performed in New York in 1883.[62] Her main material is the twenty-eight quarto leaves of Wilde's corrections; alterations listed in a pirated American edition published by Smithers in 1903; and Wilde's autograph alterations to the 1882 edition.

A clear pattern emerges from a comparison of the different versions of *Vera*. The changes between the 1880 and 1882 editions of the play and Wilde's autograph corrections to the latter edition show a careful progress towards a politically and dramatically more complex play which is simultaneously more radical in its implications. The changes made on Marie Prescott's advice for the 1883 performance, however, work in the opposite direction, suggesting a tension between Wilde's own intentions and the demands of the popular stage.[63] In 1883 the young writer willingly compromised his creation to secure an audience; in later years he was to develop more subtle methods in order to satisfy both his own tastes and those of the public.

One marked difference between the two early editions and the final 1908 version is that the earlier editions place the action of the play in 1800. The 1882 edition also includes a prologue set in 1795.[64] In his autograph corrections to the 1882 edition Wilde deleted all reference to the year the play is set in, and the 1908 edition therefore does not specify the date.

Manuscripts and Letters in the William Andrews Clark Memorial Library, compiled by John Charles Finzi (California, 1957). The notebook containing twenty-nine pages of a fragment of the first draft, written in pencil, is housed in the Beinecke Library, Yale. The twenty-eight quarto leaves in Wilde's hand are printed in Mason, *Bibliography of Oscar Wilde*, 274–81, which also prints the correspondence between Marie Prescott and Wilde regarding production details of *Vera*.

[62] *Oscar Wilde's 'Vera; or, The Nihilist'*, ed. Reed.

[63] The revisions made on Prescott's advice for the 1883 perf. in many places contradict Wilde's intentions as revealed in his previous revisions of the play, discussed below. For this reason, I have concluded that Wilde to some degree compromised his designs in order to secure a public performance of his work. I have therefore taken the 1908 edn. of *Vera* to represent most closely Wilde's final intentions.

[64] Stuart Mason incorrectly reports in his *Bibliography of Oscar Wilde*, 252, that the 1880 edn. places the action in the present day, and that the dating is altered to 1800 in the next edn. In fact both edns. place the action in 1800. Kohl, *Oscar Wilde*, 35, 38–40, repeats this mistake, writing at length on the incomprehensibility of Wilde's anachronistically redating the play from the present to the past.

Wilde's placing of the play at the beginning of the century
rather than in contemporary Russia is hard to understand. The
dating is clearly quite deliberate, for other details in the play
reinforce the first stage direction, 'Scene, Moscow. Time, 1800.'[65]
So, for example, the conspirators announce that it is 'Since the
Revolution of France, the ninth year', and refer to the newly
established Republic in France.[66] Yet the placing of the action
at the beginning of the nineteenth century results in gross historical inaccuracies elsewhere in the play. The very idea of
secret police in Moscow is anachronistic, as the first modern
political police were created by Nicholas I in 1826. Similarly,
when Alexis tells the corrupt ministers, 'If you value your lives
you will catch the first train for Paris', he is condemning them
to a long wait, since the first passenger train did not run until
1830, and then between Liverpool and Manchester.[67] Indeed,
the very term 'nihilist' was only introduced in 1861 by Turgenev
in his novel *Fathers and Sons*. The issue of political terrorism,
which lies at the heart of *Vera*, was also irrelevant to Russia at
the beginning of the nineteenth century, for the nihilists' espousal
of the dagger as their method of reform reflects a state of
affairs only relevant to a more modern Russia.[68]

Such huge inaccuracies make it clear that the date of 1800
was arbitrarily attached to a play set in contemporary Russia.
As soon as the play is moved forward to 1880, it is not Wilde's
ignorance of Russian history that is revealed but his obvious
familiarity with contemporary details. Wilde was well enough
informed on the situation in Russia to include references to
starvation and poverty, afflictions which beset the newly freed
serfs, deprived of the minimal protection of the old economic
system. Vera's lament, 'What is there of awful majesty in these
men which makes the hand unsteady, the dagger treacherous,
the pistol-shot harmless?', was especially pertinent considering
the number of unsuccessful assassination attempts that took
place in the late nineteenth century, including in 1879 an

[65] *Vera* (1880), I. 2; *Vera* (1882), I. 12.

[66] *Vera* (1880), I. 3 and 6.   [67] Ibid. IV. 46.

[68] Adam Ulam, *Russia's Failed Revolutions: From the Decembrists to the Dissidents* (London: Weidenfeld & Nicolson, 1981), dates political terrorism from the
foundation of the Land and Freedom group in 1876–7, adding: 'For all the isolated
incidents in the past . . . Russia's politics had hitherto, and remarkably so in an
autocracy, been free of terrorism' (p. 126).

attempted shooting of the tsar by Alexander Solovyov, who fired at the emperor five times and only succeeded in making a hole in his greatcoat.[69]

This combination of precise contemporary detail and gross anachronism suggests that Wilde wrote a play on modern Russian revolutionaries, displaying unfashionable sympathy with their cause, and then attempted to cover his tracks by dating the play back to the beginning of the century. If set safely in the past, *Vera* could not be regarded as dangerously revolutionary or subversive. As a commentary on contemporary Russia, Wilde's failure to present the nihilists as villainous, brutal, and corrupt assassins would make the play a remarkable apology for regicide. The fact that the London performance was indefinitely postponed in 1881 after the assassination of Alexander II suggests that even as a supposedly historical melodrama *Vera* was too hot for a respectable West End theatre to handle. Wilde's anachronistic setting of the action in 1800 suggests a rather naïve and muddled attempt to disguise the more subversive aspects of his play.

The other significant difference between the 1880 edition and its successors was the addition of the prologue. As shown above, the prologue provides Wilde's most explicit challenge to the conventional image of the nihilist as villain and sets the scene for a far more sympathetic portrayal of Russia's revolutionaries. The 1880 edition also presents the conspirators as considerably more bloodthirsty and ruthless than in the final version. So, in the first edition, when the President of the Nihilists tells Vera that Prince Paul may be useful to them, she asks what they will do with him afterwards. The President's reply is concise: 'Strangle him.'[70] This contrasts strongly with Vera's declaration in the final version that 'we have given him our word: he is safer here than ever he was in his palace'.[71]

This alteration is characteristic. The earlier edition is significantly more conventional than the later editions: Prince Paul is more despicable, the conspirators more bloodthirsty, and Alexis more heroic. In the 1880 edition Prince Paul appears as a more

---

[69] *Vera* (1908), I. 150. See also Hingley, *Nihilists*. Between late 1879 and early 1880 the 'People's Will' also made six unsuccessful attempts on the tsar's life, succeeding only in destroying a consignment of jam for his estates.
[70] *Vera* (1880), III. 34.   [71] *Vera* (1908), III. 42.

traditional theatrical villain, delivering heavy-handed threats to his less powerful colleagues:

PRINCE PAUL [*to* COUNT ROUVALOFF]. By the bye, Count, are you going to let me have those two black horses of yours for twenty thousand roubles: You remember my speaking to you about them?

COUNT ROUVALOFF. I assure you, Prince Paul, I don't want to sell them, I intend racing in the spring.

PRINCE PAUL. Ah! in the spring? [*After a pause*] I think if I were you, Count, I should sell them.[72]

Similarly, Alexis's character is made less sympathetic, becoming more arrogant and autocratic in later drafts. In an early manuscript draft of the play, when the young Czarevitch attempts to remove General Kotemkin from the conspirators' gathering he uses gentle persuasion and flattery, declaring that the General hardly looks his age and remarking how well a field marshal's uniform would suit him.[73] This exchange did not appear in any of the published editions, and Wilde's corrections to the 1882 edition remove any hint of Alexis's friendly complicity with the General; even the line 'I shall rely on you' is cut, leaving only the bare, arrogant order of the final version.[74]

By contrast, the changes which Wilde made on Marie Prescott's advice for her American production of *Vera* had the effect of rendering the play more traditionally romantic and conventional. The play was advertised not as *Vera; or, The Nihilists* but as *Vera; or, The Nihilist*: a small but significant difference which reflected the shift of interest from revolutionary politics to the more personal struggle of Vera herself, with nihilism providing little more than a backdrop.[75] A young child is added to the prologue in order that Vera may display a more charming and playful aspect to her character, and her relationship with her childhood sweetheart, Michael, is fleshed out into a comic game of flirtation and pursuit.[76] The joyful frivolity of

[72] *Vera* (1880), II. 18.

[73] MS notebook, containing fragment of first draft of *Vera*, Beinecke Library, Yale.

[74] *Vera* (1882), I. 25.

[75] See advertisements for play in the *World* (20 Aug. 1883), 7; *New York Times* (20 Aug. 1883), 7; *New York Daily Tribune* (20 Aug. 1883), 7.

[76] *Oscar Wilde's 'Vera; or, The Nihilist'*, ed. Reed, I. 6–11. For Marie Prescott's suggestions for Wilde to 'brighten Vera's character', see their correspondence printed in Mason, *Bibliography of Oscar Wilde*, 258–70.

these episodes is then brought into opposition with the terrible, inhuman world of the nihilists: in the 1882 version, knowledge of her brother's suffering immediately fires Vera with a passion for justice and revenge; in the performed version, however, Vera is horrified by the ruthless oath of allegiance that her brother urges her to swear, and is only finally persuaded by his violent persistence:

DMITRI. What! when they have tortured me! Ay, tortured me, beaten me like a dog on the roadside, branded me like a common thief; when they are bringing me away to starve in the dungeon, to rot in the mine, when—
VERA. Enough, enough! I'll take the oath.
DMITRI. You swear it?
VERA. I swear it.[77]

Little attempt is made to align the audience's sympathies with the nihilists in this version. Michael, the peasant boy turned regicide, is presented as fanatical and unbalanced to the extent that even his colleagues urge him to be calm.[78] Vera is also removed from her position as leader of the nihilists, all the lines which refer to her as 'the star of freedom' or the 'priestess' of liberty being cut.[79] The nihilists thus appear considerably more misguided and violent than in previous versions, for not only is Vera further distanced from their activities, but the Czarevitch is also presented as a far more sympathetic character. Vera's doubts as to Alexis's commitment to their cause are excised, as are the hints that Alexis may have inherited more from his father than just his crown.[80] In *Vera; or, The Nihilist* constitutional monarchy is the ideal solution.

In describing his treasured drama Wilde consistently laid emphasis on the passion for liberty displayed in it. To Clara Morris he declared that 'democracy is the note through which the play is expressed', though he was careful to add that 'the tragedy is an entirely human one'.[81] Similarly, Constance Lloyd timidly repeated to her brother what her fiancé had told her about his new play: 'Oscar says he wrote it to show that an abstract idea such as liberty could have quite as much power and be quite

---

[77] *Oscar Wilde's 'Vera; or, the Nihilist'*, ed. Reed, I. 12–13.
[78] Ibid. II. 21.   [79] Ibid. 19, 23, 24.   [80] Ibid. IV. 58, V. 69.
[81] To Clara Morris (*c*.Sept. 1880), *Letters*, 71.

as fine as the passion of love (or something of that sort).'[82] Constance's rather tentative comments are born out by Wilde's own statements. The tension between passion and the abstract love of liberty, hinted at by Constance, is set forth clearly by Wilde in an interview with the *World* in New York. As he explained to the reporter:

'Heretofore the passion portrayed in the drama has been altogether personal, like the love of a man for a woman, or a woman for a man. I have tried to show the passion for liberty. For this purpose I have chosen the extreme expression of liberty, the Nihilism of Russia...

'The prevailing idea is a conflict between liberty and love.'

'Which passion triumphs?'

'That's my fifth act', replied the aesthete smiling again.[83]

In Wilde's fifth act love wins over liberty. Vera abandons her oath and kills herself, leaving Alexis to enjoy the imperial crown. Wilde's description of Vera's struggle as one of liberty versus love implies that the final act is not simply a question of whether Vera murders her lover or spares him, but a more complex battle between passion and politics. By declaring that the conflict in the final act is between liberty and love, Wilde implies that Vera's mission to kill the Czar is not just 'assassination' or 'murder' but a political act, and a justifiable one at that. In this context Vera's passion for Alexis may be presented as a temptation rather than as the saving strength of humane emotion holding her back from a bloody deed. Wilde's presentation of a political conspiracy thus becomes subtly even more radical in the final act, rather than simply lapsing into melodramatic and romantic tragedy, as at first appears.

In the 1908 version of *Vera* the conflict between liberty and love is foreshadowed in the first act, where Vera muses to herself: 'Why does he make me feel at times as if I would have him as my king, Republican though I be?'[84] In the third act, her desire to save Alexis from the nihilists leads her to abandon her principles so far as to declare that 'The people are not yet fit for a republic in Russia.'[85] Michael hardens her resolve by reminding her that her brother was condemned under the

[82] From Constance Lloyd to Otho Holland Lloyd (23 Nov. 1883), *Letters*, 153.
[83] The *World* (New York; 12 Aug. 1883), 5.   [84] *Vera* (1908), I. 157.
[85] Ibid. III. 227.

tyrannical system they seek to destroy, and, like a self-indulgently loquacious Lady Macbeth, Vera steels herself to the deed once more.

The final act, as Wilde observed, is where the conflict between love and liberty becomes most powerful. Prince Paul's cynical judgement on the transient nature of Alexis's democratic enthusiasms is proved true as the new Czar muses on the terrible potency of the crown. Vera has already shown love to be a suspiciously undemocratic sentiment, and Alexis goes further by casting away all talk of democracy as he revels in the romantic potential of his new-found power:

> O God, you think I am a traitor, a liar, a king? I am, for love of you. Vera, it was for you I broke my oath and wear my father's crown. I would lay at your feet this mighty Russia, which you and I have loved so well; would give you this earth as your footstool; set this crown on your head. The people will love us. We will rule them by love, as a father rules his children. . . . It is men's custom in Russia to bring gifts to those they love. I said, I will bring to the woman I love a people, an empire, a world![86]

Alexis's revolutionary convictions are thus revealed to be little more than skin-deep; he accepts his place in the dynastic line and offers to crown Vera as empress 'in that great cathedral which my fathers built'.[87] Vera, however, shows that her beliefs and principles are more profoundly held, for, in spite of the fact that this is the first time Alexis has openly confessed his love for her, she 'loosens her hands violently from him, and starts up', declaring that, 'I am a Nihilist! I cannot wear a crown!'[88] Whereupon Alexis executes a perfect about-turn and offers the mirror image of his previous speech:

> I am no king now. I am only a boy who has loved you better than his honour, better than his oath. For love of the people I would have been a patriot. For love of you I have been a traitor. Let us go forth together, we will live amongst the common people.[89]

In Alexis's case there is little conflict between love and liberty, for love is not simply the stronger force, it is the only one. Alexis's enthusiasm for liberty is only an offshoot of his love for Vera. Vera, on the other hand, though she throws away the

---

[86] Ibid. 253–4.   [87] Ibid. 254.   [88] Ibid. 255.   [89] Ibid.

dagger and enters into a love duet with the Czar, at least has the self-awareness to know that she is betraying her beliefs.

That Wilde should allow even these faint hints that Vera's failure to assassinate her lover might be the result of weakness rather than strength is remarkable, especially as it directly contradicts the dramatic tradition it is written in. The love duet between Vera and Alexis which is interrupted by the cries of the nihilists outside is an obvious echo of Act III, Scene v of *Romeo and Juliet*, a play in which the power of love is set against a bloody cause, but a cause without nobility, a feud without principle or rationale against which the lovers represent life and hope. That Wilde should equate assassination with liberty and set it in the balance with love was highly unusual in dramatic terms.

As Wilde observed, the passions displayed in the theatre were as a rule personal rather than abstract. Vera is remarkable in being so strongly motivated by political and ethical convictions. Far more conventional was Victorien Sardou's treatment of a very similar conflict, and the success of Sardou's *Fédora* attests to the audience's preference for passion over politics. Sardou's heroine, Fédora, sees her fiancé assassinated and swears to avenge his death. The chief suspect is Loris Ipanoff, a man believed to be a nihilist. Fédora pursues him to Paris, where she watches him closely for any evidence of guilt. Ipanoff, however, falls in love with Fédora and she, to her confusion, finds herself loving him in return. His confession of love, however, is somewhat marred by his simultaneous confession to having shot Fédora's former fiancé, Vladimir. In vengeful fury, Fédora denounces Ipanoff to the Russian police and arranges for his kidnapping and extradition. No sooner has she done this than Ipanoff completes his story by explaining that he shot his victim not for any abstract political reasons but because Vladimir was having an affair with his wife. Fédora immediately repents her rash action in having condemned this obviously noble man, and takes poison to prove her contrition, expiring in the bewildered Ipanoff's arms. The implication of Sardou's play is that murder for political, ethical, or revolutionary motives is unforgivable, but murder motivated by jealous passion is perfectly understandable, even noble.

Marie Prescott was aware of the audience's preference for such conclusions, for among the changes that Wilde made to

Vera for the 1883 production were a number which strengthened the role of love in Vera's motivation and removed the
more subtle conflict between love and liberty which underlies
the final act. In the 1880 edition of the play, Wilde made Vera
reaffirm her determination to assassinate Alexis not because of
any abstract belief in the evil of monarchy but because Michael
has convinced her that Alexis planned to make her his mistress,
not his wife.[90] In the 1882 edition, Wilde revised this scene so
that Vera is motivated by the memory of her brother's fate,
thus merging personal emotion with abstract principle, for
Dmitri died a victim of the repressive regime she swore to
oppose. Marie Prescott clearly preferred personal passions to
abstract ones, and she emphasized this in her analysis of *Vera*,
as she wrote to Wilde: 'Then (there you show your genius Mr.
Wilde) you have the well balanced motive throughout that
through love everything begins and ends.'[91] The revisions that
Wilde made to the play for the New York performance confirm
Marie Prescott's interpretation. Vera is given a speech which
resolves the conflict between love and liberty; Alexis is presented
as a noble idealist who reaffirms his loyalty to the democratic
cause, while Vera speaks only of love:

> The past is already dead; 'tis but an empty dream from which my
> soul has awakened: now I know life's meaning and the secret of
> this life, and bent and broken on this wheel of love, bent back and
> broken on love's fiery wheel, what should I do but worship, and
> whom worship but your own self who art more dear to me than
> any thing on earth, who for my sake wouldst have stepped down
> from your high throne and given power and principality away for
> my poor love . . .[92]

These lines were Wilde's reply to Marie Prescott's request for
'a few lines that will express her loving amazement and tender
gratitude for Alexis sacrifice of his glorious power for her
love'.[93] The actress–manager knew that love, not politics, sold
tickets.

---

[90] *Vera* (1880), III. 40–1.
[91] Letter to Oscar Wilde (11 Feb. 1883), repr. in Mason, *Bibliography of Oscar Wilde*, 267.
[92] Mason, *Bibliography of Oscar Wilde*, 281. From the twenty-eight quarto leaves entirely in the autograph of the author, which appear to have been made for the performance of *Vera* in New York in 1883.
[93] Marie Prescott, letter to Wilde (9 Jan. 1883), ibid. 261.

The final 1908 version of *Vera; or, The Nihilists* is thus not the simple melodrama it has been judged to be. Wilde chose a popular theatrical form, the Russian play, for his first drama, but his treatment of its stock elements differed radically from that of his more conventional contemporaries. Wilde takes nihilist beliefs seriously, while at the same time demonstrating the complex political reality which renders their aspirations overly simplistic and ultimately redundant. Beneath *Vera*'s melodramatic surface lies a subtle and complex pattern of qualification and contradiction. Alexis is not the perfect hero he first appears and his allegiance to the ideals of democracy is too capricious to be depended upon. Yet, as Prince Paul observes, the next in line to Alexis is the Grand Duke, whose cruelty to animals and inability to keep his word would make him an excellent tsar according to the old tradition.

Yet all the subtleties of Wilde's play are lost, because their end result is confusion. No coherent subtext emerges, as too many contradictions of character and motive add up to a maze of hints below the highly theatrical surface. Wilde himself is too unsure of where his loyalties lie and what his own convictions are, and as a result *Vera* is too full of qualifications to achieve any real impact.

Nevertheless *Vera* is filled with many delicate theatrical touches, perhaps too delicate to be perceived by even the most discerning audience. Vera's last line, 'I have saved Russia!' sounds like the ultimate melodramatic ending; but it is more subtle and ambiguous than is at first apparent. As the last act reveals, Alexis's nihilist convictions are utterly dependent on Vera's influence. So with Vera dead, what chance is there of Alexis following in his father's footsteps, as Prince Paul and the other nobles predict? Vera's cry that she has saved Russia by preserving its future tsar may be tainted with a subtle and deliberate tinge of irony.

3

Lady Windermere's Fan

> The originality, I mean, which we ask from the artist, is
> originality of treatment, not of subject. It is only the
> unimaginative who ever invents. The true artist is known
> by the use he makes of what he annexes, and he annexes
> everything.[1]

ACCORDING to Wilde's theories of art, the genius of the artist
lies not in invention but in adaptation. The critic is therefore
the supreme artist, superior to the original creator; the critic
refashions the works of others, using them as raw material for
his own creative imagination. In writing *Lady Windermere's
Fan* (1892), Wilde was therefore both creator and critic. For
his first successful play Wilde appropriated the plots and conventions of numerous popular contemporary dramas, reshap-
ing and subverting their material to criticize the social principles
on which they were founded. *Lady Windermere's Fan* won
acclaim as a conventionally sentimental drama of society manners, remarkable only for its epigrammatic wit. Beneath the
surface of the play, however, Wilde had subtly remoulded the
substance of French boulevard theatre; he had taken the established cast of protective male, innocent female, and scheming
fallen woman and reversed the moral values traditionally associated with them.

Lady Windermere's Fan was a highly popular and successful
play: Wilde made £7,000 from it in 1892 alone.[2] It was produced at the St James's Theatre by George Alexander, a guarantee in itself of the play's respectability, conventionality, and

[1] Oscar Wilde, review of *Olivia* at the Lyceum, *Dramatic Review*, 1/17 (30 May
1885), 278.
[2] This was the result of a wise decision on Wilde's part. Alexander offered to
buy the play outright for £1,000, but, impressed by his offer, Wilde replied: 'A
thousand pounds! I have so much confidence in your excellent judgement, my dear
Alec, that I cannot refuse your generous offer—I will take a percentage.' George
Alexander, quoted in *Evening Standard*, 29 Nov. 1913; quoted in Ellmann, *Oscar
Wilde*, 315.

commercial success. Notably Hesketh Pearson summed up Alexander's carefully judged policy as a manager:

He produced plays that were correctly risky, and they became the talk of a social world that was correctly risky...

His dramas were triumphs of monetary speculation: they were quite innocent of mental speculation. Pinero was his god; Wilde was his rather uncertain archangel.[3]

It is easy to see how *Lady Windermere's Fan* fitted into this category, for its basic plot is reassuringly familiar and conventional. It is the tale of a young wife who, suspecting her husband of adultery, almost abandons her home and her child, but is brought to see the error of her ways and is restored to her proper place, chastened by a better understanding of her maternal duty. At the same time, it presents the return of a delinquent mother, who finally fulfils her maternal role by sacrificing herself for her child. The plot is that of a sentimental melodrama complete with moral: the duty of a mother to her child, as preached by Mrs Erlynne to her own abandoned daughter. To soften this stern message the play preaches a lesson on Christian charity. Lady Windermere is made aware of her own fallibility, and is thereby brought to look more kindly on the sins of others. She begins the play as a moral absolutist, believing that life must be lived by 'hard and fast rules', passing a life sentence on those who err.[4] She ends the play having learnt that judgement must be tempered by charity, for even the strictly virtuous like herself have a hidden capacity for sin. Lady Windermere has learnt to pity and forgive the poor sinner, to understand the weakness in others by recognizing the weakness in herself.

In addition to this moderate and orthodox morality, *Lady Windermere's Fan* criticizes the society it portrays. Lord and Lady Windermere are isolated in their idealism and virtue amidst a gallery of cynics and pragmatists. As the Duchess of Berwick manœuvres to secure the wealthy Mr Hopper for a son-in-law,

---

[3] Pearson, *Modern Men and Mummers* (London: George Allen & Unwin, 1921), 80–1.

[4] *Lady Windermere's Fan: A Play about a Good Woman* (London: Elkin Mathews & John Lane, 1893), I. 11. Cited below as *LWF*. References are to act and page number.

the society marriage is shown to be a mercenary affair. Lady Windermere is advised to accept infidelity as an inevitable part of marriage, and modern practicality is thereby shown to be little short of cynicism. This is a society in which, as the Duchess of Berwick observes, all men are bad and they reduce society to their level. She complains that: 'The most dreadful people seem to go everywhere. They certainly come to my parties—the men get furious if one doesn't ask them.'[5] But the moral tale has a happy ending. The Windermeres escape the corrupting influence of their environment: Lord Windermere does not become 'almost modern'; Lady Windermere does not sink to 'the same level as an age like this'.[6] There is nothing here which oversteps the mark of the 'correctly risky'.

The conservative critic Clement Scott, writing in the *Illustrated London News*, condemned Wilde's portrait of society as the quintessence of cynicism. But the anonymous critic of the *Daily News* defended the author from such a charge by suggesting a higher moral purpose in the play:

It will be said that all this is a perverse and debasing picture of life; but why should not the playwright be credited with a wholesome satirical object? Perhaps when society has seen itself in Mr. Wilde's looking-glass it may be disposed to mend what in its ways requires mending, and even to make a beginning in the matter of higher aims.[7]

Yet Wilde himself repudiated any such intention, not only denying any desire to reform society but disavowing the orthodox moral implications apparently contained within the play. On 26 May 1892 Wilde spoke at a meeting of the Royal General Theatrical Fund, with George Alexander in the chair. An alderman called Routledge had praised Wilde for calling a spade a

---

[5] Ibid. I. 13 and 20.

[6] Ibid. I. 7. Most modern critics have taken these to be the themes of the play. As Regenia Gagnier puts it: '*Lady Windermere's Fan* (1892) presented both a sentimental, moralised conclusion and exposed society's dominant, if self-deluded, materialism' (*Idylls of the Marketplace*, 117). Epifanio San Juan and Robert Keith Miller see it as a moral melodrama centring on Lady Windermere's education in moral duality: Miller, *Oscar Wilde* (New York: Ungar, 1982), 42–9; San Juan, *The Art of Oscar Wilde*, 139–54. Philip Cohen and Christopher Nassaar emphasize the same themes, while discussing the implied criticism of society's hypocrisy: *The Moral Vision of Oscar Wilde*, 181–92; *Into the Demon Universe*, 73–81.

[7] Clement Scott, *Illustrated London News*, 100 (27 Feb. 1892), 278; unsigned review, *Daily News* (22 Feb. 1892), 3.

spade and lashing vice in *Lady Windermere's Fan*, but Wilde rejected this interpretation of his work in favour of a disturbingly anarchic message:

I would like to protest against the statement that I have ever called a spade a spade. The man who did so should be condemned to use one. I have also been accused of lashing vice, but I can assure you that nothing was further from my intentions. Those who have seen *Lady Windermere's Fan* will see that if there is one particular doctrine contained in it, it is that of sheer individualism. It is not for anyone to censure what anyone else does, and everyone should go his own way, to whatever place he chooses, in exactly the way that he chooses.[8]

Individualism is the true doctrine of *Lady Windermere's Fan*, a doctrine subtly disguised by the surface melodrama of this work. Thus, Mrs Erlynne rejects the maternal role, preferring her freedom to the restrictive duties of a mother. She is not expelled at the end of the play as a dangerously corrupting influence, but turns her back on the narrow-minded and hypocritical confines of society, having won for herself a potentially happy marriage—the one prize conventionally denied to the fallen woman. In a dénouement of incomplete revelation, Mrs Erlynne is the only character with complete knowledge, and, beyond that, complete understanding. The fallen woman has a wit and wisdom which surpass that of the protective male and the innocent female. Lord Windermere must not know of his wife's weakness, or his love for her may die. Lady Windermere must not know of her mother's true identity, or her belief in truth and virtue may die. Mrs Erlynne alone has the breadth and strength of mind to know and accept all. Wilde thus reverses the traditional hierarchy of the fallen-woman play, challenging the moral values and social conventions on which it is based. *Lady Windermere's Fan* was subtitled *A Play about a Good Woman*, but, beneath the reassuring title, the play questions the meaning of the very terms 'good' and 'bad'.

Lady Windermere's Fan not only imitated the more conventional plays whose values it sought to undermine, it actually borrowed and transformed material from a number of other plays, which acted as 'sources' for Wilde's drama. Contemporary

---

[8] Royal General Theatrical Fund, report of speech 26 May 1892, quoted in Ellmann, *Oscar Wilde*, 347–8.

critics were quick to note Wilde's debt: A. B. Walkley, for example, noted in the *Speaker* that 'For the staleness of the incidents one has only to refer to half a dozen familiar French plays.'[9] The plays on which Wilde drew for the plot material of *Lady Windermere's Fan* have mostly fallen into obscurity, but they were familiar to contemporary critics and the links were obvious. Yet, rather than seeking to conceal his borrowings, Wilde seems to have presented the critics with a challenge to name as many sources as possible, a challenge to which they rose. The tale of a disgraced mother, believed dead, encountering her virtuous daughter was identified as deriving from *Odette* (1881) by Victorien Sardou.[10] The mother's fear that her former sin will be imitated by her daughter was traced to *Révoltée* (1889) by Jules Lemaître.[11] The structure of Wilde's first act was declared to be identical to that of *Francillon* (1887) by Alexandre Dumas *fils*, while the forced invitation of the mistress to the wife's private party was found in *L'Étrangère* (1876) by the same author.[12] Some of the theatrical links suggested by critics were tenuous and incidental. The discovery of Mrs Erlynne in Lord Darlington's rooms inevitably recalled the famous screen scene in Sheridan's *School For Scandal* (1777), as well as echoing a scene in Scribe's *Adrienne Lecouvreur* (1849) where two rivals try to protect their reputations by hiding in their lover's room. The scene also recalled a play by Haddon Chambers, *The Idler*, which had recently been performed at the same theatre, but contained no further similarity to Wilde's than the basic situation of a married woman in a bachelor's room.[13]

The critics interpreted the relationship between *Lady Windermere's Fan* and these other dramas very simply: Wilde, the novice dramatist, was carefully imitating formulas that had already proved successful. As the critic of the *Daily Graphic* put it: 'Mr. Wilde has adopted the methods of his predecessors, and carefully avoided efforts at novelty, but has hardly got his

[9] A. B. Walkley, *Speaker*, 5 (27 Feb. 1892), 257.
[10] *Daily Telegraph* (22 Feb. 1892), 3; *Punch* (5 Mar. 1892), 113.
[11] *Speaker*, 5 (27 Feb. 1892), 257–8.
[12] *Black and White*, 3 (27 Feb. 1892), 264; the *World* (24 Feb. 1892); *Punch* (5 Mar. 1892), 113; *Speaker*, 5 (27 Feb. 1892), 257–8.
[13] *Daily Telegraph* (22 Feb. 1892), 3; *Athenæum*, 3357 (27 Feb. 1892), 285–6; *Academy*, 41/1035 (5 Mar. 1892), 236–7; *Observer* (21 Feb. 1892), 6; *Black and White*, 3 (27 Feb. 1892), 264; *Speaker*, 5 (27 Feb. 1892), 257–8.

hand in yet at the game.'[14] In the opinion of these critics, Wilde's only original gesture was to have reserved the revelation of Mrs Erlynne's true identity until the last act.[15] But the relation of *Lady Windermere's Fan* to its source plays is far more sophisticated than any of the critics perceived. Wilde discreetly altered all the material he borrowed to produce a radically different play from those of his predecessors. In successive drafts, Wilde drew his play further and further from its origins.[16] The earliest handwritten draft of the play is similar in method and content to the conventional plays it mimics.[17] Later drafts show Wilde carefully altering characters and dialogue to undermine the assumptions on which the more traditional dramas were based. The final version of the play, published in 1893, is thus highly complex. On the surface it remains reassuringly conventional, but underneath this veneer, unnoticed by most audiences, lies a very different play.

The reasons for the deceptive appearance of *Lady Windermere's Fan* stretch beyond Wilde's habitual pleasure in hoodwinking the Victorian public. At a time when the very plays whose more conventional morality he was subverting had only just been passed by the censor, and when originality of treatment

---

[14] *Daily Graphic*, 9 (22 Feb. 1892), 8.

[15] *Speaker*, 5 (27 Feb. 1892), 257; *Athenæum*, 3357 (27 Feb. 1892), 285–6. After the 1st perf. Wilde revised the play, moving the revelation of Mrs Erlynne's identity forward from the fourth to the second act, a change which George Alexander had long been urging. For a discussion of these changes see below.

[16] MSS referred to here are, in order of composition: (*a*) Aut. MS BL Add. MS 37943: Acts I–IV, first draft with corrections and additions. Titled simply 'Play', the MS is handwritten by the author in ink. It is in many places incomplete. (*b*) Magdalen College, Oxford, MS 300: early typescript of Acts I and II, under the title 'A Good Woman'. Corrected in pencil throughout by the author, with many rewritten passages and additions in his hand. This typescript contains some pencil corrections in another hand than Wilde's, possibly that of 'Hill, 18 Colestown Street', whose name Wilde inscribed inside the cover. Some of the corrections are upheld in the final version, others (in Hill's(?) hand) are queried or ignored by Wilde. 69 pages. (*c*) Licensing copy no. 33, (dated 15 Feb. 1892): BL LCP Add. MS 53492H. Differs in many places from final version, most significantly in revelation of Mrs Erlynne's identity being reserved for the last act; (*d*) *Lady Windermere's Fan* (cited in n. 4 above). For a full list of the various MSS see the introduction to *Lady Windermere's Fan*, ed. Small, pp. xxviii–xxx. References below to the various versions are by act and page number.

[17] Aut MS BL Add. MS 37943.

almost guaranteed the refusal of a licence, Wilde's subtlety and circumspection were as much a necessity as an artistic indulgence. To challenge society's sexual mores openly on the Victorian public stage was impossible. Public performances were dependent on the granting of a licence from the Lord Chamberlain, and these were only grudgingly conferred on even the most orthodox and sentimental presentation of the fallen woman.

The most famous courtesan play was *La Dame aux Camélias* by Alexandre Dumas *fils*, in which Marguerite Gautier, a consumptive courtesan, falls in love with an honest young man.[18] Marguerite first sacrifices her ill-gotten riches to live in virtuous rural seclusion with Armand, then sacrifices her health to abandon Armand and return to her former dissolute life, so that Armand's innocent sister may make a respectable marriage. Marguerite dies as a result of her sacrifice, forgiven on her deathbed by Armand and his father. This play was refused a licence by the Lord Chamberlain when submitted in English translation under the title *Camille* for performance at the Drury Lane Theatre in 1853. It remained under official interdiction for a further twenty years.[19] One of its most controversial aspects was the fact that a courtesan was portrayed as capable of genuine love and selflessness. As the usually liberal critic, George Henry Lewes, commented: 'The very skill with which the young Dumas has treated it, makes his crime all the greater, because it tends to confuse the moral sense, by exciting the sympathy of an audience.'[20] The then Examiner of Plays, William Bodham Donne, went further when, in 1859, a manuscript of the play was submitted by the St James's Theatre. In his report Donne described it as 'a glorification of harlotry [which] in the last act . . . profanes the sanctity of death'.[21]

[18] *La Dame aux Camélias, Théâtre Complet de Dumas Fils*, i (Paris: Calmann Lévy, 1890). Written in 1849, but, even under the more liberal French laws, not perf. until 2 Feb. 1852, at the Théâtre du Vaudeville, Paris.

[19] John Russell Stephens, *The Censorship of English Drama, 1824–1901* (Cambridge: Cambridge University Press, 1980), 82–4.

[20] William Archer and W. H. Lowe (eds.), *Dramatic Essays: John Forster, George Henry Lewes. Reprinted from the Examiner and the Leader* (London: Walter Scott, 1896), 241–2.

[21] General Letters (Theatres) (1858–1901) LC 1: 70, 26 and 24 Mar. 1859, PRO. Quoted in Stephens, *The Censorship of English Drama*, 83.

Not only was propriety to be preserved but the strictest morality was to be observed. The fallen woman was only to be allowed on stage if the drama abided by Miss Prism's definition of fiction—the bad had always to end unhappily. So, for example, in 1867 Donne advocated that the new Parisian seduction drama, *Le Supplice d'une femme*, should be granted a licence. In his appeal to the Lord Chamberlain he stressed that the piece contained 'much that was good in principle'. The wife did pay for her sins with 'a heavy expiation', and her lover 'was not a worthless character'. More importantly, there was 'no attempt to gloss over vice, or to make wrong appear right'.[22] The Lord Chamberlain, however, declined to license the play, in spite of the fact that it begins with the revelation of the wife's adultery, and is from then on exclusively concerned with the husband's righteous punishment of the guilty and humble couple.[23]

The wit and humour which make *Lady Windermere's Fan* appear light-hearted and even frivolous would have helped Wilde's drama pass the censor. As Sir Herbert Tree reported in 1909, on having a play rejected by the Lord Chamberlain: 'I was told that it would be unacceptable—the subject was adultery—but if it could be made more comic, it would pass.'[24] Yet the most likely reason for the unchallenged licensing of *Lady Windermere's Fan* was its apparent conventionality. Harley Granville Barker's testimony to the 1909 Joint Select Committee inquiry into theatrical censorship is worth quoting at length, because he articulated perfectly the reasons which led Wilde to disguise his treatment of adultery and female virtue as an unoriginal, familiar, and harmlessly orthodox play. Granville Barker argued that:

---

[22] General Letters (Theatres) (1858–1901) 1: 85, 8 and 18 June 1868, PRO. Quoted in Stephens, *The Censorship of English Drama*, 85.

[23] *Le Supplice d'une femme* (Paris, 1865). Dumas *fils* revised and rewrote the original text by Émile de Girardin, but then repudiated the work. In its published form, the drama is ascribed solely to Girardin. *Punch* (5 Mar. 1892), 113, and *Daily Telegraph* (22 Feb. 1892), 3, both suggest that Wilde borrowed from this play for *Lady Windermere's Fan*, but there is no similarity between the two plays beyond the basic topic of adultery.

[24] Quoted in Richard Findlater, *Banned! A Review of Theatrical Censorship in Britain* (London: MacGibbon & Kee, 1967), 77.

A dramatist, in sending his play for a licence, or in having his play
sent in for a licence, is running a great risk of having his property
destroyed, and therefore the one thing that he does not want to do
is to make the Censor think about his play, and he naturally is in-
clined to send in a play which contains only such subjects, and such
a treatment of subjects, as have grown so familiar to the Licenser of
Plays that he no longer thinks about them at all. For instance, I think
it may be said without offence to the authorities that the Censor no
longer stops to think about a certain treatment of adultery on the
stage. If that treatment comes within certain dramatised limits—I
mean limits practised by dramatists—he passes it practically without
question. But the moment that any original point of view, or unusual
point of view, on any subject is put before the Censor he naturally
stops to think about it, and the process of his thinking very often
interferes with the licensing of the play.[25]

It is therefore hardly surprising that so many critics noted Wilde's
debt to other playwrights, and dismissed *Lady Windermere's
Fan* as derivative and unoriginal. Wilde had as much reason to
reveal as to conceal his sources.

The play which Wilde's drama most clearly resembles is
Odette by Victorien Sardou, in which a disgraced mother encounters the innocent daughter who believes her dead.[26] *Odette*
has been found guilty of adultery by her husband, the Count
of Clermont-Latour, who turns her out and gains custody of
their young daughter. Fifteen years later, the Count is in Nice
with his innocent daughter, Bérangère, who has been led to
believe that her mother died in a boating accident soon after
her birth. Odette, however, is in the same city, consorting with
the gamblers, cheats, and women of dubious reputation, who
inhabit the edge of society. Bérangère is in love with an eminently suitable young man, but the match is forbidden by his
mother, who knows Odette's history and will not consent to
link their families together while Odette continues to soil the
name of Clermont-Latour by dragging it through the dirt of the
demi-monde. The Count therefore begs his delinquent wife to
accede to the demands of the future mother-in-law, to give up

---

[25] Quoted in John Palmer, *The Censor and the Theatres* (London: T. Fisher
Unwin, 1912), 217–18.
[26] Sardou, *Odette, Théâtre Complet*, vi (Paris: Albin Michel, 1935), 1st perf.
Théâtre du Vaudeville, 17 Nov. 1881. An English version of *Odette* by Clement
Scott was produced at the Haymarket Theatre, London, 2 Apr. 1882.

her married name, and to leave France for ever. Odette agrees only on condition that she be allowed to meet her daughter, clearly hoping for a tearful reunion. She is introduced to Bérangère as an old friend of her dead mother, but her attempts at self-revelation are foiled as her daughter's incredible purity forces her to acknowledge the insuperable gulf between them. Bérangère's suitor then announces that his mother, hearing more of Odette's activities in France, has now decreed that the marriage cannot take place while Odette is alive. Overcome by remorse, Odette has taken leave of her daughter, without having revealed her true identity. A commotion is heard outside the window, and the tragic news is announced: Odette has just drowned in a boating accident. 'How sad!' exclaims the innocent daughter, 'Just like my mother!' The curtain descends on the Count and his daughter praying at the bedside of the conveniently expired sinner.

The differences between *Odette* and *Lady Windermere's Fan* reflect precisely the differences between Wilde's treatment of his themes and the more conventional attitudes displayed by other contemporary playwrights. The major issues may be summed up as follows: the presentation of the fallen woman as dissolute, depraved, and deserted; the fallen woman's repentance for her sin and nostalgia for her lost innocence; the delinquent mother's desire to reclaim her maternal role; the superiority of the innocent and sheltered girl to the tainted woman; the superiority of the male characters both to the innocent woman whom they seek to protect and to the depraved woman they seek to exclude. These themes were well worn, and a comparison between *Lady Windermere's Fan* and other plays on similar subjects reveals the radical nature of Wilde's treatment.

Sardou's *Odette* is a perfect example of the theatrical stereotype of the fallen woman. Weak-minded, shallow, and insufficiently principled, she falls into a sordid and empty adulterous affair. The daughter of a woman of dubious reputation and morals, Odette has no intrinsic qualities to keep her from degenerating once she is set adrift from the moral influence of polite society.[27] Fifteen years after being expelled by her husband, she

---

[27] In Scott's English version, Odette's loose morals were explained by Scott's leaving her as the only French character among an otherwise virtuous and English cast. *Odette* (BL LCP Add. MS 53270).

is consorting with divorced women, swindlers, and cheats, dulling her distaste for her sordid life with regular doses of morphine. The weakness and viciousness of Odette's character which lead her to fall inevitably into sin are typical of the theatrical fallen woman. Augier's impure adventuress, Olympe Taverny, for example, cannot escape from her own corrupt nature.[28] Olympe tricks her way into a respectable marriage, but, like Odette, is too frivolous to recognize the true values of family life and destroys her chances of redemption by entering into an adulterous affair.

The Mrs Erlynne of the first manuscript version is obviously moulded along the lines of Odette. Introduced by the Duchess of Berwick as 'really quite wicked', her right to the name of 'Mrs Erlynne' is immediately questioned, and her milieu defined as that of Odette's shady *demi-monde*: 'Not that ladies call on her, dear, except very fast women who gamble—but she has a great many men friends, very disreputable I believe.'[29] Mrs Erlynne's entrance in Act II does nothing to dispel this impression. Lady Windermere's description of her unwelcome guest, though of course coloured by her suspicions, gives an impression of Mrs Erlynne as a full-blown harlot: her daughter condemns her as 'That vile painted woman whose very sight is a degradation, whose touch an infamy.'[30] All references to Mrs Erlynne as a 'painted woman' are excised in a subsequent typescript.[31] The stage direction for Mrs Erlynne's long-awaited entry in the final version contrasts strongly with earlier impressions: she enters 'very beautifully dressed and very dignified', and as her daughter greets her coldly she 'bows to her sweetly in turn'.[32]

The charm, wit, and elegance of the final Mrs Erlynne all contradict the conventional expectations of the audience. Her self-control, intelligence, and resourcefulness, however, could link her to another adventuress, Dumas's Suzanne, the scheming central character of *Le Demi-Monde* (1855).[33] Suzanne, like

---

[28] Émile Augier, *Le Mariage d'Olympe, Théâtre Complet de Émile Augier*, iii (Paris: Calmann Lévy, 1897), 1st perf. Théâtre de Vaudeville, Paris, July 1855.
[29] Aut. MS BL Add. MS 37943: I. 10–12.   [30] Ibid. II. 47.
[31] Typescript of Acts I and II, Magdalen College, Oxford, MS 300: II. 22.
[32] *LWF* II. 47.
[33] Alexandre Dumas *fils, Le Demi-Monde, Théâtre Complet*, ii (Paris: Calmann Lévy, 1890); 1st perf. Théâtre du Gymnase-Dramatique, 20 Mar. 1855. Also perf.

Mrs Erlynne, is strong-minded, self-assured, and always ready
with a plausible explanation for unfavourable appearances, but,
unlike Mrs Erlynne, she possesses no heart. Informed that the
man she has been scheming to marry is dead, it takes her only
seconds to transfer her affections to another. Earlier versions of
Mrs Erlynne display a similar insensibility. Even in the relatively late version submitted to the Lord Chamberlain for licensing, Mrs Erlynne coldly informs her son-in-law that 'The worries
of other people can hardly be supposed to interest a woman
like me.'[34] The final Mrs Erlynne, by contrast, is marked by the
generous, though impulsive, emotions which enable her to accept
rather than judge the weaknesses of others.

The portrayal of a fallen woman with a heart could, however, be as conventional as the other stereotype of the painted
and scheming harlot. An adventuress who belatedly discovered
her truer and worthier self, realizing this self through sacrifice,
was no challenge to the moral conventions of the Victorian
age. Mrs Erlynne may be fitted into this mould: prompted by
previously neglected maternal impulses, she sacrifices herself
for her daughter, and thus redeems herself from her state of
sin. This commonly accepted interpretation of Mrs Erlynne's
role makes *Lady Windermere's Fan* little more than a sentimental melodrama.[35] Yet Wilde quite specifically emphasized
the originality of her character. In a letter to George Alexander
he declared that the chief merit of his last act was 'the revelation of a character as yet untouched by literature'.[36] He

by the Comédie-Française at the Gaiety Theatre, London, 9 and 19 June 1879, as
part of their visiting season. Wilde was in London in June 1879, and paid homage
to the talents of Sarah Bernhardt, who played in the Comédie-Française's productions of *Phèdre* and *L'Étrangère*. For a full account and list of plays performed,
see E. Got, *La Comédie-Française à Londres (1871–1879): Journal inédit de E.
Got et F. Sarcey*, with an introduction by Georges d'Heyli (Paris: Ollendorff,
1880).

[34] BL LCP Add. MS 53492 H: IV. 64.

[35] Alan Bird presents exactly this interpretation in his study, *The Plays of Oscar
Wilde*, where he comments that Mrs Erlynne's 'morality is as conventional as that
of her daughter and her son-in-law' (p. 108). Epifanio San Juan defines the centre of
the play as Mrs Erlynne's redemption, finding herself in an existential moment
of maternal love and sacrificing herself to avoid a repetition of the past (*The Art of
Oscar Wilde*, 140–54). Similarly Philip Cohen concludes that Mrs Erlynne 'rather
belatedly . . . fulfils the obligations to God, her daughter, and her own heart that
redeem her and guarantee her authenticity' (*The Moral Vision of Oscar Wilde*, 191).

[36] To George Alexander (mid-Feb. 1892), *Letters*, 309.

repeated this claim in a letter to an unidentified admirer, announcing that 'the fourth act is to me the psychological act, the act that is newest, most true'.[37] The originality to which Wilde refers is Mrs Erlynne's refusal to perform the rituals of repentance and reform which mark the redemption of the magdalen. Wilde's adventuress scorns the well-trodden path of her predecessors:

> I suppose, Windermere, you would like me to retire into a convent, or become a hospital nurse, or something of that kind, as people do in silly modern novels. That is stupid of you, Arthur; in real life we don't do such things—not as long as we have any good looks left, at any rate. No—what consoles one nowadays is not repentance, but pleasure. Repentance is quite out of date. And besides, if a woman really repents, she has to go to a bad dressmaker, otherwise no one believes in her. And nothing in the world would induce me to do that.[38]

In the first draft of the play, Wilde made his repudiation of dramatic conventions even more explicit, as Mrs Erlynne mocked the idea that she should 'retire to a convent or something of that kind as people do in plays'.[39]

Late nineteenth-century drama was brim-full of repentant and dying magdalens. As Jerome K. Jerome observed of the adventuress in his satirical *Stage-Land: Curious Habits and Customs of its Inhabitants* (1889):

> It is repentance that kills off the bad people in plays. They always repent, and the moment they repent they die. Repentance, on the stage, seems to be one of the most dangerous thing[s] a man can be taken with. Our advice to Stage wicked people would undoubtedly be 'Never repent. If you value your life, don't repent. It always means sudden death!'[40]

Gilberte, the heroine of *Frou-Frou* (1869) by Henri Meilhac and Ludovic Halévy, provides a perfect model for Jerome's satire and Mrs Erlynne's mockery.[41] Like Lady Windermere,

---

[37] To an unidentified correspondent (postmark 23 Feb. 1893), *Letters*, 332.
[38] *LWF* IV. 120.   [39] Aut. MS BL Add. MS 37943: IV. 106.
[40] *Stage-Land: Curious Habits and Customs of its Inhabitants* (London: Chatto & Windus, 1889), 37.
[41] Meilhac and Halévy, *Frou-Frou, Théâtre de Meilhac et Halévy Complet*, i (Paris: Calmann Lévy, 1899), 1st perf. Théâtre du Gymnase, Paris, 30 Oct. 1869.

Gilberte wrongly believes her husband guilty of adultery and responds by abandoning her hearth, home, and young child for the arms of a lover. The wronged husband kills the lover in a duel and Gilberte is left to see the error of her ways. She does so, demonstrating her remorse by visiting the poor and nursing the sick, from whom she contracts the illness which kills her a few seconds after she has begged forgiveness of her husband. Gilberte symbolically displays her repentance by giving up the silk gowns, whose rustling sound earned her the nickname of the title, and wearing instead 'une méchante petite robe noire qu'elle ne quitte jamais' [an ugly little black dress which she never takes off].[42] She obviously shares Mrs Erlynne's sartorial distaste for such outfits, however, since her dying wish is to be buried in a more becoming rose-patterned white dress.[43] Dumas's Marguerite Gautier had set the fashion in deathbed absolution, and her followers were numerous. Henry Arthur Jones's contribution to the genre was *Saints and Sinners* (1884), in which a minister's daughter, Letty Fletcher, succumbs to an unscrupulous seducer.[44] She earns forgiveness through a life of poverty and suffering, accompanied by social ostracism. Even this exemplary career is cut short by death—she contracts the obligatory fatal disease from one of the patients she selflessly nurses.

Another example of the plays whose code of behaviour Mrs Erlynne rejects is *Illusion* (1890) by Pierre Leclerq.[45] The heroine

---

[42] *Frou-Frou*, V. ii. 156.   [43] Ibid. V. v. 164-5.

[44] Jones, *Saints and Sinners* (London: Macmillan, 1891), 1st produced Theatre Royal, Margate, 22 Sept. 1884, and Vaudeville Theatre, London, 25 Sept. 1884. This play is a likely object of Wilde's scorn, as he once declared: 'There are three rules for writing plays. The first rule is not to write like Henry Arthur Jones; the second and third rules are the same.' Hesketh Pearson, *The Life of Oscar Wilde* (London: Methuen, 1946), 221.

[45] *Illusion*, by Pierre Leclerq. 1st produced Strand Theatre, July 1890 (BL LCP Lic. No. 133. Add. MS 53453G). Despite his French name, Leclerq was English, a member of a family of celebrated actors. His sister, Rose, would be the original Lady Bracknell. I am indebted for the discovery of this play to Kerry Powell's excellent study, *Oscar Wilde and the Theatre of the 1890s*, 22-32. Professor Powell speculates that Wilde may have attended a matinée performance of *Illusion*, concluding that 'Wilde's play holds more in common with Leclerq's *Illusion* than with any other play of the kind' (p. 22). The plot of *Illusion* is sufficiently similar to that of *Lady Windermere's Fan* to suggest it was a possible source for Wilde's plot; there is, however, no definite evidence. No contemporary critics noted the similarity, and all notable plot elements, such as the return of the 'dead' mother, are also present in plays such as *Odette* and *Révoltée*. Professor Powell notes Wilde's use of contemporary plays, but he limits Wilde's originality to the surprise of the last act, where Mrs Erlynne rejects both motherhood and repentance.

of *Illusion*, like Lady Windermere, suspects her husband of infidelity, when he is actually protecting her from the dreadful knowledge that her supposedly dead mother is living a life of notoriety and sin. Like Mrs Erlynne, *Illusion*'s errant mother, La Faneuse, encounters her innocent young daughter, but, unlike Mrs Erlynne, she is prompted by her daughter's innocence to repent of her wicked ways and redeem herself through good deeds. La Faneuse moves from one stereotype of the fallen woman to another. She is first introduced as 'a woman who has ruined ... wealthy men as a business—poor ones as a pastime'.[46] Her first entrance presents the gaudy spectacle which Mrs Erlynne avoids: '*She is dressed in a dazzlingly rich ball or dinner dress. She carries a fan and is ablaze with diamonds.*'[47] The transformation from one convention to the other, from the hardened harpy to the repentant magdalen, takes place when La Faneuse comes in contact with her daughter. Una's purity and faith destroy her mother's happiness by awaking her conscience, as the sinful mother declares: 'I seem to feel her pure blood tingling in my veins.'[48] Repentance, grief, and humility complete the metamorphosis. Having given away all her ill-gotten gains 'to found a home for others who have been as I have been, who would be as I *will* be', she dons the costume appropriate to her new role: '*she is dressed as a nurse with a long black cloak and a particularly long veil ... and wears no jewelry whatever.*' This is, she announces, 'My costume till I die!' The curtain slowly descends on her heroic resolution: 'My past is black! my future shall whiten it!'[49]

La Faneuse's division of her life into two entirely separate phases, the sharp contrast she presents between the fallen and redeemed woman, and her intense regret for her lost virtue are all typical of the fallen woman play. The tainted woman's anguished longing for her former innocence provides the moral force of these plays, the warning to all who are tempted to stray. Similarly, the strong contrast between the degenerate fallen woman and the sexually pure innocent emphasizes the gulf between them: they are two separate breeds and, no matter what efforts the fallen may make to reform, such they will remain. Thus even Pinero's *The Second Mrs Tanqueray* (1893), a play which was greeted at the time as a radical examination

[46] *Illusion*, I. 15.   [47] Ibid. III. 50.   [48] Ibid. 59.   [49] Ibid. 62–4.

of the fallen-woman question, offers the same conservative moral.[50] Pinero's Paula Tanqueray is an intelligent, warm-hearted, and impulsive woman, a world away from her brassy and brainless friend, Lady Orreyed, a woman with an equally dubious past. Yet, in spite of the sympathetic light in which Paula Tanqueray is presented, she is nevertheless condemned to realize that her fall is irretrievable. She marries Aubrey Tanqueray but her past resurfaces in the form of her step-daughter's fiancé, a former lover of her own, and the play ends with Paula's remorseful suicide. Much of the play's tension lies in Paula's attempts to win the affection of her innocent step-daughter, who in turn coldly rebuffs her. In a key scene, Aubrey opens his wife's eyes to her own unsuitability as a companion for his daughter. He reminds Paula of the innocent young school-girl she once was and points out the gulf between the pure girl and the corrupt woman. Paula *'drops on the ottoman in a paroxysm of weeping'*, crying, 'Oh God! A few years ago!'[51]

A very similar scene is played out in Sardou's *Odette*. The delinquent mother expresses suitable nostalgia and regret for her lost virtue; her favourite fantasy is that she never sinned but is still the faithful wife, pouring tea by the fire while her husband reads and her daughter sews.[52] Foolishly, Odette still dreams of regaining her former position; she hopes that a meeting with her daughter will give her the opportunity to reveal her true identity and to be reunited with her family. She is soon disillusioned: Bérangère's happy chatter about her dead mother—how loving she was, how virtuous, how much her father loved her—forces Odette to recognize the impassable distance which lies between her present and former selves. The final touch is added when Bérangère sympathizes with Odette's tale of a woman who erred and had her child taken from her. The daughter's answer is simple: the woman should reform and repent so that no one can help but forgive her. Odette withdraws, defeated by a sense of her own unworthiness. It is the myth of the dead mother which overcomes Odette; the delinquent mother cedes her place to her fictional counterpart.

---

[50] A. W. Pinero, *The Second Mrs Tanqueray* (London: Heinemann, 1895), 1st perf. St James's Theatre, London, 27 May 1893. See e.g. William Archer's review in the *World* (31 May 1893).

[51] *The Second Mrs Tanqueray*, III. 127.   [52] *Odette*, III. iv. 372–3.

Bérangère shows Odette the only picture she has of her mother, a miniature painted when Odette was only 13. This image is the touchstone against which Odette is judged, and presents the true ideal of the play. So Odette bids a final farewell to her daughter, advising her: 'Cette image de votre mère que vous avez là dans votre cœur, conservez-la toujours aussi belle, aussi pure! Elle sera la gardienne de votre vie!' [This image of your mother which you carry in your heart, keep it always just as beautiful, just as pure! It will be the guardian-angel of your life!][53] It is Odette and not the dead mother who is the false image, the distortion of reality, and Odette can only atone for her error by imitating the death of her fictional counterpart.

Wilde replays this scene in *Lady Windermere's Fan*, but subverts the material he borrows from Sardou to present a very different evaluation of the fallen woman. Lord Windermere scornfully prepares the ground for Mrs Erlynne's obligatory lament for her lost innocence by reminding her of the girl she once was. But Wilde's *aventurière* is made of sterner stuff:

LORD WINDERMERE. I wish that at the same time she would give you a miniature she kisses every night before she prays.—It's a miniature of a young innocent-looking girl with beautiful *dark* hair.

MRS ERLYNNE. Ah, yes, I remember. How long ago that seems! It was done before I was married. Dark hair and an innocent expression were the fashion then, Windermere![54]

Mrs Erlynne mocks Lord Windermere's smug certainties; the miniature, she suggests, may be as deceptive as her present appearance. Lord Windermere wishes to shame her with the gulf between her former and present selves. Mrs Erlynne replies by hinting that there is no such gulf, that all her life she has adapted her exterior to suit the social superficialities of the time.[55]

---

[53] Ibid. IV. v. 423.   [54] *LWF*, IV. 118–19.

[55] Wilde here anticipates Shaw's appeal for a more accurate portrayal of the fallen woman. After viewing *The Second Mrs Tanqueray* in 1893, Shaw objected to Paula's shame and regret when her husband reminded her of her innocent girlhood. As he wrote: 'One can imagine how, in a play by a master-hand, Paula's reply would have opened Tanqueray's foolish eyes to the fact that a woman of that sort is already the same at three as she is at thirty-three, and that however she may have found by experience that her nature is in conflict with differently constituted people, she remains perfectly valid to herself' (*Saturday Review*, 79, 23 Feb. 1895, 249–50). Mrs Erlynne thus anticipates Shaw's Mrs Warren, his own attempt to portray such a woman.

Mrs Erlynne thus does not redeem herself through repentance and reformation as was expected of any fallen woman who was not a thoroughly heartless and hardened harpy. She does not, as so many critics claim, atone for her former sin by rediscovering her proper role of self-sacrificing mother.[56] As Wilde said, 'if there is one particular doctrine contained in [*Lady Windermere's Fan*], it is that of sheer individualism'.[57] Mrs Erlynne follows the precepts set forth in 'The Soul of Man under Socialism' by rejecting self-sacrifice in favour of self-realization.[58] She does not wish to be a mother nor to be trammelled by the moral strictures of English society. Mrs Erlynne very deliberately contradicts the conventional, sentimental moral, rejecting the role of mother as it interferes with her freedom. So she reassures her son-in-law:

> Oh, don't imagine that I am going to have a pathetic scene with her, weep on her neck and tell her who I am, and all that kind of thing. I have no ambition to play the part of a mother. Only once in my life have I known a mother's feelings. That was last night. They were terrible—they made me suffer—they made me suffer too much. For twenty years, as you say, I have lived childless—I want to live childless still.[59]

It is with this rejection of motherhood that Wilde presented his most radical challenge to Victorian theatrical stereotypes and to the moral values they upheld. In the second act Wilde had cheated his audience's expectations by presenting not a vulgar and degenerate fallen woman but a character possessed of considerable charm and poise. In the third act the audience is reassured: Mrs Erlynne's self-sacrifice marks her out not, like

---

[56] See e.g. San Juan, *The Art of Oscar Wilde*, 140–54; Miller, *Oscar Wilde*, 42–9; Cohen, *The Moral Vision of Oscar Wilde*, 181–92.

[57] Quoted in Ellmann, *Oscar Wilde*, 347–8.

[58] Cf. 'It is to be noted also that Individualism does not come to man with any sickly cant about duty, which merely means doing what other people want because they want it; or any hideous cant about self-sacrifice, which is merely a survival of savage mutilation . . .': 'The Soul of Man', 315.

[59] *LWF* IV. 119. In 'The Soul of Man', 300, Wilde offers Jesus as the perfect individualist, adding that he 'rejected the claims of family life'. Mrs Erlynne also realizes Shaw's suggestions (derived from Ibsen's *A Doll's House*) for women's pursuit of individual liberty: 'The sum of the matter is that unless Woman repudiates her womanliness, her duty to her husband, to her children, to society, to the law and to everyone but herself, she cannot emancipate herself.' *The Quintessence of Ibsenism* (London: Walter Scott, 1891), 43.

Dumas's Suzanne or Augier's Olympe, as the fallen woman as dangerous harpy, but rather as the fallen woman as magdalen, like Dumas's Marguerite Gautier or Jones's Letty Fletcher. Yet, in the final act, Mrs Erlynne not only refuses to act according to the audience's expectations, she even mocks those very expectations. Wilde declared that 'the fourth act is to me the psychological act, the act that is newest, most true'.[60] Through Mrs Erlynne, Wilde not only subverted all the conventions governing the behaviour of the fallen woman, but dared to question the sacred status of motherhood as woman's greatest ambition.[61]

Once again, Odette presents the tradition from which Mrs Erlynne dissents. Thus, in Scott's English translation, Odette begs her estranged husband not to speak to her of Bérangère, because:

> Every word you speak revives the embers of my long-smouldering love: you give me back my child in fancy only once more to deny me the reality. There is only one way of curing such women as I am—distressed, harassed, heart-broken women—by the priceless example of a pure life. We find the world a mockery, an empty sham, a hollow lie, and we would return as prodigals, if led home by our children. For me there is but one hope left in all the world, the absolution of maternity, after the penance of separation.[62]

Wilde's delinquent mother looks for no such absolution. What Odette yearns for is within Mrs Erlynne's grasp (she is, after all, a master of the art of plausible explanation), but she rejects it; she prefers to maintain her independence rather than submit to the demands of motherhood. It was precisely this which outraged those reviewers who were willing to take the play seriously. When the critic and translator Clement Scott reviewed *Lady Windermere's Fan,* he articulated Wilde's cynical intentions thus: 'I will prove to you by my play that the very instinct of maternity—that holiest and purest instinct with women—is

---

[60] To an unidentified correspondent (postmark 23 Feb. 1893), *Letters*, 332.

[61] Cf. e.g. Joseph Shillito's tribute to the maternal role in *Womanhood: Its Duties, Temptations and Privileges* (London: Henry S. King & Co., 1877): 'And what to be a mother? To give birth to young immortals! To guide and train the opening minds of those who shall influence the coming generation.... Sacred, blessed motherhood! is not yours a high and holy mission?' (p. 13).

[62] *Odette* trans. Clement Scott, 1st produced Theatre Royal, Haymarket, 1882 (BL LCP Add. MS 53270: II. 62–3).

deadened in the breast of our English mothers.'[63] Scott also
dismissed *Lady Windermere's Fan* as lacking the pathos of
Odette, pointedly comparing the behaviour of the two mothers:

Odette, as guilty, as frivolous, as worldly as any Mrs Erlynne ever
painted, was still woman enough to choke with suppressed sobs, and
on departing into space, unrecognised and unloved by her daughter,
to kiss the fair tresses of her maiden hair. But the cynical modern
dramatist dismisses his adventuress from her daughter's presence with
a mocking laugh on her lips . . .[64]

Mrs Erlynne's behaviour is, indeed, emphatically unmaternal.
Whereas La Faneuse fondly reminisces about the tiny infant arms
which she once unwound from her breast, and Odette recalls
the golden curls and smiling eyes of the young Bérangère, Mrs
Erlynne remarks calmly of her long-lost daughter: 'She's grown
quite pretty. The last time I saw her—twenty years ago, she
was a fright in flannel. Positive fright, I assure you.'[65]
    The family reunion, for which other delinquent mothers long,
holds no promise for Mrs Erlynne; it is, rather, a threat of confinement from which she escapes. Mrs Erlynne's rejection of the
maternal role provides yet another example of Wilde subverting
the traditional theatrical climax. Odette redeems herself by
abandoning all thoughts of reclaiming her daughter, but other
guilty mothers, who repent and perform suitable acts of self-
sacrifice, in time are forgiven and receive the ultimate reward
of reunion with their family. Thus the fallen heroine of *Frou-
Frou* devotes herself to the poor and sick, and as a reward
is allowed to spend the last ten minutes of her life in the
bosom of her family. *Révoltée* by Jules Lemaître, a play from
which Wilde clearly borrowed plot material, offers a similar
dénouement.[66] Lemaître's heroine, Madame de Voves, has had
an illegitimate daughter who grew up in a convent, knowing
nothing of her mother's identity. The delinquent mother learns

---

[63] Clement Scott, *Illustrated London News*, 100 (27 Feb. 1892), 278.
[64] *Daily Telegraph* (22 Feb. 1892), 3.
[65] *Illusion*, III. 55–6; *Odette*, IV. v. 414; *LWF* II. 63.
[66] Jules Lemaître, *Révoltée* (Paris: Calmann Lévy, 1889), 1st perf. Théâtre de
l'Odéon, Paris, 9 Apr. 1889. Wilde ordered from France copies of Lemaître's
Impressions de Théâtre iv, which included a long review of *Révoltée* by the author;
see Merlin Holland, 'Plagiarist or Pioneer?', in George Sandalescu (ed.), *Rediscovering Oscar Wilde* (Gerrards Cross: Colin Smyth, 1994), 206–7.

that her now-married daughter is contemplating an affair with another man. This threatened repetition of the past prompts a horrified soliloquy from Madame de Voves just as it does from Mrs Erlynne. Madame de Voves reveals the truth to her legitimate son, who challenges the prospective lover to a duel but is seriously wounded himself. Overcome by remorse at learning of her half-brother's injury, the errant daughter repents and begs forgiveness. The play ends with a family tableau at the son's bedside. The only moment at which Lemaître's play breaks out of its sentimental conventions is when Madame de Voves first reveals her true identity to her daughter, Hélène. Rather than running into her mother's arms with a cry of delighted recognition, Hélène responds thus:

> Ma mère? . . . Ma mère? . . . Non, rien . . . Comment cette révélation me laisse-t-elle si tranquille? J'ai peur de paraître impie et abominable, mais c'est ainsi . . . Pourquoi me l'apprendre? Vous vous figuriez, sans doute, que j'avais là, tout prêts pour vous, des trésors de tendresse qui déborderaient subitement, ou que je concevrais, comme cela, tout d'un coup, que vous ne vous êtes pas donné la peine de m'inspirer . . . Eh bien, non, non, je ne sens rien. Et c'est horrible.[67]

> [My mother? . . . My mother? . . . No, nothing. . . . How can this revelation leave me so unmoved? I fear to seem blasphemous, loathsome, but there it is. . . . Why tell me? No doubt, you imagined that I had gems of tenderness all ready for you, which would suddenly burst forth, or that I would conjure up feelings, just like that, which you never took the trouble to inspire in me. . . . But, no, no, I feel nothing. And it is horrible.]

Hélène's rebellion is, however, short-lived and presents no challenge to the traditional values of family duty and affection. Hélène's rejection of her mother only serves to demonstrate how hard-hearted and selfish she has become; Mrs Erlynne's rejection of her daughter is not inspired by any lack of heart but rather by her adherence to an unorthodox and independent system of values.

The challenge presented by Mrs Erlynne to the popular conventions governing the behaviour of the fallen woman were the

---

[67] *Révoltée*, III. vii. 80.

result of careful revision on Wilde's part. In the first autograph version of the play, Mrs Erlynne approximates more closely to the traditional delinquent mother. The first Mrs Erlynne talks with regret of the family ties she has lost; as she says to Lady Windermere: 'I am afraid we shall never meet again. Our lives lie too far apart. You have so much in life—a husband who loves you—a child who loves you[.] I am—well, something of the Bohemian is in my veins. I have none of these things.'[68] But neither is she a true Bohemian, for her freedom is indistinguishable from loneliness: 'You see, I am quite alone in the world Lady Windermere. I have no relations, or ties of any kind. I have my freedom. It is rather like freedom in the desert—but it is freedom, I suppose.'[69] The first Mrs Erlynne is an altogether weaker and more conventional character. Like Odette, she clearly desires to fulfil the role of mother but denies herself even the attempt to gain it, too aware of her own unworthiness. The generosity and compassion which prompt the mother to sacrifice herself to save her daughter are an integral part of the final Mrs Erlynne; in the last act she treats both daughter and son-in-law with restrained tolerance and understanding. The moment of self-sacrifice and the feelings which prompted it are, however, clearly an exceptional impulse for the first Mrs Erlynne. So she muses to the uncomprehending Lord Windermere: 'I wonder why I did it now. Suddenly there awoke in ones nature feelings that one thought were dead, or that one thought one never had at all. They wake in one's nature, and then they die.'[70] Like Odette, she redeems herself with one fleeting impulse, while her basic character is condemned as frivolous and selfish. Leaving her daughter, she reverts to type: 'Those who live for pleasure, as I do, should have no hearts. It spoils one's game.'[71] All that this woman can offer the Windermeres is the trite philosophy of the fallen: 'Believe me, my dear Arthur, you take life too seriously—and so does Violet. Nothing matters very much, except want of money.'[72] The first Mrs Erlynne is thus considerably closer to the conventional stereotype. When she rejects the role of mother she simply

---

[68] Aut MS BL Add. MS 37943: IV. 98.   [69] Ibid. 97.
[70] Ibid. 103.   [71] Ibid. 106.
[72] Ibid. Lady Windermere is called Violet, not Margaret, in this MS, while Mrs Erlynne and her grandchild are, with rather heavy-handed irony, named Angela.

proves her own inadequacy; when the poised, generous, and self-possessed Mrs Erlynne of the final version rejects the role of mother, however, her actions challenge the traditional estimation of motherhood as the highest condition that woman could aspire to.

Wilde jealously oversaw the theatrical birth of his unconventional heroine, instructing the harassed George Alexander over small but significant details: 'Also, would you remind Lady Plymdale to say "That woman!" not "That *dreadful* woman." We must not make Mrs E. look like a cocotte. She is an adventuress, not a cocotte.'[73] The prime source of conflict between Wilde and Alexander was, however, the question of when Mrs Erlynne was to reveal her true identity. Alexander urged a conventional structure whereby the audience is in full possession of the facts in the first, or at the latest second, act. Wilde clung tenaciously to his more unusual fourth-act revelation. After the first performance, Wilde gave in to Alexander's pressure and moved the disclosure back from the final act to the end of the second. Alexander greeted Wilde's acquiescence with relief and even wrote to thank Clement Scott for his contribution to the fight: Scott knew of Wilde's recalcitrance, and in his *Daily Telegraph* review of the first performance of the play he had strongly criticized Wilde for keeping the audience so long in the dark.[74]

Wilde had originally insisted on delaying the disclosure of Mrs Erlynne's true identity because he felt that the mystery served to maintain the focus on the *aventurière* rather than her daughter: 'When they learn it, it is after Lady Windermere has left her husband's house to seek the protection of another man, and their interest is centred on Mrs Erlynne, to whom dramatically speaking belongs the last act.'[75] Wilde feared that Mrs Erlynne would appear conventionally hard and debased were her true identity known too early. Had he intended to let out the secret, he explains to Alexander, 'I would have written the play on entirely different lines. I would have made Mrs Erlynne

[73] To George Alexander (mid-Feb. 1892), *More Letters*, 113.

[74] Correspondence between George Alexander and Clement Scott, repr. in Joel H. Kaplan, 'A Puppet's Power: George Alexander, Clement Scott, and the Replotting of *Lady Windermere's Fan*', *Theatre Notebook*, 46/2 (1992), 59–73.

[75] To George Alexander (mid-Feb. 1892), *Letters*, 308–9.

a vulgar horrid woman.'[76] The reason for his altering the play was not, as he emphasized in a letter to the editor of the *St James's Gazette*, the critics' dislike of the play's unconventionally mysterious structure, but that he had finally been persuaded that the new structure would not undermine but strengthen the psychology of his drama. Ignoring the artistic strictures of the old, he bowed to the opinions of the young, because

I am bound to state that all my friends, without exception, were of opinion that the psychological interest of the second act would be greatly increased by the disclosure of the actual relationship existing between Lady Windermere and Mrs Erlynne.[77]

Wilde accepted the revision only once he had been reassured that the originality of Mrs Erlynne's character was thereby emphasized, not destroyed. The knowledge that Mrs Erlynne is saving her own daughter explains the fallen woman's noble self-sacrifice in the third act—the audience is no longer puzzled by the sudden 'good' actions of the 'bad' woman. But the revision may render the last act more shocking: the element of suspense is lifted and attention is focused on 'the revelation of a character as yet untouched by literature'.[78]

Instead of enduring a painful death, poverty, or the rigours of hospital nursing, Wilde's fallen woman not only leaves the stage in perfect health, impervious to the moral strictures which demanded her repentance and conversion, but also ends the play in possession of a husband. This was Wilde's final and most sacrilegious offence in the eyes of his critics. So Clement Scott, already outraged by Mrs Erlynne's turning down the role of mother, was further shocked that Wilde, 'the cynical modern dramatist', should allow his heroine 'to go downstairs after parting from her child and to frivol with a "middle-aged masher"

---

[76] To George Alexander (mid-Feb. 1892), *Letters*, 308–9.

[77] To the editor of the *St James's Gazette* (26 Feb. 1892), *Letters*, 313.

[78] To George Alexander (mid-Feb. 1892), *Letters*, 308. Joel Kaplan defines the placement of Mrs Erlynne's revelation as 'a political act, one that would determine whether the play would reinforce or disrupt the sensibilities of Alexander's public' ('A Puppet's Power', 68). He thus argues that the early disclosure is a victory for the forces of conformity. Yet Clement Scott, who was fully aware of Mrs Erlynne's identity, was also the most critical of the play's unorthodox morality. See Scott's review, *Daily Telegraph* (22 Feb. 1892), 3.

who is accepted as her second husband under the very roof of her abandoned daughter!'[79] Wilde subverted theatrical conventions by rewarding his fallen woman with the ultimate prize of a husband.

For a fallen woman to marry and thereby re-enter society was unthinkable. Augier contemplated the possibility of such an event in *Le Mariage d'Olympe*, and concluded that the father-in-law of such a woman would have no choice but to shoot her like a dog. Pinero was slightly more charitable in his consideration of the theme: his fallen heroine is allowed to shoot herself. Most plays, however, were concerned with the need to prevent such an immoral misalliance occurring in the first place. Thus, in Dumas's *Le Demi-Monde* the clever courtesan, Suzanne, schemes to win the hand of the naïve Raymond de Nanjac. Her chief opponent is Olivier de Jalin, a former lover, who tells de Nanjac of Suzanne's past and even shows him the love-letters she once sent him. The far-sighted Suzanne, however, successfully denies authorship of the letters— she had persuaded a friend to write them for her. Suzanne, having outmanœuvred de Jalin several times, is allowed to voice a brief protest:

> Admettons, et il faut l'admettre, puisque c'est vrai, que je ne sois pas digne, en bonne morale, du nom et de la position que j'ambitionne, est-ce bien à vous, qui avez contribué à me rendre indigne, à me fermer la route honourable où je veux entrer?[80]

> [Let us admit, and it must be admitted, because it's true, that I am not worthy, in moral terms, of the name and the position to which I aspire. Is it really for you, who have helped to make me unworthy, to bar me from the honourable path I wish to take?]

In reply, de Jalin admits that his motives did include jealous revenge and acknowledges his debt to Suzanne, but adds: 'Cependant, à ma place, il n'est pas un honnête homme qui n'eût agi comme moi.' [However, there is not a single honest man who, in my place, would not have acted as I did.][81] De Jalin's code is indeed proved to be the only acceptable one, as, when

[79] *Daily Telegraph* (22 Feb. 1892), 3.
[80] *Le Demi-Monde*, III. xi. A minor character in *An Ideal Husband* is also named the Vicomte de Nanjac.
[81] Ibid.

he finally manages to scotch Suzanne's plans, he is rewarded with the hand of a suitably innocent and pure maiden as his wife. The final judgement on him is that of de Nanjac, who tells the young girl: 'Vous serez heureuse, mademoiselle; vous épousez le plus honnête homme que je connaisse.' [You will be happy, mademoiselle; you are marrying the most honest man I know.][82]

By the 1880s, in the novel, fallen heroines might be treated with greater liberality: in George Gissing's *The Unclassed*, for example, a reformed prostitute, Ida, wins love and a proposal from the hero, Waymark; and in *A Terrible Temptation* by Charles Reade a fiery courtesan, 'La Somerset', makes an advantageous marriage and embarks on a new career as a lay preacher.[83] On stage, however, fallen heroines fared extremely unhappily in the marriage stakes. Exceptions were rare and grudging. In *John O'Dreams* (1894) the fact that an angelic reformed prostitute is granted the hand of the man she loves is somewhat tarnished by the fact that he is an unreformed alcoholic and drug addict.[84] In Wilkie Collins's *The New Magdalen* (1873), the fallen heroine, Mercy Merrick, is allowed to marry the noble Julian Gray, the man whose preaching first inspired her to reform.[85] This marriage is, however, very specifically a reward for her repentance, humility, self-sacrifice, and self-abasement. Mrs Erlynne breaks every rule, for she scorns repentance, rejects motherhood as demanding too great a sacrifice of self, and yet, in spite of all this, ends the play triumphantly in possession of a husband.[86]

[82] *Le Demi-Monde*, V. v.

[83] George Gissing, *The Unclassed* (1st pub. London, 1884; rev. edn. London: Lawrence & Bullen, 1895). Charles Reade, *A Terrible Temptation* (London: Chapman & Hall, 1871).

[84] Haddon Chambers, *John O'Dreams*, 1st perf. Haymarket Theatre, London, 1894 (BL LCP Add. MS 53560R).

[85] *The New Magdalen*, 1st perf. Olympic Theatre, London, 19 May 1873. Published by the author, London, 1873. Adapted from Collins's novel of the same title. For all the traditional moral emphasis on reform, repentance, and Christian charity, *The New Magdalen* prompted an American correspondent to write to *The Daily Graphic*: 'The author . . . has opened a recruiting office for prostitutes . . . a play so utterly vicious, so shamefully profligate in its teaching, has never before been produced at a New York theatre.' Quoted in Catherine Peters, *The King of Inventors: A Life of Wilkie Collins* (London: Secker & Warburg, 1991), 362–3.

[86] Wilde may well have hesitated before committing himself to so radical an ending, as the first autograph MS breaks off at Mrs Erlynne's exit with Lord Augustus.

Wilde not only defies the conventional form, he turns it on its head. In the sub-plots to *Odette* and to Dumas's *Le Demi-Monde, Francillon*, and *La Dame aux Camélias*, an old roué who has had a number of affairs and has led a carefree bachelor life wins the love of a young, unspoiled girl, frequently about half his age. In *Lady Windermere's Fan*, Mrs Erlynne, the woman with a considerable past behind her, wins the hand of Lord Augustus, who, though by no means young, is still undoubtedly the only true innocent left in his society.

A central theme in Victorian theatrical treatments of the fallen woman was the insuperable gulf between the errant woman and the innocent maiden. In Leclerq's *Illusion*, for example, the fallen mother, La Faneuse, exclaims in wonder at her daughter's purity: 'What a sweet flower from so vile a plant!'[87] Even when the sinful mother is reunited with her daughter, every precaution must be taken to avoid contamination: La Faneuse puts on her gloves and pulls down her ankle-length veil before daring to embrace her daughter. Lord Windermere subscribes to exactly these values, telling Mrs Erlynne that he hates to see her next to her daughter, because 'You sully the innocence that is in her.'[88] But Lord Windermere's judgement is proved to be inadequate, for Wilde presents the fallen woman as superior in knowledge, understanding, and generosity to her unsullied daughter.

Fighting to prevent a repetition of her own past, Mrs Erlynne first offers her daughter all the conventional moral arguments—the horror of being an outcast, the wife's duty to her husband, the mother's duty to her child—but the basis of her argument is later revealed to be anything but conventional:

> I may have wrecked my own life, but I will not let you wreck yours. You—why, you are a mere girl, you would be lost. You haven't got the kind of brains that enables a woman to get back. You have neither the wit nor the courage. You couldn't stand dishonour![89]

Overcome by her mother's arguments, Lady Windermere falls naturally into the role of infant, needing guidance and support from the stronger adult: 'Take me home', she cries to her mother, '*holding out her hands to her, helplessly, as a child might do.*'[90]

---

[87] *Illusion*, III. 59.   [88] *LWF* IV. 115.
[89] Ibid. III. 82.   [90] Ibid. 83.

Mrs Erlynne's adult superiority is sustained to the end of the play. Fallen mothers like Odette and La Faneuse relinquished their children, aware of their own unworthiness for the role of mother; Mrs Erlynne abandons all attempts to reclaim her daughter when she understands the limitations to Lady Windermere's maturity and understanding. Like Odette before her, Mrs Erlynne asks a few probing questions and concludes that revelation is impossible:

MRS ERLYNNE. You are devoted to your mother's memory, Lady Windermere, your husband tells me.
LADY WINDERMERE. We all have ideals in life. At least we all should have. Mine is my mother.
MRS ERLYNNE. Ideals are dangerous things. Realities are better. They wound, but they're better.
LADY WINDERMERE. If I lost my ideals, I should lose everything.
MRS ERLYNNE. Everything?
LADY WINDERMERE. Yes.[91]

These lines signal the limits of Lady Windermere's education. She has learnt to reject the 'hard and fast rules' that she first subscribed to, as she tells her husband:

I don't think now that people can be divided into the good and the bad as though they were two separate races or creations. What are called good women may have terrible things in them, mad moods of recklessness, assertion, jealousy, sin. Bad women, as they are termed, may have in them sorrow, repentance, pity, sacrifice.[92]

She has moved beyond a puritan morality of absolutes, but she still divides and labels humanity. She now separates the world into not two but four categories: not just good and bad, but also good-with-bad and bad-with-good. Her essential standards of judgement are unchanged. Thus, when Lord Windermere says wonderingly to Lord Augustus, 'Well, you are certainly marrying a very clever woman!', Lady Windermere corrects him: 'Ah, you are marrying a very good woman!'[93] This final line is subtly ironic: were she to know Mrs Erlynne's true identity she would undoubtedly consider her anything but 'good', while the labelling of women as 'good' or otherwise is precisely what Mrs Erlynne herself had rejected.

[91] *LWF* IV. 124.   [92] Ibid. 109.   [93] Ibid. 132.

Mrs Erlynne realizes the narrowness of her daughter's understanding, that she cannot cope with the ambiguities and confusions of reality but must retain her false ideals as the basis
of her faith. So she lets her daughter preserve the myth of her
dead mother, like a reassuring teddy-bear, symbolizing the limits of her maturity. Wilde thus rewrites the scene from Sardou's
Odette, where the supposedly dead mother withdraws, leaving
her mythical counterpart to reign supreme. Odette is overcome
by shame when confronted with the purity of her daughter and
the imaginary mother she worships. She therefore departs, having
advised Bérangère to preserve her 'dead' mother's image as the
guardian angel of her life. Wilde reverses Sardou's standards:
the dead mother is not a symbol of purity and goodness, but
of failed understanding, of the false idealism which prevents
true compassion and acceptance.[94]

Wilde's reversal of the traditional relationship between the
fallen woman and the innocent maiden was even reflected in
the casting of the first production. Marion Terry, an actress
described as 'the embodiment of dramatic innocence and theatrical guilelessness', played Mrs Erlynne, while Lily Hanbury
was cast as Lady Windermere.[95] More than one critic expressed
their surprise, and their comments clearly reflect the simple
categorization of women that Wilde's play challenged. So A. B.
Walkley refers to Lady Windermere as 'the opposite type' to
Mrs Erlynne, while the critic of the *Daily Telegraph* asks, 'when
. . . did good woman ever play bad woman so well?'[96]

By presenting the fallen woman as superior in judgement to
the innocent and sheltered female, and by showing how Lady

---

[94] *Odette*, IV. v. 423. Mrs Erlynne's preference for reality over illusion may also
provide a direct rebuke to Leclerq's *Illusion*, where 'illusion' is continually associated with virtue, hope, and happiness, while 'reality' is synonymous with cynicism, pain, and despair, as for example when the heroine, showing her husband the
mark of where he hurt her, declares, 'The bruise is the true emblem of reality!'
(*Illusion*, I. 18).

[95] *Truth*, 31 (25 Feb. 1892), 386.

[96] A. B. Walkley, *Speaker*, 5 (27 Feb. 1892), 258; *Daily Telegraph* (22 Feb.
1892), 3. The costumes of the first production also reflected Wilde's unusual
characterization: mother and daughter both wore similarly stylish and restrained
costumes of mushroom brown in Act IV, for example, reflecting the essential
similarity between 'good' and 'bad' woman. For a full account of the costuming
see Joel Kaplan and Sheila Stowell's superb study, *Theatre and Fashion: Oscar
Wilde to the Suffragettes* (Cambridge: Cambridge University Press, 1994), 11–20.

Windermere's moral sense and understanding mature through her contact with the seamier side of life, Wilde challenged the literary and social convention that women must be sheltered if they were to remain pure. As a protective mother put it succinctly in Charles Reade's novel, *A Terrible Temptation*, 'Complete innocence means complete ignorance: and that is how all my girls went to their husbands.'[97] Thus, in Sardou's *Odette*, every male in the play, from Bérangère's father to her young suitor, gathers round to protect the innocent girl from any corrupting knowledge of the world. The protective Lord Windermere sees himself in just such a role, but his wife challenges his assumptions. Lord Windermere views the fallen and unfallen woman as races apart, divided by the hallowed ignorance of the latter. So, he declares, smiling as he strokes his wife's hair:

LORD WINDERMERE. Child, you and she belong to different worlds. Into your world evil has never entered.

LADY WINDERMERE. Don't say that, Arthur. There is the same world for all of us, and good and evil, sin and innocence, go through it hand in hand. To shut one's eyes to half of life that one might live securely is as though one blinded oneself that one might walk with more safety in a land of pit and precipice.[98]

Wilde does not merely question this careful sheltering of women from the harsher realities of life, he openly mocks it. The Duchess of Berwick ensures that her daughter's observation of the world is limited to photograph albums, sunsets, and maps of Australia. Lady Agatha is a comic caricature of the innocent young girl, the dutiful daughter, who utters no words but 'Yes, Mamma'. Wilde's Agatha is the comic version, Henry James's Aggie the tragic.[99]

Wilde further subverts the convention of sheltering young women from knowledge of the world by challenging the role of the protective male. Lord Windermere clearly believes that he is fulfilling the role of all-knowing guardian to his wife, but this very presumption only serves to emphasize his lack of understanding at the end of the play. As one reviewer remarked of Lord Windermere: 'He is made to do various silly things

---

[97] *A Terrible Temptation*, vol. i, ch. 8, p. 151.   [98] *LWF* IV. 130.
[99] See James's *The Awkward Age* (1899). James was present at the 1st perf. of *Lady Windermere's Fan*.

in the interests of justice, and evinces throughout the play
the knowledge of the world of the average country curate.'[100]
In *Odette* all the male characters band together to defend
Bérangère, while excluding the evil influence of Odette. In *Lady
Windermere's Fan*, Lord Windermere believes he is playing the
same role, but it is the fallen woman who is protecting him,
while the innocent female, his wife, achieves a better understanding of events than he does. Lord Windermere actually
regresses through the play. He ends the play regretting the
second chance he gave to Mrs Erlynne, and believing in the
hard-and-fast rules that Lady Windermere has learnt to reject.
He divides women clearly into good and bad, assuming that
Mrs Erlynne and his wife belong to entirely different worlds. It
is for this reason that Mrs Erlynne sees that he must never
know of his wife's weakness. Lord Windermere, blinkered by
his ideas of female virtue, must be protected from full knowledge of the facts, for he could never truly forgive his wife,
blind as he is to the complexities of human motive and impulse
which contradict the simple categories of virtuous and sinful
womanhood. As Mrs Erlynne observes, 'Love is easily killed.'[101]

This unusual dramatic hierarchy—the fallen woman being supreme, the innocent wife next in line, and the usually dominant
male left to be protected by both women—was largely the
result of Wilde's revision of the successive manuscript drafts.
In the final version Lady Windermere begins the play as a combination of naïve puritan and childlike rebel—her flight from
her husband is both desperate and defiant; she ends the play
maturer in judgement and capable of questioning her husband's
views—the final line is, after all, a challenge to his opinions. In
the first manuscript version, however, Lady Windermere begins
the play as a self-assured and determined woman and ends it
subdued and chastened, knowledge of her own weakness hum-
bling her before her husband.

The first Lady Windermere is a strident, assertive, and morally stringent woman. Her strict condemnation of sinners is not
based on the idealism which comes of innocence, for she is
clearly well acquainted with the weakness of others and the

ways of the world. When she is first informed of Mrs Erlynne's existence, she is only surprised that such a woman has dared to invade her territory: 'I didn't know people of that kind lived in our part of town. I thought they lived north of the Park.'[102] Discovering her husband's perfidy, she retains sufficient self-command to utter aphorisms on modern morality: 'What a hideous romance that has the cheque-book for its basis—a nineteenth-century romance. A romance of foulness.'[103] Where the final Lady Windermere quails before such a terrible revelation, her predecessor greets it as a challenge, an opportunity to display the unbending principle on which she prides herself: 'We have been too lax. We must make an example. I propose to begin with Mrs Erlynne. I think it would be rather dramatic.'[104] Her plan to strike Mrs Erlynne is not the desperate threat of the final version, but a more deliberate and vindictive act of self-righteous revenge. She delights in a cruelly ironic exchange with Lord Augustus, glorying in her self-appointed role of moral crusader: 'Good evening, Lord Augustus. I am very glad you've come. Theres someone coming here tonight whom you know. At least the Duchess tells me you know her. Her debut into good society will be interesting, and I don't think its likely to be forgotten.'[105] Lord Windermere begs his wife to behave graciously to Mrs Erlynne, and his wife answers him as his equal, if not his superior. Her defiance has none of the childlike desperation which marks her later incarnation; it is the coolly reasoned stance of the puritan:

> She is your mistress, and if a man brings his mistress to his wife's house he insults his wife publicly. And the wife has a right to defend herself. Remember the insult began with you. By hitting her across the face with my fan, I will be merely paying it back. Women have stood this sort of thing from their husbands too long. We are going to have a new regime in these matters.[106]

In his revisions, Wilde carefully excised Lady Windermere's knowledge of the world, so that the remaining statements represent the trusting idealism of youth rather than the pronouncements of a steel-edged morality. So, for example, in conversation with Lord Darlington, her criticism of modern marriage is cut. The exchange first stands as:

---

[102] Aut. MS BL Add. MS 37943: I. 24.   [103] Ibid. 20.
[104] Ibid. 30.   [105] Ibid. II. 37.   [106] Ibid. 39.

LORD DARLINGTON. You think the age very bad.

LADY WINDERMERE. From some points, yes. From the point of view of marriage, yes, I assure you, I shudder at half the people I meet. The modern husband goes one way, the modern wife another. Their paths divide, and if the two ever meet it must be with haggard faces and with shameful eyes. Nowadays people seem to look on life as a speculation. It is not a speculation. It is a sacrament. Its real presence is Love. Its purification is sacrifice.[107]

Once Wilde's pencil has been at work, the tone is radically altered, and the voice of the trusting *ingénue* is heard:

LORD DARLINGTON. You think the age very bad.

LADY WINDERMERE. I do, Lord Darlington. Nowadays people seem to look on life as a speculation. It is not a speculation. It is a sacrament. Its real presence is Love. Its purification is sacrifice.[108]

The effect of Wilde's revisions is to change the basic implications of the play. In the early version the focus is upon Lady Windermere, who is converted from stringent moral absolutism to a more charitable view of the world, while Mrs Erlynne serves as a demonstration of the good within the bad—a refined version of the whore with a heart of gold. Lady Windermere learns to regard the sins of others with more indulgence and to trust in her husband to guard her own weakness. Thus the first Lady Windermere runs from the frightening new life she now perceives and seeks instead the shelter of her husband's strong arms:

LORD WINDERMERE. We'll go away next week.

LADY WINDERMERE. Oh! before that. I want peace. I'm bewildered with life. It terrifies me. It terrifies me.

LORD WINDERMERE. Poor darling—we'll go away today, if you like.[109]

Lady Windermere abandons her defiant and confrontational tone, and instead plays the child under Lord Windermere's paternal guidance. In the final version, however, Lord Windermere's treatment of his wife as little more than a child seems inappropriately patronizing in view of her new knowledge. The final Lady Windermere does not run from life, and is no more

---

[107] Magdalen College MS 300: I. 6.

[108] Ibid. This is the version of the play shown by Wilde's autograph corrections, and is retained in the final 1893 published version.

[109] Aut. MS BL Add. MS 37943: IV. 91.

in need of protection from its harsher facts than her husband. She begins the play as the familiar childish figure, but it is her mother who appropriates the conventionally male role of teacher.

This emphasis on Lady Windermere's moral growth and independence from her husband's narrower system of values inverts the more traditional endings of plays from which Wilde probably borrowed material. Thus, in Lemaître's *Révoltée*, the reckless young wife ignores the admonishments of her newly revealed mother, and is only prevented from committing adultery by the intervention of her half-brother. The rebel of the title, however, ends the play suitably subdued, kneeling to ask forgiveness from her brother and her husband. In another contemporary play, *The Glass of Fashion* (1883) by Sydney Grundy, a wife is humbled into admitting her own inferiority to her husband.[110] In Grundy's play, Colonel Trevanion knows that his wife, Nina, was born illegitimately and that her younger sister, born after their parents' marriage, will inherit the family estate. Trevanion goes to considerable lengths to shield Nina from this terrible knowledge, accidentally leading his wife to believe that he has squandered all the money she supposedly inherited. Strong-willed and rebellious, Nina reacts to her husband's attempts to assert his authority by becoming entangled with a confidence trickster, and is only rescued from scandal by the resourcefulness of her younger sister, in a scene of concealment and discovery similar to the third act of Wilde's play. Nina finally discovers the truth, and bows in shame before her husband. Parentage is less important in Grundy's play than property: while Nina believes that she has brought considerable wealth into their marriage, she persists in giddily pursuing the world of fashion and neglecting her duty to her husband. Suitably humbled by knowledge of her economic dependency she meekly accepts her husband's declaration that 'I will no longer be the husband of Mrs Trevanion, you shall be Colonel Trevanion's wife'.[111] Lady Windermere, by contrast, may be

---

[110] Sydney Grundy, *The Glass of Fashion* (1883) (BL LCP Add. MS 53291L). I am again indebted for the discovery of this play to Kerry Powell's *Oscar Wilde and the Theatre of the 1890s*, 17–18. Grundy accused Wilde of plagiarizing his work, but there are no elements in *The Glass of Fashion* that are not common to other plays such as *Révoltée*, *Odette*, or Haddon Chambers's *The Idler*.

[111] *The Glass of Fashion*, II. 57.

led to a better understanding of her duty to her child, but she is exalted, not humbled, by the events of the play. In a neat reversal of the dramatic conventions, the errant wife ends the play at her husband's side, not meekly accepting his moral lessons but quietly correcting his narrowly absolute judgement.

Lady Windermere's Fan has often been seen by critics as an awkward combination of two types of drama. Regenia Gagnier talks of Wilde's society plays as based on the conflicting elements of 'social satire and melodramatic sentimentality', while Epifanio San Juan makes the same point more caustically when he comments: 'If one strips the play of its verbal pyrotechnics, and such "mindless chatter" as that of the Duchess of Berwick, one gets the residue of cheap melodrama.'[112] As shown above, far from being a cheap or sentimental melodrama, *Lady Windermere's Fan* borrows the language and characters of melodrama only to subvert them. The play is also surprisingly coherent and unified. Wilde painstakingly edited the play until every apparently irrelevant exchange or careless epigram contributed to the play as an artistic whole, echoing, elaborating, or questioning its themes. The 'sentimental melodrama' of Lady Windermere and her delinquent mother challenges conventional ideas of the good and bad woman, while the apparently idle chatter of Wilde's dandies develops and questions accepted notions of virtue and vice.

The all-male dialogue in Act III, for example, centres on the theme of male and female virtue. Believing themselves alone, the men cynically reject society's demands for purity and question its desirability; as Cecil Graham puts it: 'A man who moralises is usually a hypocrite, and a woman who moralises is invariably plain.'[113] The dandy undermines any simple moral dichotomy between good and bad, emphasizing instead the practical uses of a reputation for virtue in the case of women, and its lower market value in the case of men. So Graham comments to Lord Darlington: 'My dear fellow, what on earth should we men do going about with purity and innocence? A carefully thought-out buttonhole is much more effective.'[114] Graham's comment not only highlights the different standards

---

[112] Gagnier, *Idylls of the Marketplace*, 106; San Juan, *The Art of Oscar Wilde*, 143 n.
[113] *LWF* III. 90. [114] Ibid. 94.

applied to each sex, it also hints that female virtue may be
valued for its 'effectiveness' in the marriage market, not for any
intrinsic moral worth—a hint supported by the Duchess's ruthless chaperoning of her daughter. The more subversive touches
in this dialogue are developed through successive drafts. Thus,
in the first autograph version of the play, Graham remarks
that: 'That is the worst of women. They always want one to be
good. And if we're good when they meet us they don't love us
at all. They like to find us bad, and to leave us good.'[115] This
is simply a reference to the orthodox role of woman as reforming influence, as man's moral guardian. In the final version of
the play, however, Wilde pokes fun at precisely this conceit,
mocking the idea of reform and questioning the sexual effectiveness of virtue. So Graham comments instead that 'They like
to find us quite irretrievably bad, and to leave us quite unat-
tractively good.'[116]

In the final version of the play Lord Darlington is Wilde's
vehicle for much of this unorthodox morality. It is Darlington
who first questions Lady Windermere's hard-and-fast rules, and
who expounds the Wildean philosophy that 'life is far too
important a thing ever to talk seriously about'.[117] In Act II he
urges Lady Windermere to reject all society's values and to live
instead according to the dictates of individualism, realizing
herself in spite of the world. This unconventional philosophy is
later practised by Mrs Erlynne, while Darlington betrays his
own principles by first seeking to influence Lady Windermere
(influence being a major crime according to the creed of individualism) and then by subscribing to exactly the values he
questioned by worshipping her as the embodiment of female
virtue. Wilde's own sympathy with the individualist philosophy
that Darlington expounds is clear from his criticisms of Maurice
Barrymore's interpretation of the part in the American production. As he wrote to his New York agent:

I hear Barrymore dresses the part badly, and does not see that Darlington is *not* a villain, but a man who really believes that Windermere

---

[115] Aut. MS BL Add. MS 37943: III. 84.
[116] *LWF* III. 92. This is revised from the licensing copy, where men are referred
to as 'hopelessly good' (BL LCP Add. MS 53492H: III. 49). The whole issue of
male and female innocence is further developed by Wilde in *An Ideal Husband*.
[117] *LWF* I. 15.

is treating his wife badly, and wishes to save her. His appeal is not
to the weakness, but to the strength of her character (Act II).[118]

Once again, the moral ambiguity of Lord Darlington's character is the result of careful revision. In the first autograph version, Darlington is a cardboard villain redeemed only by love
for a good woman. As he tells Lady Windermere: 'People say
I am wicked—but I love you—that I am heartless—Ah! I love
you—love you as I have never loved any living thing.'[119] Even
in as late a version as that submitted to the Lord Chamberlain,
Lord Darlington still plays the traditional sensual villain, whose
rooms are sinisterly described as 'oriental and luxurious', and
whose entry in Act II significantly interrupts any attempt at
reconciliation between husband and wife.[120] While Darlington
is the conventionally depraved adulterer, he reinforces the simple moral structure of the play, presenting an immoral counterpart to Lord Windermere, the upright and protective husband.
When Darlington becomes a more ambiguous character, he
serves to develop the moral complexities set forth in the final
version of the play.

Similarly Wilde uses the Duchess of Berwick to demonstrate
the hypocrisy and materialism of society, the opposite side of the
coin to Lady Windermere's puritanism. The relations between
Mrs Erlynne and Lord Windermere reflect the links between
property and propriety on which their society is based; Lord
Windermere hopes that by paying money to Mrs Erlynne he
can maintain the illusions of morality on which his wife's faith
is founded. The Duchess of Berwick, like Lady Bracknell after
her, is an embodiment of society's standards. Her role was
probably modelled on that of Thérèse in Dumas's *Francillon*.[121]
The first act of *Lady Windermere's Fan* bears a marked resemblance to the first act of *Francillon*, in which a young wife,
Francine, learns of her husband's infidelity and is advised by an
older friend, Thérèse, to accept and ignore this as part of married
life. In Dumas's play, Thérèse is not just the voice of society,
she is the voice of reason; Francine claims to have revenged

---

[118] To Elisabeth Marbury (Feb. 1893), *More Letters*, 119.
[119] Aut. MS BL Add. MS 37943: II. 49–50.
[120] BL LCP Add. MS 53492H: III. 40 and II. 24.
[121] Alexandre Dumas *fils*, *Francillon*, *Théâtre Complet*, vii (Paris: Calmann Lévy,
1890), 1st perf. Théâtre Français, Paris, 17 Jan. 1887.

herself on her husband by committing a similar act of infidelity, but Thérèse saves her friend's marriage and reputation by
tricking her into a confession of innocence. The Duchess of
Berwick propounds society's strictures with equal complacency,
but the effect of her advice is not to underline society's wisdom
but to undermine it. Her pronouncements on the inevitable
inequality of marriage would seem comically cynical but for
the hint of personal tragedy which underlies them; when Lady
Windermere protests that she and her husband married for
love, the Duchess replies: 'Yes, we begin like that.'[122]

It is through the Duchess that Wilde emphasizes the materialism that lies beneath society's stern morality. She keeps her
daughter ignorant to ensure her marriageability, and quite bla-
tantly treats her son-in-law as a commodity; as she tells him,
'Ah! we know your value, Mr Hopper. We wish there were
more like you. It would make life so much easier.'[123] It is
property alone which guarantees propriety; so she reproves her
daughter: 'No nice girl should ever waltz with such particularly
younger sons! It looks so fast!'[124] The Duchess's priorities are
conveyed by subtle hints, the result of careful revision. Thus,
for example, in the first manuscript version, she comments that
her faithless husband 'never gave away large sums of money—
I am sure he didn't. He is so economical by nature.'[125] In the
final version, she declares instead: 'I am bound to say he never
gave away any large sums of money to anybody. He is far too
high-principled for that!'[126]

Lady Windermere's Fan is thus a far more radical and coherent
play than it is generally judged to be. Through painstaking,
detailed revision, Wilde used the plot mechanisms and characters
of the traditional dramas of the fallen woman and delinquent
mother to challenge the values on which those dramas were
based. *Lady Windermere's Fan* is heavily indebted to other contemporary plays, yet Wilde did not simply borrow material but

---

[122] *LWF* I. 20.   [123] Ibid. II. 39–40.
[124] Ibid. 37. The satire here is softened from the Duchess's more blatant boast
in an earlier typescript that 'Agatha has never waltzed with any thing under £5,000
a year' (Magdalen College MS 300: Act I, autograph addition on sheet inserted at
p. 11).
[125] Aut. MS BL Add. MS 37943: I. 15.   [126] *LWF* I. 19.

inverted and subverted it to produce a considerably more complex and revolutionary play than those of his predecessors.[127]

Wilde's radical subversion of dramatic conventions was not just a comment on the popular drama of his contemporaries, for the implications of *Lady Windermere's Fan* reach beyond the stage itself. The relevance of Wilde's comedy to contemporary society was emphasized by the elaborately realistic detail of the scenery and costumes; the characters on stage were to mirror those in the audience.[128] Wilde again emphasized the link between stage and reality, the hypocrisy of society and the antics of his actors, when he wrote to the editor of the *Daily Telegraph* just before his play opened, 'For anybody can act. Most people in England do nothing else. To be conventional is to be a comedian.'[129] At the opening night Wilde implicated his audience still further. Standing before the curtain, cigarette in hand, he carelessly reversed the respective roles of actors and audience:

Ladies and gentlemen: I have enjoyed this evening immensely. The actors have given us a charming rendering of a delightful play, and your appreciation has been most intelligent. I congratulate you on the great success of your performance, which persuades me that you think almost as highly of the play as I do myself.[130]

[127] Kerry Powell has also noted Wilde's use of contemporary plays, but he limits Wilde's originality to the surprise of the last act, where Mrs Erlynne rejects both motherhood and repentance. He thus sees *Lady Windermere's Fan* as essentially a far more conventional and less original play. As he writes: 'In a sense *Lady Windermere's Fan*, like many of Wilde's works, is an epigram writ large, whose force and wit derive from the antithesis of expectation. But epigrams are incompatible with sentiment and convention, and intrusions of that sort give Wilde's first comedy an ambivalence which in the final analysis injures it—but not mortally. Its final act completes a clever, but hesitating reversal of a retrograde theatrical genre. Wilde thereby fleshes out, from the dry bones of forgotten plays like *Illusion* and *The Glass of Fashion*, a work that is, in a strangely limited sense, his own' (*Oscar Wilde and the Theatre of the 1890s*, 31–2).

[128] George Alexander's wife, Florence, remembers that 'I arranged the flowers; in those days we had so much detail, and I loved to make things look real.' Quoted in A. E. W. Mason, *Sir George Alexander and the St James's Theatre* (London: Macmillan, 1935), 227. The store that Wilde set by such details is revealed in a letter to Grace Hawthorne (5 Oct. 1894), where he writes that his plays require 'artistic setting on the stage . . . beautiful dresses, a sense of the luxury of modern life, and unless you are going out with a management that is able to pay well for things that are worth paying for, and to spend money in suitable presentation, it would be much better for you not to think of producing my plays' (*Letters*, 374).

[129] To the editor of the *Daily Telegraph* (19 Feb. 1892), *Letters*, 311.

[130] Speech according to George Alexander. Quoted in Ellmann, *Oscar Wilde*, 346.

Predictably, the public remained oblivious to all but surface appearance; they were outraged, not by anything that Wilde said but by the fact that he had failed to extinguish his cigarette before ladies. As Mrs Erlynne mockingly observed to Lord Windermere: 'Manners before morals!'[131]

---

[131] *LWF* IV. 113.

4

A Woman of No Importance

As far as the serious presentation of life is concerned, what we require is more imaginative treatment, greater freedom from theatric language and theatric convention. It may be questioned, also, whether the consistent reward of virtue and punishment of wickedness be really the healthiest ideal for an art that claims to mirror nature.[1]

LADY WINDERMERE'S FAN ends with the triumph of the dandyesque Mrs Erlynne; A Woman of No Importance, Wilde's second successful society drama, first performed only fourteen months later, ends with the joint triumph of an evangelical puritan and a reformed magdalen, while the dandyesque Lord Illingworth is discarded as 'a man of no importance'.[2] The plot of the latter play seems to lack all the moral complexity of its predecessor: where the 'bad' Mrs Erlynne departed in proud possession of a husband, the wicked Lord Illingworth is left ignominiously deprived of his son, while virtue, in the form of his abandoned mistress, is rewarded with wealth and happiness in the new Eden of America. 'Repentance is quite out of date', declared Mrs Erlynne. Mrs Arbuthnot, the fallen woman of 'no importance', performs all the acts of repentance that her predecessor eschewed: she conscientiously attends church, visits the poor and the sick, and leads a life of secluded virtue. Wilde thus appears to contradict the conclusions of his earlier work.

A Woman of No Importance appears to be a conventional melodrama of seduction and judgement, a play whose only originality is to plead for greater leniency for repentant fallen women and harsher punishment for fallen men. By 1893 there was nothing particularly remarkable about such a message—it

[1] Wilde, commenting on an article by Mrs Craik on the condition of the English stage, 'Literary and Other Notes', WW (Dec. 1887), 85.
[2] A Woman of No Importance (London: John Lane, 1894), IV. 154. Dedicated 'To Gladys, Countess de Grey'. Cited below as WNI; references are to act and page number.

lies at the heart of H. A. Jones's *Saints and Sinners* (1884) and Pinero's *The Profligate* (1889), two successful plays written by establishment playwrights.[3] Yet, in spite of its conventional appearance, *A Woman of No Importance* is as radical a drama as its predecessors. The basic plot of the play is melodramatic and unoriginal, but, as with *Lady Windermere's Fan*, this very familiarity served to disguise Wilde's more controversial concerns. When Herbert Beerbohm Tree, the actor–manager who first produced the play and acted the part of Lord Illingworth, complimented Wilde on the success of his work, Wilde nonchalantly replied:

> Plots are tedious. Anyone can invent them. Life is full of them. Indeed one has to elbow one's way through them as they crowd across one's path. I took the plot of this play from *The Family Herald*, which took it—wisely, I feel—from my novel *The Picture of Dorian Gray*. People love a wicked aristocrat who seduces a virtuous maiden, and they love a virtuous maiden for being seduced by a wicked aristocrat. I have given them what they like, so that they may learn to appreciate what I like to give them.[4]

As this suggests, Wilde exploited the seduction drama to his own ends. Contemporary critics noted similarities between Wilde's play and a wealth of popular dramas dealing with seduction and illegitimacy: Dumas the younger's *Le Fils naturel* (1858), Sardou's *Les Vieux Garçons* (1865), Augier's *Le Fils de Giboyer* (1862) and *Les Fourchambault* (1878), and H. A. Jones's *The Dancing Girl* (1891).[5] Like these plays, *A Woman of No Importance* offered the theatrical clichés of the vulnerable woman who becomes a victim of male depravity, the humble and self-sacrificing mother, and the noble son who honours and protects her in spite of her shame. But Wilde subtly recast these conventional elements in order to question the sexual and social mores on which they were based.

    A number of contemporary critics accepted the play entirely at face value. Reviewers in *Black and White* and *The Athenæum*

---

[3] A. W. Pinero, *The Profligate* (London: Heinemann, 1891), 1st perf. Garrick Theatre, 24 Apr. 1889.

[4] Quoted in Hesketh Pearson, *Beerbohm Tree: His Life and Laughter* (London: Methuen, 1956), 67.

[5] See e.g. reviews in *Daily Graphic* (20 Apr. 1893), 7; *Athenæum*, 3417 (22 Apr. 1893), 515; *St James's Gazette* (20 Apr. 1893); *Observer* (23 Apr. 1893), 6.

complimented Wilde on producing such a moral play, and a writer in the *Illustrated Church News* went as far as to declare: 'A living sermon is being preached nightly at the Haymarket on the hollowness of the *fin-de-siècle* society code.'[6] Other reviewers who had accepted the play as a conventional moral tale found themselves perplexed by the less familiar elements of Wilde's treatment. An anonymous critic wrote in the *Saturday Review*:

Truth to tell, Gerald Arbuthnot is far from interesting, and Hester Worsley is, like him, something of a bore and a prig. Indeed, Mr. Wilde does not shine as a depictor of candour and innocence. His enthusiasms are flat and his moralizings tedious. Gerald's interest in his patron appears to be prompted by his hope of advancement, and the whole force of the strong, if not very novel, situation at the end of the third act is completely destroyed by the fact that his bold intervention, when his sweetheart has been insulted by Illingworth, follows on his mealy-mouth comment on his mother's story.[7]

W. B. Yeats noted the same curious imbalance in the apparently familiar melodramatic format. Reviewing the published text of the play, Yeats commented on the way in which the audience's sympathies were led away from the drama's ostensible heroes and towards its apparent villains:

There is something of heroism in always being master enough of oneself to be witty; and therefore the public of to-day feels with Lord Illingworth and Mrs Allonby much as the public of yesterday felt, in a certain sense, with that traditional villain of melodrama who never laid aside his cigarette and his sardonic smile. The traditional villain had self-control. Lord Illingworth and Mrs Allonby have self-control and intellect; and to have these things is to have wisdom, whether you obey it or not . . . [T]he tragic and emotional people, the people who are important to the story, Mrs Arbuthnot, Gerald Arbuthnot and Hester Worsley, are conventions of the stage. They win our hearts with no visible virtue, and though intended to be charming and good

[6] Unsigned reviews in *Black and White*, 5 (29 Apr. 1893), 318; *Athenæum*, 3417 (22 Apr. 1893), 515–16; *Illustrated Church News* (27 May 1893), 556. Wilde seems to have been amused by such reactions, writing to his publisher that the published version 'should have a good sale at Liverpool where it has been lectured on and formed a text for reckless sermons': letter to John Lane (Aug. 1894), *More Letters*, 124.

[7] Unsigned review, *Saturday Review*, 75 (6 May 1893), 482–3.

and natural, are really either heady and undistinguished, or morbid with what Mr. Stevenson has called 'the impure passion of remorse'.[8]

These reviewers divided the characters into two camps—the good (Hester, Gerald, and Mrs Arbuthnot) and the bad (Lord Illingworth and Mrs Allonby)—and then observed that while the plot presented the triumph of the first camp, all the best tunes belonged to the second. A perceptive critic in *Black and White* explained this apparent contradiction by observing that Wilde's writing operated on more than one level, the more sophisticated elements of the drama combining with the crassly familiar in order to please the unthinking masses:

As long as the pits of our theatres are filled with one kind of audience and the galleries with another, plays must exist to please both. There is a *Family Herald* sort of audience in the upper regions of the theatre, that asks for the triumph of virtue and the humiliation of vice, and cares nothing for art, and wit, and true comedy and Mr. Wilde flings the two or three bits of claptrap in his play to the 'Gods'.[9]

A skit on *A Woman of No Importance* published in the *Theatre* also highlighted the number of broadly melodramatic moments clearly designed to placate a simple-minded gallery. So in a parodic 'Condensed Drama' the climax at the end of Act III is picked out as a deliberate piece of audience manipulation:

HESTER [*enters in a state of great indignation, followed by Lord Illingworth*]. Gerald, I love you; Lord Illingworth has insulted me. I was walking with him in the dark with his arm round my waist, when suddenly and without first asking my permission, he kissed me.

GERALD. Villain! [*Gallery wakes up.*] I was told that you were a profligate, and I esteemed you. I heard that you had ruined many happy homes and I reverenced you; but now that you have bestowed an unsolicited salute upon an American citizen I propose to thrash you within an inch of your life [*gallery wide awake and expectant*], so clear a ring, mother, and hold my coat.

MRS ARBUTHNOT [*to herself*]. Now for an effective curtain. [*With pardonable pride*] This, I think, is *my* situation.

GERALD [*squaring up to Lord Illingworth*]. Come on!

---

[8] W. B. Yeats, 'An Excellent Talker', *Bookman* (Mar. 1895), pp. vii–viii, 182. Review of publication of *A Woman of No Importance* in Oct. 1894.
[9] *Black and White* (6 May 1893), 318.

MRS ARBUTHNOT [*throwing herself between them in the approved fashion*]. Gerald, forbear! If thou wouldst strike anything let it be an attitude, for he, Lord Illingworth, is thy father!
[*Sensation, group and curtain.*][10]

Modern critics, such as Alan Bird and Norbert Kohl, have similarly ascribed the more melodramatic elements of the play to the limitations of Wilde's skill and his willingness to compromise his art to the demands of popular taste.[11] Kerry Powell too, while noting some differences between Wilde's play and those from which he borrowed the substance of his plot, is forced to conclude that, ultimately, *A Woman of No Importance* 'fails because it never frees itself of such uninspiring ancestors as *The Dancing Girl* and *Madame Aubert*. Its good moments are freakish appendages, not saving graces.'[12] Where Wilde's contemporaries were puzzled by his failure to elicit more admiration and sympathy for his good characters, modern critics have tended to explain this by presenting the play as less a conflict between good and evil than between dandyism and puritanism, logic and emotion, or aristocrats and commoners.[13] Two notable exceptions are Christopher Nassaar and Patricia Behrendt, both of whom find incest at the heart of the play. Nassaar interprets it as a parable of inverted morality where Mrs Arbuthnot is the most sinister character, seeking to secure her son for her own unnatural passions.[14] Behrendt argues that Lord Illingworth has sexual designs on Gerald, designs which are in no way altered by knowledge of his parenthood.[15]

---

[10] *Theatre*, 21 (June 1893), 330.
[11] See e.g. Bird, *The Plays of Oscar Wilde*, 114–34; Kohl, *Oscar Wilde*, 224–54.
[12] Powell, *Oscar Wilde and the Theatre of the 1890s*, 72.
[13] Rodney Shewan, for example, interprets the play as a battle between dandyism and puritanism (*Oscar Wilde*, 168–77); Epifanio San Juan emphasizes a struggle between male logic and female emotion (*The Art of Oscar Wilde*, 154–69); Peter Raby divides the cast into aristocrats and non-aristocrats (*Oscar Wilde*, 91–6). Philip Cohen, however, views the play in simple moral terms as a conflict between good and evil, the good Mrs Arbuthnot regaining her lost paradise, while the 'satanic' Lord Illingworth is banished (*The Moral Vision of Oscar Wilde*, 192–203).
[14] Nassaar, *Into the Demon Universe*, 109–22.
[15] Behrendt, *Oscar Wilde*, 147–58. Behrendt quotes with approval Lytton Strachey's summary of the play after seeing the 1907 revival: 'Mr. Tree is a wicked lord, staying in a country house, who has made up his mind to bugger one of the guests—a handsome young man of twenty. The handsome young man is delighted; when his mother enters, she sees his Lordship and recognises him as having copulated with her twenty years before, the result of which was—the handsome young

Wilde's successive manuscript revisions of the play show him carefully moving away from the more conventional dramas to which he owed much of his play's plot and situation. *A Woman of No Importance* is not based on simple contrasts, whether between good and evil, logic and passion, or aristocrat and commoner, for it is less concerned with binary oppositions than with the power structure which underlies and creates such dichotomies. The play does more than offer a stereotypical battle between wicked aristocrat and seduced maiden; it questions the social and sexual customs which produced those stereotypes. It is less a matter of whether Lord Illingworth or Mrs Arbuthnot be the guiltier party, than whether terms of innocence and guilt should be applied to human, and more specifically sexual, behaviour. As Wilde commented to an interviewer:

Several plays have been written lately that deal with the monstrous injustice of the social code of morality at the present time. It is indeed a burning shame that there should be one law for men and another law for women. I think that there should be no law for anybody.[16]

Wilde began work on *A Woman of No Importance* in July or August 1892. He wrote to Herbert Beerbohm Tree, the manager of the Haymarket Theatre to whom the play was promised: 'I have written two acts, and had them set up by the typewriter: the third is nearly done, and I hope to have it all ready in ten days or a fortnight at most. I am very pleased with it so far.'[17] On 13 October 1892 Wilde signed over to Tree the rights of his new play. The success of *Lady Windermere's Fan* had clearly put Wilde in a strong negotiating position, for the contract secured him a considerable percentage of the play's takings, in spite of the fact that it was not yet completed.[18]

Once again, Wilde took *A Woman of No Importance* through several different drafts before arriving at the version performed

man. She appeals to Lord Tree [*sic*] not to bugger his own son. He replies that it is additional reason for doing it (oh! he is a very *wicked Lord*).' (p. 156)

[16] Quoted in Pearson, *The Life of Oscar Wilde*, 251.
[17] To Herbert Beerbohm Tree (*c*.1 Sept. 1892), *Letters*, 320.
[18] Signed copy of contract in Herbert Beerbohm Tree Collection, Drama Dept., University of Bristol, repr. in *More Letters*, 118. For a comparison of Wilde's royalties with those of other contemporary playwrights, see John Russell Stephens, *The Profession of the Playwright: British Theatre 1800–1900* (Cambridge: Cambridge University Press, 1992), ch. 3.

at the Haymarket Theatre on 19 April 1893. The version performed can be reconstructed with more than usual accuracy
thanks to a prompt-book and rehearsal scripts preserved by
Tree.[19] These rehearsal copies, however, differ from the version
of the play published by John Lane in October 1894, and it is
thus the published edition which must b⌐ taken as the final
version of the play as Wilde intended it.[20] The development of
the play through its successive drafts offers insights into Wilde's
intentions, as the drama moves away from its conventional
roots to achieve its final complex and subversive form.[21] Wilde
sent typescripts of the play to Tree at different stages in its development, seeking the advice of a fashionable actor–manager.
Looking back on this partnership more than twenty years later,
Tree portrayed himself as a much-needed mentor:

You know 'A Woman of No Importance' was written for me. Wilde
had the idea of the character of Lord Illingworth for me and he came
to me with it. I was playing in Belfast when he wrote the play, and
he came there so that I could help him. In those days I used to work
a great deal with the dramatists who wrote for me, a practice not
indulged in so frequently now. I remember sitting up night after night
in our rooms at the hotel, drinking porter and eating roast beef, while
the play was in process of formation.[22]

This retrospectively rosy version of their collaboration is contradicted not only by the fact that Wilde actually composed the

---

[19] Herbert Beerbohm Tree Collection, Bristol. This includes several typescripts
and carbon copies with pencil and ink corrections, actors' parts, drafts of the
contract between Wilde and Tree, property lists, and diagrams of sets. For a complete list of the contents of this collection see Russell Jackson and Ian Small, 'Some
New Drafts of a Wilde Play', *English Literature in Transition*, 30/1 (1987), 7–15.

[20] *WNI.*

[21] MSS referred to in this chapter are listed here in chronological order. (*a*) Aut.
MS draft entitled 'Mrs Arbuthnot', BL Add. MS 37944. (*b*) Typescript, corrected
in author's hand, entitled 'Mrs Arbuthnot'. BL Add. MS 37945. (*c*) Typescript of
A Woman of No Importance submitted to the Lord Chamberlain's Office. BL Add.
MS 53524N. (*d*) First edn. *A Woman of No Importance* (London, 1894). See nn.
61–3 below for details of various working copies of the play. For a more detailed
account of the play's composition and for a complete stemma of the play, see,
Jackson and Small, 'Some New Drafts of a Wilde Play', and introduction to *A
Woman of No Importance*, in *Two Society Comedies*, ed. Small and Jackson, pp.
ix, 2–9. All references are to act and page number.

[22] 'Behold the First Lord Illingworth; Sir Herbert Tree, New York's Busiest
Actor, Reminisces Distractedly of the Beginnings of *A Woman of No Importance*',
New York Times (30 Apr. 1916), sect. 2, 7.

play in Cromer, but by Tree himself, who told his biographer, Hesketh Pearson, that he produced *A Woman of No Importance* 'With the interference of Wilde'.[23] The version Tree's company performed was not precisely the version which Wilde published a year later, a fact which suggests that Wilde's own intentions and the demands of the popular commercial stage were not always in accord.[24]

The sentimental plot of *A Woman of No Importance* centres on Mrs Arbuthnot, the fallen woman of the title who is thus casually dismissed by her former lover. She is a woman who, having borne an illegitimate child and failed to persuade the father to marry her, sentences herself to a life of charity and humble seclusion in atonement for her past sin. She is threatened with further suffering when her former seducer returns and attempts to alienate her son's affections from her and claim the boy as his own. Good triumphs, however, and she is finally rewarded for her virtue when the son not only forgives his mother's past transgression but offers her a happier life, living abroad with himself and his pure young wife. This plot was familiar to Wilde's audiences not only through sentimental fiction, as Wilde suggested with his claim to have borrowed it from the *Family Herald*, but through numerous other dramas of illegitimacy and seduction.

Wilde's play closely paralleled Dumas's *Le Fils naturel*, and the similarity was noted by a number of contemporary critics.[25] In Dumas's play a young aristocrat, Charles Sternay, seduces Clara, a household servant, who bears him a son and then waits patiently for him to marry her. Only when she hears that Sternay is about to take a rich wife to further his career does

[23] Pearson, *Beerbohm Tree*, 69. The first acts were begun in London and Babbacombe and the last two were written in Norfolk, from where the names Hunstanton and Brancaster originate.

[24] This is not to portray Tree as purely a fashionably commercial manager. Wilde's play was preceded by H. A. Jones's *The Dancing Girl*, but it was also succeeded by matinées of Ibsen's *An Enemy of the People*. Pearson, *Beerbohm Tree*, 72.

[25] Alexandre Dumas *fils*, *Le Fils naturel*, *Théâtre Complet*, iii (Paris: Calmann Lévy, 1890), 1st perf. Paris, Théâtre du Gymnase-Dramatique, 16 Jan. 1858. Perf. by the Comédie-Française, Gaiety Theatre, London, 4 June 1879. For reviews commenting on the similarity of Wilde's play, see e.g. *Daily Graphic* (20 Apr. 1893), 7; *Athenæum*, 3417 (27 Apr. 1893), 515–16.

Clara lose faith in him, rejecting the money he offers and leaving the neighbourhood. Twenty years later their son Jacques applies for the hand of Hermine, Sternay's niece, and is rejected by his own father on the grounds of his illegitimacy. Sternay gives a number of logical but cowardly reasons for his refusal, pointing to the public shame which would be visited upon himself and his niece if it were known that he had accepted as a son-in-law the man whom he had refused to recognize as his son. Sternay's arguments are, as Jacques observes, 'la froide logique de l'égoïsme social' [the cold logic of society's self-interest].[26] Sternay's reasoning undergoes a change, however, when Jacques becomes a national hero, having used his diplomatic skills to prevent the outbreak of a major European war. Sternay now openly boasts of his fatherhood and prepares to welcome his famous son into the bosom of his aristocratic family. Jacques, however, firmly rejects his offer; he refuses to abandon his mother and ignore her years of noble sacrifice by exchanging her name for that of his calculatedly selfish father. Sternay again declares that he therefore may not marry Hermine. Jacques thereupon outmanœuvres his ambitious father. He will not honour Sternay's name by assuming it himself, but he will give his father a nobler title; Jacques has asked only one favour of the grateful minister in return for his services—that his father be granted the title of count that he has always desired. Sternay accepts the title and acknowledges his son's moral and strategic victory:

STERNAY. Vous vous vengez noblement, Jacques; mais si vous ne voulez pas m'appeler votre père, vous me permettrez bien de vous appeler mon fils?
JACQUES [*en souriant*]. Oui, mon oncle.[27]

[STERNAY. You avenge yourself nobly, Jacques; but if you do not wish to call me your father, will you allow me to call you my son?
JACQUES [*smiling*]. Yes, uncle.]

Despite the similarity in situation between Dumas's unmarried mother and Wilde's, there are significant differences in their character and behaviour. Clara is constantly humble, self-sacrificing, and timid. She has been careful not to press Sternay

---

[26] *Le Fils naturel*, II. iv.   [27] Ibid. IV. ix.

into granting her the marriage which she so desperately desires for the sake of her son. Coming from a humbler rank than her lover, she is afraid of appearing to have trapped him into matrimony by becoming pregnant. Clara is self-effacing to the point of being ready to commit suicide if that would facilitate her son's marriage. Aware that her fallen status is a constant reminder of Jacques's illegitimacy, she offers to leave the country, to disappear from his life for ever and live in lonely poverty rather than impair his future standing.

Clara's entire identity and existence are bound up in her son. She greets him on his glorious return:

> Mais pensais-tu quelquefois combien je devais être heureuse, plus encore que ne le serait une autre mère? Car tu es tout pour moi, Jacques; je n'ai ni père, ni mère, ni mari. Tu es tout mon passé, tout mon présent, tout mon avenir. Tu es mon seul raison d'être dans ce monde. Si tu mourrais, je mourrais![28]

> [But have you sometimes thought how happy I must be, happier than any other mother would be? Because you are everything to me, Jacques; I have neither father, nor mother, nor husband. You are all my past, all my present, all my future. You are my only reason for living in this world. If you died, I would die!]

This total absorption is also to be found in Mrs Arbuthnot, but, her devotion to her son is a form of maternal possessiveness. Clara, however, does not regard her son as an extension of herself, but herself as subservient to him. The self-seeking Sternay and his proud mother, the Marquise d'Orgebac, exploit Clara's humility to their own ends. They need ask nothing of her, for she always eagerly anticipates their egotistical plans. When Jacques learns that his father now plans to adopt him, he asks his mother whether his aspiring family has demanded yet more sacrifices of her. She replies:

> Non, ils ne m'ont rien demandé. C'est moi qui ai réfléchi, qui songe à ta position, qui me dis que, pour ton avenir, le nom de ton père te sera plus utile que le mien, et, pour cette jeune fille qui t'aime, et qui t'a été patiente et dévouée, le nom et le titre de sa famille seront préférables.[29]

> [No, they have asked nothing of me. It's I who have reflected, I who think of your position, who say to myself that, for the sake of

your future, your father's name will be of more use to you than mine, and, for this young girl who loves you, and has waited devotedly for you, the name and title of his family will be preferable.]

In contrast to Clara Vignot, Wilde's unmarried mother fights fiercely against her former lover for sole possession of their son. Her absorption in her son does not lead her to deny her own desires but to place them before the wishes of her child. She tells Lord Illingworth that she will not allow her son to become secretary to the man who has caused her so much suffering in the past. 'My dear Rachel', replies Lord Illingworth, 'I must candidly say that I think Gerald's future considerably more important than your past.' The mother's reply denies her son any independent existence: 'Gerald cannot separate his future from my past.'[30] Mrs Arbuthnot even attributes this opinion to Gerald—an opinion that he has patently never expressed since he still knows nothing of her past.

Both Clara Vignot and Rachel Arbuthnot have speeches in which they reminisce about their son's boyhood. These speeches, though apparently similar, have very different implications. Clara talks of how her tiny son would put his arms about her as she worked through the night, his love giving her the strength to continue, while he dreamt aloud of how he would look after her when he was rich. At the end of her speech, mother and son fall into each other's arms crying. Mrs Arbuthnot's speech, by contrast, reveals a tension between the demands of the mother and the uncomprehending independence of the son:

[B]oys are careless often, and without thinking give pain, and we always fancy that when they come to man's estate and know us better they will repay us. But it is not so. The world draws them from our side, and they make friends with whom they are happier than they are with us, and have amusements from which we are barred, and interests that are not ours; and they are unjust to us often, for when they find life bitter they blame us for it, and when they find life sweet we do not taste its sweetness with them . . .[31]

Where Clara, ashamed of her fallen status and the stain she has visited upon her son, sees her only role in life as one of humble self-abasement, Mrs Arbuthnot asserts a greater hold over her son thanks to her status as single parent. Unlike the conventional

[30] *WNI* II. 79.   [31] Ibid. IV. 135.

stage-mother, Mrs Arbuthnot rejects the standard association of maternity and self-sacrifice. Mrs Erlynne rejected motherhood as too exacting; Mrs Arbuthnot simply redefines the mother's role, demanding instead that the son sacrifice himself to her.

In more conventional dramas than Wilde's the role of the unmarried mother is uniquely one of self-sacrifice, humility, and self-effacement. In Émile Augier's *Les Fourchambault* Madame Bernard was abandoned by her lover because his unscrupulous father had led him to doubt the paternity of their child.[32] Yet Madame Bernard never blames him for his lack of faith. She accepts her fate and lives a life of virtuous and obscure humility. Only when her former lover faces financial ruin does she reveal his identity to their son, and then only to urge Bernard to save his father from the dishonour of bankruptcy. Her money saves the man who once abandoned her, but she remains quietly in the background, winning admiration for her proper and dignified retreat from a world she is no longer entitled to enter. Her reputation for virtue, like Clara's, rests entirely on her modesty and reserve.

Ostensibly, Mrs Arbuthnot fits into this role: she wears black, hides away from the bustle of society, and devotes herself to religion and charity. Yet when she describes this life of piety and atonement to Gerald it is in tones far from conventional:

> And you thought that I didn't care for the pleasant things of life. I tell you I longed for them, but did not dare to touch them, feeling I had no right. You thought I was happier working amongst the poor. That was my mission, you imagined. It was not, but where else was I to go? The sick do not ask if the hand that smooths their pillow is pure, nor the dying care if the lips that touch their brow have known the kiss of sin. It was you I thought of all the time; I gave to them a love you did not need; lavished on them a love that was not theirs . . .[33]

Mrs Arbuthnot is no quietly resigned magdalen but a passionate woman whose strict moral sense is constantly at war with

---

[32] Émile Augier, *Les Fourchambault, Théâtre Complet de Émile Augier*, vii (Paris: Calmann Lévy, 1897), 1st perf. Paris, Théâtre Français, 8 Apr. 1878. Perf. by the Comédie-Française, Gaiety Theatre, London, 20 June 1879.
[33] *WNI* IV. 135–6.

her own deepest emotions. More conventional treatments of
the unmarried mother theme like *Le Fils naturel* allow the
audience to sympathize with a fallen woman by presenting her
as a passive victim, a woman whose fall was the fault of another and who may thus, without contradiction, play the role
of virtuous and pure mother to her illegitimate offspring, while
leading a life of modest atonement for her former sin. Wilde
breaks this mould by creating a woman who is no cardboard
saint but all too palpably flesh and blood. As a young girl,
Rachel Arbuthnot's passions overruled her strict moral upbringing and she left home with her lover. Later she condemns
herself according to her inherited moral code, while continuing
to find her emotions in conflict with orthodox social and moral
laws. She rejects marriage to the father of her son, explaining:

> you were always in my heart, Gerald, too much in my heart. For,
> though day after day, at morn or evensong, I have knelt in God's
> house, I have never repented of my sin. How could I repent of my
> sin when you, my love, were its fruit. Even now that you are bitter
> to me I cannot repent. I do not. You are more to me than inno-
> cence. I would rather be your mother—oh! much rather!—than
> have been always pure. . . . Oh, don't you see? Don't you under-
> stand! It is my dishonour that has made you so dear to me. It is my
> disgrace that has bound you so closely to me. It is the price I have
> paid for you—the price of soul and body—that makes me love you
> as I do. Oh, don't ask me to do this horrible thing. Child of my
> shame, be still the child of my shame![34]

Mrs Arbuthnot, like Mrs Erlynne before her, eschews repentance, yet, unlike Mrs Erlynne, she does not reject the morality
which condemns her but rather continues to wrestle with laws
too restrictive to allow room for her own natural passions. Mrs
Arbuthnot is more typically female in her rebellion, for as Lord

[34] Ibid. 136. Wilde here smuggles in under melodramatic covering views which
provoked outrage when more baldly stated over a decade later in St John Hankin's
play, *The Last of the De Mullins* (London: Martin Secker, 1908). Hankin's heroine
also rejects marriage to the father of her illegitimate child and celebrates the joys
of motherhood, with or without marriage. The play was performed before the
Stage Society at the Haymarket Theatre, 6 and 7 Dec. 1908, and its reception
caused Shaw to remark: 'The play will have to fight its way like *A Doll's House.*'
Bernard Shaw's Letters to Granville Barker, ed. C. B. Purdom (New York: Phoenix
House, 1956), 143.

Illingworth observes: 'Every woman is a rebel, and usually in wild revolt against herself.'[35]

It is primarily the fierceness of Mrs Arbuthnot's passions that sets her apart from her literary predecessors. Mrs Arbuthnot's sexuality and the intensity of her emotions remain uncurbed, while fallen heroines like Mrs Gaskell's Ruth and Nathaniel Hawthorne's Hester Prynne earn forgiveness by learning to distrust and repress their instinctive passions. In her novel *Ruth* (1853), Mrs Gaskell pleads for greater charity towards fallen women, basing her argument on the tale of a young girl who is seduced without ever understanding her situation. Ruth, once she has been properly educated in the tenets of her society and its religion, becomes a model of piety, humility, and generosity.[36] She is the perfect example of the unmarried mother: she visits the poor and tends to the sick but with none of the thwarted passion which torments Wilde's heroine. Nor does Ruth find any conflict between her love for her child and her love of God:

Her whole heart was in her boy. She often feared that she loved him too much—more than God himself—yet she could not bear to pray to have her love for her child lessened. But she would kneel down by his little bed at night . . . and tell God what I have now told you, that she feared she loved her child too much, yet could not, would not, love him less; and speak to Him of her one treasure as she could speak to no earthly friend. And so, unconsciously, her love for her child led her up to love of God, to the All-knowing, who read her heart.[37]

Nathaniel Hawthorne's Hester Prynne, heroine of his novel *The Scarlet Letter* (1850), has an illegitimate daughter 'named . . . "Pearl", as being of great price,—purchased with all she had,—her mother's only treasure!'[38] Wilde directly echoes Hawthorne when his heroine muses: 'It may be that I am too bound to [Lord Illingworth] already, who, robbing me, yet left me richer, so that in the mire of my life I found the pearl of price, or what I thought would be so.'[39] Hester, like Mrs

---

[35] *WNI* III. 94.   [36] *Ruth*, 3 vols. (London: Chapman & Hall, 1853).
[37] Ibid. ii. 130–1.
[38] Nathaniel Hawthorne, *The Scarlet Letter* (Cambridge: Riverside Press, 1879), 102.
[39] *WNI* IV. 134.

Arbuthnot, is threatened with having her child taken from her and suffers from her Pearl's limited affection. When the puritan magistrate suggests taking the child, Hester responds fiercely:

> 'God gave me the child!' cried she. 'He gave her in requital of all things else, which ye had taken from me. She is my happiness!—she is my torture none the less! See ye not, she is the scarlet letter, only capable of being loved, and so endowed with a million-fold the power of retribution for my sin?'[40]

Pearl links her mother to God, reminding her of her sin, but keeping her from despair and preserving her capacity for love. Indeed, it is suggested in the novel that Hester Prynne is closer to the true Christian religion than the narrow-minded, retributive New England community from which she is excluded.

Mrs Arbuthnot is also an exile from her society, but, unlike Hester, her exclusion is self-imposed; none of her neighbours are aware of her actual status. It is not the inhabitants of Hunstanton who impose rigid standards of female purity; Mrs Allonby, who at a generous estimate ran away only once before her marriage, is welcome there. The American heiress is drawn to Mrs Arbuthnot precisely because she keeps to the strict moral code which Hunstanton society, to Hester Worsley's disgust, frequently waives. Mrs Arbuthnot separates herself, and, bearing her sin with what verges on pride, she deliberately rejects any connection with the rest of her sex:

> I owe nothing to other women. There is not one of them who will help me. There is not one woman in the world to whom I could go for pity, if I would take it, or for sympathy, if I could win it . . . I am a tainted thing. But my wrongs are my own, and I will bear them alone. I must bear them alone. What have women who have not sinned to do with me, or I with them? We do not understand each other.[41]

Mrs Arbuthnot's absolute morality and self-immolation serve another purpose, for, if both mother and son are to bear the badge of shame and to be excluded from society, then she is left in sole possession of him. So, when Gerald tells her of his love for Hester Worsley, she remembers the American girl's harshly moral declarations, and cruelly informs her son: 'I fear

---

[40] Hawthorne, *The Scarlet Letter*, 128.   [41] *WNI* IV. 132–3.

you need have no hopes of Miss Worsley. I know her views on
life. She has just told them to me.'[42]

The Mrs Arbuthnot presented in earlier manuscript versions
of the play is a softer, more pliable and conventional character.
She is a woman who has been taught to look more kindly on
others through knowledge of her own weakness, and who therefore displays little of the stern absolutism of her successor. So,
in the first manuscript version, Gerald comments to his mother:

> I have often heard you say that we should all be more charitable
> one about another.... And you have always been so charitable
> yourself about people, mother. You have always said that it is
> unfair to judge people by their pasts. And if anyone has done
> anything wrong, you have always been the one to find excuses for
> them, and to say that they are going to lead a better life and that
> sort of thing.[43]

In spite of her strong love for her son, the first Mrs Arbuthnot
puts his needs before her own. So she recalls Gerald's childhood: 'And then you began to grow up, and became stronger,
oh! much stronger, and ran about, and wanted playmates. And
I felt you would be happier at school than you were at home.
It was dull for you here, with only me to talk to, and so I sent
you to school.'[44] The first Mrs Arbuthnot thus plays a role
much closer to that of Dumas's Clara Vignot. Indeed, an exchange between Gerald and his mother in an early manuscript
draft virtually reproduces situations from *Le Fils naturel*, presenting a cowed and self-effacing Mrs Arbuthnot, significantly different from her final version. So, in *Le Fils naturel*, when Jacques
first learns of his true parentage he reproaches his mother:

> quand j'aurais été en âge de comprendre et de travailler, il fallait
> m'avouer toute la vérité et faire de moi un ouvrier obscur, sans
> autre ambition que son pain de chaque jour ... il ne fallait pas faire
> de moi un faux gentilhomme affeublé d'un nom d'emprunt, vivant
> sans pudeur et sans honte d'un double déshonneur.[45]

---

[42] *WNI* III. 112.

[43] Aut. MS BL Add. MS 37944: III. 204–5. Written in black ink in four MS
books, each containing one of the four acts. After the first eight pages, the booklet
containing the fourth act has been turned upside-down so that the page-numbering
is reversed. Corrections have been made to this MS by Wilde in lead pencil and
red pencil. After the preliminary sketch-book, sold at auction in New York, this
is the earliest version of the play.

[44] Aut. MS BL Add. MS 37944: IV. 252.   [45] Dumas, *Le Fils naturel*, II. vi.

[... when I was old enough to understand and to work, you should have told me the whole truth and made me a humble labourer, with no other ambition than earning my daily bread.... you should not have made me a false gentleman, handicapped by a borrowed name, living without modesty or shame under a double dishonour.]

Gerald's reaction to the same news in the first draft of Wilde's play is similar: 'We had no right to be here at all, with a false name, a false position, a false life. I know you never wanted to go into society and that sort of thing, mother. But still it would have been better if we had lived somewhere with poor common people.'[46] Mrs Arbuthnot's reply is crucial. Rather than indignantly asserting her own integrity before Gerald's orthodox morality as the final Mrs Arbuthnot does, she cowers before his reproaches:

I will go anywhere you wish, and live as you choose. Work if it is necessary to work, starve if one of the two must starve. If there is ignominy it shall be mine. If there is disgrace it shall be mine also. Or if you think it would be wiser for you to be by yourself, well, I don't mind living alone ... if you will let me see you, from time to time, Gerald. You needn't let people know that I'm your mother, if you don't wish it.[47]

The final Mrs Arbuthnot may talk of repentance, but it is self-assertion not self-effacement which comes naturally to her.

A similar transformation takes place with Lord Illingworth. Where Mrs Arbuthnot's original type is the repentant and humble fallen woman, Lord Illingworth's original type is the moustache-twirling villain of traditional melodrama, the cynical and stylish aristocrat who looks on with heartless contempt as his victim suffers. The autograph manuscript presents a figure very close to the corrupt and witty Lord Henry Wotton of *The Picture of Dorian Gray*—Wilde himself pointed out the similarity.[48] Lord Henry preached a doctrine of individualism and self-perfection while manipulating Dorian, leading him not to discover his own true character but simply to reflect Lord Henry's own jaded view of life. The first Lord Illingworth similarly seeks to mould the character and views of his prospective secretary to form a mirror-image of himself. As he comments

---

[46] Aut. MS BL Add. MS 37944: IV. 263.
[47] Ibid. 262.   [48] Wilde, quoted in Pearson, *Beerbohm Tree*, 67.

to Mrs Allonby: 'It is always pleasant to have a slave to whisper in one's ear that, after all, one is immortal. But young Arbuthnot is not a disciple ... as yet.'[49] Mrs Allonby later observes that Lord Illingworth intends Gerald to be 'an exact replica of himself, for the use of schools'.[50] In early drafts, Illingworth is quite deliberately presented as a rake, a man who has the callous bad taste to speak to the mother of his child of the numerous love-letters he has exchanged with other mistresses.[51] He clearly seeks to undermine Mrs Arbuthnot's standing with her son and to persuade Gerald to set aside all consideration of her; he speaks not only of her ignorance of the world, but emphasizes her failure to perform the expected rites of maternal self-sacrifice.[52]

The subtlety of Wilde's final presentation of the relation between Lord Illingworth and Mrs Arbuthnot is best demonstrated by examining the scene in Act II where seducer and seduced confront each other over the past. William Archer singled out this scene in his enthusiastic review of the play, declaring that:

> I do not hesitate to call [this] scene ... the most virile and intelligent—yes, I mean it, the most intelligent—piece of English dramatic writing of our day. It is the work of a man who knows life, and knows how to transfer it to the stage. There is no situation-hunting, no posturing. The interest of the scene arises from emotion based upon thought, thought thrilled with emotion. There is nothing conventional in it, nothing insincere. In a word, it is a piece of adult art.[53]

The originality of the scene derives primarily from the character of Lord Illingworth. Eschewing the melodramatic cynicism of the conventional villainous seducer, he answers Mrs Arbuthnot's histrionic accusations with the cool voice of reason:

MRS ARBUTHNOT. Are you talking of the child you abandoned? Of the child who, as far as you are concerned, might have died of hunger and want?

---

[49] Aut. MS BL Add. MS 37944: I. 46. Mrs Allonby's name is in this draft spelt 'Allenby', but for clarity's sake the final spelling is used throughout this chapter. Similarly, Gerald Arbuthnot is first named 'Alec' and Hester 'Mabel', but only their final names are used.

[50] Aut. MS BL Add. MS 37944: IV. 270.   [51] Ibid. 229.
[52] Ibid. III. 153.
[53] Archer, *The Theatrical World for 1893* (London: Walter Scott, 1894), 107–8.

LORD ILLINGWORTH. You forget, Rachel, it was you who left me. It was not I who left you.[54]

Mrs Arbuthnot attempts to claim the superiority of wounded virtue, playing the conventional melodramatic role of the seduced maiden. Lord Illingworth, however, does not respond in kind, but undercuts her posturing with an even-handed detachment entirely at odds with the traditional seduction drama. The result is not the usual confrontation between virtue and vice but a far more unusual and realistic conflict where seduced maiden and wicked aristocrat are finally allotted an equal share of the blame. So Lord Illingworth answers his former lover that, far from having been an experienced and worldly-wise seducer, he was hardly older than she was when the affair started. Mrs Arbuthnot is undeterred:

MRS ARBUTHNOT. When a man is old enough to do wrong he should be old enough to do right also.
LORD ILLINGWORTH. My dear Rachel, intellectual generalities are always interesting, but generalities in morals mean absolutely nothing. As for saying I left our child to starve, that, of course, is untrue and silly. My mother offered you six hundred a year. But you wouldn't take anything. You simply disappeared, and carried the child away with you.[55]

Wilde took care to give Lord Illingworth as strong a hand as possible: in the first draft Mrs Arbuthnot is offered only £250.[56] The final Lord Illingworth also stands squarely by his own interests rather than passing the blame on to his absent mother: where the first Lord Illingworth explains his failure to marry his mistress as 'my mother's doing', in the final version he calmly answers: 'I had no expectations then.'[57]

The final Lord Illingworth is a man with a coherent philosophy of life, who expresses genuine affection for his son, seeking not to steal him from his mother but proposing rather that they share their offspring on a six-monthly basis. He is not a cynical, selfish, and hypocritical manipulator in the mould of Dumas's

[54] *WNI* II. 77.
[55] Ibid. 78. In the 1st production, Mrs Arbuthnot's adoption of the role of repentant magdalen was further complicated by the form-fitting bodice and plunging neckline of Mrs Bernard Beere's black dress. Kaplan and Stowell, *Theatre and Fashion*, 26.
[56] Aut. MS BL Add. MS 37944: II. 129.   [57] Ibid. 128–9; *WNI* II. 78.

Charles Sternay, but neither is he a sentimentalized and romanticized version of the wicked aristocrat, like Jones's Duke of
Guisebury in *The Dancing Girl*, a role in which Beerbohm Tree
himself had achieved considerable popularity.[58] Jones's Duke
of Guisebury seduces a Quaker maiden, Drusilla Ives, who,
unlike Mrs Arbuthnot, takes to her new life like a duck to
water and proceeds to become a fully-fledged *femme fatale*.
Drusilla suffers the standard fate of the fallen woman, dying in
a foreign country from no diagnosable cause other than having
danced on a Sunday. Guisebury on the other hand is revealed to
be a sentimental hero with too little regard for social propriety.
Overcome with remorse for his past misdemeanours, he is saved
from committing suicide by Sybil, a young girl whose life he
once heroically saved. Under Sybil's reforming influence, Guisebury ends the play devoted to improving the lives of his tenants.

Tree proposed to cast himself in the role of Lord Illingworth
on the basis of his success as the Duke of Guisebury. Wilde
responded tersely: 'Before you can successfully impersonate the
character I have in mind, you must forget that you ever played
Hamlet; you must forget that you ever played Falstaff; above
all you must forget that you ever played a Duke in a melodrama by Henry Arthur Jones . . . Because this witty aristocrat
whom you wish to assume in my play is quite unlike anyone
who has been seen on the stage before.'[59] In spite of this, the
Observer's critic was to observe that 'Mr Beerbohm Tree's Lord
Illingworth is nothing more or less than his *Dancing Girl* Duke
grown older and more steadfast in vice.'[60] This may well have
been due to Tree's own impulse to soften and sentimentalize
Illingworth's character.

A typescript marked 'Prompt Copy', which seems to have
been used as a working copy during rehearsals for the 1893 production, containing some corrections in Wilde's hand along with
numerous corrections, additions and stage-directions in other
hands, has been preserved in the Beerbohm Tree Collection
at Bristol.[61] Another typescript in this collection includes the

[58] Jones, *The Dancing Girl* (London: Samuel French, 1907), 1st perf. Haymarket
Theatre, London, 15 Jan. 1891, starring Herbert Beerbohm Tree and Julia Neilson.
[59] Pearson, *Beerbohm Tree*, 65.   [60] *Observer* (23 Apr. 1893), 6.
[61] Four-act typescript entitled 'Mrs Arbuthnot', marked 'Prompt Copy', with
notes, stage directions and corrections in Wilde's and other hands. Catalogued as
HBT 18/1 in Jackson and Small's summary, 'Some New Drafts of a Wilde Play',
7–15. Cited below as HBT 18/1; references are to act and page number.

casts of the 1893 production and the 1905 revival pencilled against the list of characters on the second leaf of the first act. This script was used as a working prompt-copy for the 1905 and, possibly, for the first production, and therefore provides a probable guide to Tree's staging of the play.[62] A third type-script is marked 'As revived at His Majesty's Theatre May 22nd 1907', and may therefore be assumed to be Tree's ap-proved version of the play.[63] To draw any clear conclusions from these typescripts is extremely problematic, as it is very difficult to know which corrections were made at what time, and which were made with Wilde's or Tree's approval. Yet numerous changes made to the 'Prompt Copy' and the later working prompt-copy were not retained in the 1894 edition of the play, suggesting that they did not receive Wilde's full ap-proval, while they do appear in the script marked for use in Tree's 1907 revival, thus suggesting that they represent Tree's favoured version of the play. A number of these corrections, rejected by Wilde and kept by Tree, have the effect of softening and romanticizing Tree's character. So in the 'Prompt Copy' Illingworth's cynical comment that 'Men marry because they are tired; women because they are curious. Both are disap-pointed' is cut, and in its place is added, in another hand than Wilde's, the reflection that, 'I was very nearly marrying once— but I changed my mind. Or rather other people changed it for me.'[64] The copy marked for the 1907 revival retains both the original epigram and the added romantic reminiscence.[65] Again mellowing Illingworth's character, in the 1893/1905 prompt-copy, in the second-act confrontation between the two parents over Gerald's future and their past, Mrs Arbuthnot begs Illingworth to retire from Gerald's life with 'her hand on his shoulder', and Illingworth responds by 'taking her hand'.[66] Wilde

---

[62] Typescript with two sets of corrections, with property list and diagrams of sets, entitled 'A Woman of No Importance'. Postdates HBT 18/1, as it incorporates a number of corrections made in the previous typescript. Catalogued by Jackson and Small, and cited below, as HBT 18(a)/1; references are to act and page number.

[63] Carbon copy of typescript, entitled 'A Woman of No Importance'. Incorpo-rates ink corrections made to HBT 18(a)/1. Later corrected in pencil. Includes stage directions and business. Catalogued by Jackson and Small, and cited below, as HBT 18(a)/5; references are to act and page number.

[64] HBT 18/1: III. 5.   [65] HBT 18(a)/5: II. 5.

[66] HBT 18(a)/1: II. 19. These directions are corrections to the typescript, which originally had Mrs Arbuthnot kneel, and Lord Illingworth attempt to raise her.

did not retain these directions in the published edition. Similarly, in the 'Prompt Copy', when Lord Illingworth offers to
marry Mrs Arbuthnot he no longer adds the ungentlemanly
comment, 'And that will show you that I love my son at least
as much as you love him. For when I marry you, Rachel, there
are some ambitions I will have to surrender, high ambitions
too, if any ambition is high.'[67] This speech is cut and added on
the facing page in another hand than Wilde's is the inscription,
'?Bring in here about something wanting in his life.—Put it
strongly.'[68] Lord Illingworth is thus brought much closer to
the apparently wicked but essentially soft-hearted and self-tor-
turing character of Jones's Duke. Once again, though there is
no sign of Wilde having written the lines requested, the cut is
preserved in the 1907 revival copy but restored in Wilde's
1894 edition.[69]

   Wilde's final version of Lord Illingworth is neither a melodramatic villain nor a romanticized wicked hero in Jones's mould
but a coolly rational man, ready to take his share of the blame
but no more. Mrs Arbuthnot takes on the role of wronged
innocent, thereby seeking to place the entire burden of responsibility upon Lord Illingworth and to keep Gerald to herself. In
their encounter at the end of Act II, Lord Illingworth undercuts
the role she adopts, neither accusing nor justifying but answering her declarations with calm common sense. Similarly, when
she tells her son the sad and cliché-ridden tale of an innocent
maiden tricked out of her virtue by the dastardly Lord Illingworth, Gerald denies her claim to absolute moral superiority
just as effectively as his father does, answering: 'I dare say the
girl was just as much to blame as Lord Illingworth was.—After
all, would a really nice girl, a girl with any nice feelings at all,
go away from her home with a man to whom she was not
married, and live with him as his wife?'[70] Mrs Arbuthnot's real
triumph is that she finally goads Lord Illingworth into acting
out precisely the role in which she has all along sought to cast
him: when she tells him he has lost Gerald for ever, Lord

<hr>

[67] HBT 18/1: IV. 16.   [68] Ibid., verso.   [69] HBT 18(a)/5: IV. 16.
[70] *WNI* III. 116. In the aut. MS Gerald's response is even more heavily ironic,
commenting in the hackneyed voice of middle-class morality: 'I should fancy it was
extremely probable the young lady in question was no better than she should have
been.' Aut. MS BL Add. MS 37944: III. 209.

Illingworth retaliates in the caddish style of the traditional villain, addressing her as 'one's mistress and one's—', thereby earning his dismissal as 'A man of no importance.'[71]

The transformation of Lord Illingworth and Mrs Arbuthnot from the wicked aristocrat and seduced maiden of traditional melodrama into the more complex and ambiguous characters of the final version transforms the play from a simple struggle between good and evil into a more realistic and intricate struggle between two individuals. In the early manuscript version Mrs Arbuthnot's battle to keep hold of her son is presented as the struggle of the virtuous against the corrupt, much like that of Mrs Gaskell's Ruth, who rejected marriage to her seducer, declaring forthrightly: 'You shall have nothing to do with my boy, by my consent, much less by my agency. I would rather see him working on the roadside than leading such a life— being such a one as you are.'[72] So, in the autograph manuscript, Lord Illingworth seeks to make a disciple of Gerald and to undermine his mother's influence, while Mrs Arbuthnot represents a strong but charitable morality. In the final version the moral conflict between villain and heroine is less clearly defined.

Wilde plagiarized his own previous work for a number of Illingworth's *bons mots*, and the ambiguous position of his Lord is indicated by the fact that he echoes both the corrupt Lord Henry Wotton of *Dorian Gray* and the flamboyantly provocative Wilde of 'The Soul of Man under Socialism'.[73] Yet, above all, Lord Illingworth's amoral detachment serves as a counterbalance to the judgemental puritan morality espoused by Mrs Arbuthnot and Hester Worsley. In a long speech, which Tree persuaded him to cut, Lord Illingworth was to explain to Gerald that,

> the profligate, the wildest profligate who spills his life in folly, has a better, saner, finer philosophy of life than the Puritan has. He, at any rate, knows that the aim of life is the pleasure of living, and does in some way realise himself, be himself. Puritanism is the

[71] *WNI* IV. 153–4.   [72] *Ruth*, ii. 321.
[73] Cf. *WNI* I. 16–17 and III. 88 with *The Picture of Dorian Gray* (London: Ward Lock & Co., 1891), ch. 3; cf. also *WNI* I. 18–19 and II. 80 with 'The Soul of Man', 294, 317, 292, and 315–16. Wilde also informed Tree that 'Indeed, if you can bear the truth, [Illingworth] is MYSELF.' Pearson, *Beerbohm Tree*, 65.

hideous survival of the self-mutilation of the savage, man in his madness making *himself* the victim of his monstrous sacrifice.[74]

In the final version Illingworth simply comments that 'The future belongs to the dandy.'[75] The essential conflict between puritanism and the dandy philosophy remains, but it is impossible to place Wilde's own sympathies or the play's argument precisely. The puritans triumph, but the audience, as contemporary reviews demonstrated, found the 'bad' characters' amoral wit more attractive than the 'good' characters' histrionic moralizing. Complex moral ambiguity undermines any straightforward taking of sides.[76]

Wilde deviated further from the melodramatic tradition by disregarding the role of the illegitimate son himself, reducing Gerald to a passive trophy over which others fight. Both Augier and Dumas focus their interest on the illegitimate child who must find his own way in the world, winning fame or fortune through his own exertions. Illegitimate himself, Dumas created Jacques Vignot, a nameless social outcast who not only wins honour and respect but saves his country from a European war. Augier's Bernard similarly triumphs against adversity, becoming a renowned businessman, wealthy enough to rescue his own father from bankruptcy.

Gerald Arbuthnot is by contrast little more than a stage prop in the confrontation between his parents. Beyond the minimal attributes of naïvety and boyish enthusiasm, he is virtually characterless. Indeed, Wilde deliberately reduced Gerald to a cipher. In the earlier manuscript versions he is equally innocuous but he is at least possessed of his own minimal moral sense; he is capable of being influenced and corrupted, whereas the final Gerald jumps from one posture to another without ever expressing a viewpoint at all. So, in the autograph manuscript, Gerald is attracted by his father's philosophy, remarking to his mother: 'I suppose you think him bad because he doesn't believe all the old conventionalities one has been taught about life. He is perfectly right. There is not one of them that is not

[74] BL Add. MS 37945: III. 138.   [75] *WNI* III. 90.
[76] Philip Cohen analyses the play in terms of straightforward moral dichotomy, characterizing Lord Illingworth as 'satanic', and points to the verbal hint of 'ill' in Illingworth's name. (*The Moral Vision of Oscar Wilde*, 199). This may, however, be countered by the pun on 'worse' in Hester Worsley's name.

unsound, illogical, ridiculous.'[77] In this version, Hester and Mrs Arbuthnot win Gerald back to their absolute morality by presenting themselves as victims of Lord Illingworth's villainous advances, but the play still ends with a darker hint that Gerald will never again be the same artless innocent. Having been struck in the face by Mrs Arbuthnot, Lord Illingworth departs after one final thrust: 'You are the woman whom I did the honour of asking to be my wife. How foolish the wisest of us are at times. But someday your son may call you by a worse name. He has my blood in his veins as well as yours.'[78] It is doubtful whether the final Gerald Arbuthnot has any blood running in his veins at all. It is the unmarried mother who hogs the limelight, while the illegitimate son is consigned to the wings.

Just as Gerald is patently and deliberately inadequate as the young romantic lead, so his sweetheart, Hester, is equally ill cast as the *jeune première*. According to the play's conventional scheme, Hester's is the pure note of goodness and virtue; hers is the voice of moral rightness which cuts through the hypocrisy and injustice of corrupt English society. The unmasking of Lord Illingworth, the saving of Gerald, and the reunion of mother and son are all due to her. But a humourless New England puritan, who preaches the merits of stern morality and punishment, is an unlikely heroine for Wilde. The playwright's attitude to his young heroine is suitably ambiguous; Hester's dramatic poses, like Mrs Arbuthnot's, are deliberately undercut, producing a more complex moral pattern than is first perceived.

Hester's character is based upon a number of contradictions. She is easy prey for the satirist. A parodic 'Condensed Drama' of *A Woman of No Importance* has her introduce herself thus: 'I am an unconventional American. I have no accent and I despise the aristocracy; that is why I am staying with them. [*To Gerald*] Let us flirt.'[79] Hester does indeed condemn loose English morals while making a rapid bid for Gerald, denounce the class system while enjoying the hospitality of the nobility, and criticize the English for thinking too much of money while she herself is the orphan inheritor of her father's millions.

In earlier drafts of the play Hester's role is considerably

[77] Aut. MS BL Add. MS 37944: III. 203.   [78] Ibid. IV. 226.
[79] The *Theatre*, 21 (June 1893), 327.

more straightforward: she is the champion of the good Mrs
Arbuthnot and the downfall of the wicked Lord Illingworth,
while simultaneously acting as Wilde's mouthpiece for a number
of social criticisms. No partisan, she recognizes the evils in her
own country as well as in England: 'money is thought far too
much of there, as it is here, and we also have foolish people
who pride themselves on the accident of family and birth.'[80]
She speaks less of morality and more of economics, declaring,
for example, that in America:

> We are trying to reconstruct society on other foundations than
> those of luxury and pride, of selfishness and of sin. For it is sin that
> allows others to starve that it may surfeit, and lives in idleness itself
> on the work of weak hands and the toil of wretched days.[81]

In response to this speech Mrs Allonby exclaims: 'What bad
form to talk like that.'[82] The shallowness and inadequacy of
her response steer the audience's sympathies away from the
female dandy and towards the young social reformer. In the
final version, however, Hester's wider social criticisms have
been excised, leaving only her moral pronouncements; nor is
the audience necessarily being led to sympathize with these
tirades. The final Hester preaches her gospel of judgement:
'And till you count what is shame in a woman to be infamy in
a man, you will always be unjust, and Right, that pillar of fire,
and Wrong, that pillar of cloud, will be made dim to your eyes,
or be not seen at all, or if seen, not regarded.'[83] But her rhetoric
is immediately deflated when, in a brilliant display of theatrical
undercutting, Lady Caroline politely enquires, 'Might I, dear
Miss Worsley, as you are standing up, ask you for my cotton
that is just behind you?'[84]

Hester advocates the same harsh New England morality that
is portrayed in *The Scarlet Letter*, and as such is an unlikely
focus for Wilde's sympathies. As observed above, *A Woman of*

---

[80] Aut. MS BL Add. MS 37944: II. 88.   [81] Ibid. 90–1.
[82] Ibid. 92.   [83] *WNI* II. 61–2.
[84] Ibid. 62. In the 1st production, the audience's response was further complicated by the fact that Hester was played by Julia Neilson, who had previously
appeared as Drusilla Ives, the Quaker turned *femme fatale* of Jones's *The Dancing
Girl*. Neilson delivered Hester's diatribe against luxury and wealth, dressed in a
luxurious gown of white satin, entirely veiled by silver-spangled tulle. Kaplan and
Stowell, *Theatre and Fashion*, 25.

No Importance has clear links with the American novel, links which were deliberately emphasized when Wilde changed his young puritan's name from Mabel to Hester.[85] *The Scarlet Letter* portrays precisely the moral community that Hester Worsley recommends: the father and the illegitimate child are condemned along with the errant woman, and the result is shown by Hawthorne to be that man, woman, and child are all destroyed by the burden of guilt—suffering which Hawthorne suggests is essentially unnecessary. Wilde's Hester does change her mind in the course of the play, deciding that 'I was wrong. God's law is only Love', but this love is not to be extended to Lord Illingworth.[86] Hester continues to subscribe to punitive moral laws, simply shifting the burden of responsibility and punishment onto the man. Hester and Mrs Arbuthnot join together at the end of the play, still embracing an absolute morality which speaks of sin and punishment, good and evil, purity and innocence.

The play's sentimental happy ending is rendered subtly ambiguous. Gerald has been saved from the dubious influence of his father only to become the absolute property of his mother and Hester; he has found a better career than that of Lord Illingworth's secretary, that of Hester Worsley's husband. Mrs Arbuthnot's obsessive and possessive love has won the battle, but the victory is not simply that of good over evil. The questionable nature of her love is emphasized when she herself describes the dark duality which underlies her unbending morality: 'We women live by our emotions and for them. By our passions and for them, if you will. I have two passions, Lord Illingworth: my love of him, my hate of you. You cannot kill those. They feed each other.'[87]

Mrs Arbuthnot retains power over Gerald and defeats Lord Illingworth by casting herself in the role of the weak and defenceless woman. She portrays herself as the martyred victim of Lord Illingworth's unscrupulous seductive powers, ostracized

---

[85] The name Mabel is used in Aut. MS BL Add. MS 37944 and in the first three acts of Add. MS 37945. 'Hester' is first used consistently in the typescript under the title of *Mrs Arbuthnot*, which is now held in the Humanities Research Center, University of Texas. See *A Woman of No Importance*, in *Two Society Comedies*, ed. Jackson and Small, 2–8.
[86] *WNI* IV. 140.   [87] Ibid. 149.

by the hypocritical laws of her society. It is for the sake of her image as martyr that she maintains her isolation and claims a superior morality to that of her society. This subtle power game is not unique to Mrs Arbuthnot, for Wilde, the opponent of all laws, shows how social and sexual laws designed to subjugate women are often used by them to their own advantage. As Lord Illingworth tells Gerald: 'The history of women is the history of the worst form of tyranny the world has ever known. The tyranny of the weak over the strong. It is the only tyranny that lasts.'[88]

In a letter to Oswald Yorke Wilde described *A Woman of No Importance* as 'a woman's play'.[89] The play is ruled by a covert matriarchy of different female character-types: Lady Caroline, Lady Stutfield, Lady Hunstanton, Mrs Allonby, and Mrs Arbuthnot are all clearly drawn and distinctly different portraits of womanhood. Lady Hunstanton, for example, is possibly the only character in the play to abide by Wilde's code of tolerance and kindly non-interference, giving everybody the benefit of the doubt. Lord Belton died of joy, or was it gout? Lady Kelso's feet were too big, or was it her family?[90] Facts are irrelevant, a source of passing interest or amusement but never a matter for judgement. Lady Hunstanton's confusions are comical because she sees no essential difference between extremely disparate actions and attitudes; the details she regards as interchangeable would normally be seen as polar opposites, calling for extremes of approval and disapproval. Eschewing moral judgement, Lady Hunstanton views the world simply as a marvellous museum of unlabelled curiosities. The absent Mrs Daubeny, the archdeacon's wife, is one of Wilde's finest creations, a delicate study of the slow decay of body and mind, built up through an accumulation of tiny asides. This tragic picture of dissolution is rendered hilariously grotesque by being offset against the stiff-upper-lip ethos of stoic suffering. It is a fascinatingly modern exercise in black comedy. Evelyn Waugh could easily have used Mrs Daubeny as his model for Tangent in *Decline and Fall* (1928), whose progress from a bizarre sports field injury to the sanatorium and finally to hospital,

---

[88] *WNI* III. 93.   [89] To Oswald Yorke (late Feb. 1893), *Letters*, 335.
[90] *WNI* I. 7 and 10.

where he dies of gangrene, is narrated in a series of careless asides. So Mrs Daubeny's headaches, her isolation, her inability to eat anything but jellies, her failing eyesight, and, above all, her unremitting cheerfulness, combine to draw a harshly comic caricature of woman as martyr. But even Mrs Daubeny, surely the most powerless of women, still rules her husband's life; the archdeacon hurries home early, because 'Tuesday is always one of Mrs Daubeny's bad nights.'[91] This faint hint of a woman using her illness wilfully as her final weapon is strengthened by Lady Hunstanton's sympathetic enquiry as to whether her absence was due to a 'headache, as usual'.[92]

Lord Illingworth declares that women are not the victims but the arbiters of society, for: 'No man has any real success in this world unless he has got women to back him, and women rule society. If you have not got women on your side you are quite over. You might as well be a barrister, or a stockbroker, or a journalist at once.'[93] Life is a hidden power-struggle between men and women, a struggle in which women are given little material or visible power and must therefore use more subtle and less detectable means.

This conflict between the sexes was more obviously presented in the earlier manuscript versions of the play. As the women talk together after dinner, they discuss the supposedly stronger sex in tones less than reverent. Mrs Allonby comments that:

Man, poor, lumbering, awkward, reliable, unattractive man belongs to a sex that has been rational for millions and millions of years. His tradition is to be tedious. He can't help himself. It is in his race. The caveman began it, in order to annoy his wife, I have no doubt.[94]

Veiling this sexual antagonism in the final draft, Mrs Allonby instead describes man as 'poor, awkward, reliable, necessary man'.[95] The change is small but significant. The earlier Lord Illingworth also displays a more contemptuous view of the opposite sex than his later counterpart. When Gerald asks him if women are awfully clever, he answers, 'One should always tell them so', adding. 'But, as a mere matter of fact they are not.'[96]

---

[91] Ibid. III. 105.   [92] Ibid. II. 69.   [93] Ibid. III. 92.
[94] Aut. MS BL Add. MS 37944: II. 76.   [95] WNI II. 52
[96] Aut. MS BL Add. MS 37944: II. 160.

He voices the dismissive platitudes of his society: 'Good women are invariably ignorant women. Ignorance is the price a woman pays for being good.'[97] Yet the first Lord Illingworth's cynical view of women is simply the bitterness of the vanquished. The women are so clearly in control that the idea of male mastery appears not as a social reality, but rather as a form of sexual *frisson* to enliven a marriage. Lady Caroline, the domineering wife, sighs: 'It certainly would be a good thing if modern husbands lost their temper a little more often. They are far too easy going. They have no spirit.'[98]

In the final version of the play women still rule, but their power is less easily perceived, disguising itself as weakness. So Lady Caroline, a farcical caricature of the helplessly nagging wife, actually rules her husband with a rod of iron; Sir John complies with her every command. Lady Caroline is a woman for whom marriage has become a profession. Her disapproval of single men is not simply moral—the danger posed to women by these prowling loners—but commercial. Like the Duchess of Berwick, she regards men as a precious commodity in an under-supplied market. Mrs Allonby is a similarly powerful figure. Unlike Lady Caroline, she does not choose to exercise her power over her husband. Displaying his pitiful inferiority from the first, the unfortunate Ernest has revealed that he is less sexually experienced than his wife; having forfeited all the attractions of superiority, he is cast aside, and Mrs Allonby defies the conventions of marriage, declaring herself a free agent. Matching Lord Illingworth in the production of risqué comments and witty epigrams, she throws down the gauntlet both intellectually and sexually. The tight moral laws of society apparently pose little obstacle to a woman clever and unscrupulous enough to evade them.

Mrs Allonby's speech on the Ideal Man is a perfect essay on the tyranny of the weak. The man's duty is to perpetuate the myths of female weakness and incapacity:

> Oh, the Ideal Man should talk to us as if we were goddesses, and treat us as if we were children. He should refuse all our serious requests, and gratify every one of our whims. He should encourage us to have caprices, and forbid us to have missions . . . He should

[97] Aut. MS BL Add. MS 37944: III. 161.   [98] Ibid. II. 73, facing page.

never believe that we know the use of useful things. That would be unforgivable.[99]

This is the classic picture of female frailty and incompetence, the defenceless and incapable being who must be protected and ruled by the stronger, superior male. Yet the myth of female vulnerability is the root of the woman's power. While treating the woman like an idiot child and thereby preserving the air of power which makes him sexually attractive, the man is little more than a slave, at the mercy of the woman's every whim. He is, as Lady Caroline observes, 'to do nothing but pay bills and compliments'.[100] This is simply another example of the myth of female innocence being exploited to female advantage. Just as Mrs Arbuthnot casts herself as the helpless, seduced maiden, so Mrs Allonby archly reveals how the unquestionable virtue of the woman keeps the man in her thrall:

> then, if his conduct has been quite irreproachable, and one has behaved really badly to him, he should be allowed to admit that he has been entirely in the wrong, and when he has admitted that, it becomes a woman's duty to forgive, and one can do it all over again from the beginning, with variations.[101]

The originality of this portrayal of woman's position in society and of the power at her command can be demonstrated by comparing Wilde's play with other contemporary works. Dumas's *La Princesse Georges* (1871) was a possible influence on Wilde for it, too, contained a scene in which a group of women discuss marriage, love, and society, while waiting for the men to return from dinner.[102] Whereas Wilde's women speak with confidence, treating the opposite sex with affectionate pity, Dumas's women bemoan their powerlessness. Dumas's play itself treats of the Princess's helplessness in the face of her husband's infidelity. When the Princess asks her mother if society, like herself, regards infidelity as a crime which merits the death penalty, her mother's calm reply underlines the Princess's own powerlessness:

> Si c'est la femme qui trahit, oui, [la trahison mérite la mort]; si c'est l'homme, jamais, jamais! Ces messieurs ont profité de ce que nous

[99] *WNI* II. 53–4.   [100] Ibid. 54.   [101] Ibid. 55.

[102] Alexandre Dumas *fils*, *La Princesse Georges, Théâtre Complet*, v (Paris: Calmann Lévy, 1890), 1st perf. Paris, Théâtre du Gymnase-Dramatique, 2 Dec. 1871.

les avons laissés faire les lois, ils les ont faites en faveur du masculin. Crois-moi donc, chère mignonne, ne te fais pas de chagrin. Le monde, et surtout le nôtre, est organisé comme ça; nous n'y pouvons rien changer, ni toi, ni moi.[103]

[If it is the woman who is unfaithful, yes [infidelity deserves the death penalty]; if it is the man, never, never! Men have taken advantage of the fact tht we have let them make the laws, and they have designed the law in man's favour. Trust me then, my dear sweet child, do not cause yourself grief. The world, above all our world, is arranged like that, we can change nothing, neither you, nor I.]

The other women in the play suffer the same frustrating impotence, with the exception of Sylvanie, Dumas's image of a powerful woman: unscrupulous, greedy, sexually voracious, emotionally cold, untrustworthy, and thoroughly devious. Her power is entirely sexual. She is not quite human and not really a woman, as Berthe describes her type:

Elles n'ont ni nos vertus, ni nos faiblesses, ni nos chagrins, ni nos joies. Elles sont d'un sexe à part. Quand je vois la comtesse avec son regard impassible, son sourire fixe et ses éternels diamants, il me semble voir une de ces divinités de glace des religions polaires sur lesquelles le soleil darde et reflète ses rayons sans pouvoir jamais les fondre. Ces femmes-là sont sur la terre pour le désespoir des femmes et le châtiment des hommes. Elles nous humilient, c'est vrai; mais elles nous vengent; c'est une consolation.[104]

[They have neither our virtues, nor our weaknesses, neither our sorrows, nor our joys. They belong to a separate sex. When I see the countess with her impassive look, her fixed smile and her eternal diamonds, I seem to see one of those polar ice-goddesses which reflect back the shafts of the sun without ever being melted by them. These women are put on earth to the despair of women and the punishment of men. They humiliate us, it is true; but they avenge us; that is our consolation.]

The Princess wins back her husband, but her victory is a purely passive one: the Prince discovers that his lover has been seeing another man, and returns contrite to his virtuous wife.

---

[103] *La Princesse Georges*, I. ii. Wilde's women regard man-made laws as a challenge, not a restriction: 'LADY STUTFIELD. Ah! The world was made for men and not for women. / MRS ALLONBY. Oh, don't say that, Lady Stutfield. We have a much better time than they have. There are far more things forbidden to us than are forbidden to them.' *WNI* I. 11.

[104] *La Princesse Georges*, II. i.

Where Dumas's play limits female power to the unscrupulous use of sexual wiles, Augier's *Les Fourchambault* shows woman's sole power to be financial. Madame Bernard is able to save the father of her child from bankruptcy thanks to her own wealth and business sense. Yet her financial abilities have only been developed because she has been exiled from society and forced to fend for herself, adopting the man's role. As she explains to her son:

> Je me suis faite homme le jour où je suis devenue ton père. L'infériorité des femmes vient de l'habitude de vivre en tutelle. On ne développe que les forces dont on a besoin. J'avais besoin de toutes les miennes, n'ayant devant moi que les devoirs: ton existence, ton éducation, ton avenir.[105]

> [I made myself a man the day when I became your father. Women are inferior because of their protected lives. One only develops the powers one needs. I needed all mine, having nothing but duties ahead of me: your existence, your education, your future.]

Madame Bernard uses her unique powers only for others' benefit, and does so anonymously, remaining quietly and modestly in the background and asking nothing in return.

Madame Bernard is favourably contrasted with Madame Fourchambault, who is guilty of constantly demanding power. Madame Fourchambault continually demands a deciding vote in everything because she brought a large dowry with her when she married M. Fourchambault. Rudely disillusioned as to the size and economic importance of her dowry, she immediately becomes silent and humble, relinquishing all claims to power. Woman's only weapon is money, and even this brings no real authority or rights.[106] Where other playwrights presented women as the helpless victims of male law-makers, Wilde showed them as skilled operators, who exploit social and sexual conventions to their own ends.[107]

---

[105] *Les Fourchambault*, II. i.

[106] For another example of women at the mercy of man-made laws, see H. A. Jones, *Mrs Dane's Defence* (London: privately printed, 1900), 1st perf. Oct. 1900, where Sir Daniel discovers that Mrs Dane is not the widow she claims to be but a fallen woman. Mrs Dane is sent into the wilderness and Sir Daniel, a man with his own dubious past, defends this sexual double standard on financial grounds: 'A man demands the treasure of a woman's purest love. It's what he buys and pays for with the strength of his arm and the sweat of his brow.' IV. 82.

[107] Behrendt reaches opposite conclusions in her analysis, accusing Wilde of misogyny and characterizing the women in the play as 'intellectually inferior' and 'strangely ignorant of the realities of their own world'. *Oscar Wilde*, 127–47.

A Woman of No Importance effectively argues against all sexual laws and restrictions, showing them to be both ineffectual against the power of passion and impulse, and a potent weapon in the hands of those who choose to exploit them. Mrs Arbuthnot struggles with an absolute morality which denies all her true instincts as a woman, finding in the melodramatic role of injured innocent both a relief from her own guilt and a means of retaining possession of her son. Meanwhile, the women of Hunstanton take advantage of their supposedly weaker status to manipulate the men around them. The ostracism of the fallen woman is a matter of convenience to these married women. Their power within society, as Wilde shows, depends upon their reputation for virtue. The fallen woman must be exiled in order that (at least outwardly) virtuous women may retain control of their husbands and their society. Even the mild-mannered Lady Hunstanton dismisses the ruin of another woman's life as 'very sad, no doubt', regarding the matter satisfactorily settled by the provision of 'admirable homes where people of that kind are looked after and reformed'.[108] Wilde's sympathies do not obviously lie with either sex. The subtle and intricate pattern of power he reveals simply reflects the hypocrisy and manipulation that result from the imposition of any law upon human behaviour.

A Woman of No Importance was thus on one level a successfully sentimental play apparently pleading for greater leniency towards fallen women who were but the helpless victims of unscrupulous male depravity. Yet below the surface lay a far more complex moral pattern, a criticism not just of the sexual double standard but of all laws governing the sexes. No one in the play is wholly virtuous or wholly corrupt. Every motive is mixed, and the happy ending has sinister undertones. A character no sooner strikes a righteous attitude than Wilde undermines it. Mr Kelvil, the lecturer on purity, styles himself the champion of female intellect and virtue: 'I have never regarded woman as a toy. Woman is the intellectual helpmeet of man in public as well as in private life. Without her we should forget the true ideals.'[109] Lady Caroline's enquiries then reveal Mr

---

[108] *WNI* III. 102.   [109] Ibid. I. 24.

Kelvil to be the father of *eight* children, whose care is cur-
rently the burden of the absent Mrs Kelvil; it is clearly not his
wife's intellectual qualities of which Mr Kelvil has been taking
advantage.[110]

Whoever quotes a law or advocates an ideal has more than
one reason for so doing. Characters strike poses to cover their
real motives, just as Wilde presents the front of a conventional
melodrama to conceal the more challenging play beneath. There
are no wicked aristocrats and innocent maidens; instead there
are ordinary flawed human beings in conflict with social and
moral laws. The true centre of *A Woman of No Importance* is
this interaction between human nature and the laws which seek
to confine it.

[110] Ibid. 25.

5
An Ideal Husband

> It was written for ridiculous puppets to play, and the
> critics will say, 'Ah, here is Oscar unlike himself!'—though
> in reality I became engrossed in writing it, and it contains
> a great deal of the real Oscar![1]

INTERVIEWED by a reporter from the *Sketch* a week after *An Ideal Husband* opened at the Haymarket, Wilde provocatively dismissed the role of the public in judging the success of his play:

'Are you nervous on the night you are producing a new play?'
  'Oh, no, I am exquisitely indifferent. My nervousness ends at the last dress rehearsal; I know then what effect my play, as presented upon the stage, has produced upon me. My interest in the play ends there, and I feel curiously envious of the public—they have such wonderful fresh emotions in store for them.'[2]

In a more serious tone, Wilde explained his belief that drama is rightly a private form of art:

'the critics have always propounded the degrading dogma that the duty of the dramatist is to please the public ... We shall never have a real drama in England until it is recognised that a play is as personal and individual a form of self-expression as a poem or a picture.'[3]

An Ideal Husband was as deceptive a play as its predecessors, its superficial conservatism concealing its more subversive implications from the common playgoer.

Reviews ranged from the confused to the patronizing. Reviewers were virtually unanimous in dismissing Wilde's plot as excessively familiar and contrived. The *Theatre* declared Wilde had regressed since his 'Norwegian'-style play, *A Woman of No Importance*, by setting out in *An Ideal Husband* 'deliberately

---

[1] Wilde, quoted by Charles Ricketts, in *Charles Ricketts Self-Portrait, Taken from the Letters and Journals of Charles Ricketts, RA*, collected and compiled by T. Sturge Moore, ed. Cecil Lewis (London: Peter Davies, 1939), 124.
[2] Gilbert Burgess, *Sketch*, 8 (9 Jan. 1895), 495.   [3] Ibid.

to imitate the examples set by Scribe and M. Sardou'.[4] Clement
Scott accused Wilde of having simply 'embroidered a well-
known Sardou play', and enumerated the links between Wilde's
play and Sardou's *Dora*.[5] The play's wealth of epigrams and
witticisms were dismissed as inverted commonplaces. While
critic upon critic demonstrated the supposedly simple trick of
constructing such *bons mots*, Shaw mocked their complacency:

As far as I can ascertain, I am the only person in London who cannot
sit down and write an Oscar Wilde play at will. The fact that his
plays, though apparently lucrative, remain unique under the circumstances, says much for the self-denial of our scribes.[6]

Another reviewer, familiar with the varied layers of sophisticated
wit and broad theatricality in Wilde's dramatic work, summed
up *An Ideal Husband* as an excessively clever melodrama:

The story, which is presumably adapted from the *Family Herald*, is
so full of high-class virtue and vice that the gallery is kept in state of
subdued enthusiasm, while the stalls are puzzling over the paradoxes . . . If some accomplished dramatist—Mr G. R. Sims, for instance—would only straighten out Mr Wilde's English into robust
intelligibility, an audience on the Surrey side might enjoy the familiar
flavour of this genteel melodrama.[7]

Apparently undisturbed by the contradictions and complications they themselves noted in the play's moral scheme, contemporary critics complacently dismissed *An Ideal Husband* as
predictable and old-hat. A. B. Walkley denounced Wilde as
profoundly commonplace, a writer who 'presents [the public]
with a false picture of life which it likes to fancy true, thinks
its thoughts, conforms to its ideals'. Yet Walkley simultaneously remarked upon the puzzling and contradictory moral
conclusion to the play: 'The great thing is not to be found out;
indeed, the whole play is designed to fill us with joy over the

[4] Unsigned review, *Theatre*, 25 (1 Feb. 1895), 104.

[5] *Illustrated London News*, 106 (12 Jan. 1895), 35. Scott's recognition of the
links between the two plays is unsurprising, since he himself collaborated on an
English version of *Dora*, entitled *Diplomacy*, which opened at the Prince of Wales
Theatre, London, in Jan. 1878.

[6] *Saturday Review*, 79 (12 Jan. 1895), 44. For dismissals of Wilde's wit, see e.g.
A. B. Walkley, *Speaker*, 11 (12 Jan. 1895), 43–5; *Sketch*, 8 (9 Jan. 1895), 496;
Clement Scott, *Illustrated London News*, 106 (12 Jan. 1895), 35.

[7] Unsigned review, *Lika Joko*, 13 (12 Jan. 1895), 244.

escape of a sinner from the penalty of his sin through a trick with a diamond bracelet.[8] With unshakeable confidence, reviewers recorded their dissatisfaction with the fates meted out to the various characters. They indicated the discrepancy between their own sympathies and the conventionally appropriate response to such characters. Not once did they stop to question whether this should be understood as part of Wilde's intention, rather than as a failure of his art. So one reviewer declared: 'We do not look, in Mr Wilde's plays, for any subtlety of plot', and yet found himself led into the expression of distinctly unconventional moral sympathies: 'I shall always think kindly of a great public man in the future if I hear that he has been suddenly found to have been all along a masterpiece of moral error. I shall put his drawbacks down to the fact that he must have got an abnormally good wife.'[9]

It was left to the more intelligently appreciative Shaw to recognize the peculiar essence of Wilde's dramatic writing, the capricious, deceptive, and deliberately intriguing nature of his plays:

In a certain sense Mr. Wilde is our only thorough playwright. He plays with everything: with wit, with philosophy, with drama, with actors and audience, with the whole theatre . . . It is useless to describe a play which has no thesis: which is, in the purest integrity, a play and nothing less. The six worst epigrams are mere alms handed with a kind smile to the average suburban playgoer; the three best remain secrets between Mr. Wilde and a few choice spirits.[10]

Modern critics, less distracted by the surface of the play, have noted Wilde's critical attitude to the society he portrays: the richness of scenery, costume, and props demanded by the play visually emphasize the values which are paramount in this society.[11] Taking more notice of Wilde's own comments on his play than his contemporaries did, modern analyses tend to

---

[8] *Speaker*, 11 (12 Jan. 1895), 43–5.
[9] *Pick-Me-Up*, 13 (19 Jan. 1895), 246–7.
[10] *Saturday Review*, 79 (12 Jan. 1895), 44–5.
[11] See e.g. Bird, *The Plays of Oscar Wilde*, 135–59; Gagnier, *Idylls of the Marketplace*, 117–29. A rare exception is Epifanio San Juan, who sees the play as essentially conservative and supportive of the *status quo*: 'The image of a stable society prevails in the end, as the conventions of marriage, family life, and public office are severally confirmed.' *The Art of Oscar Wilde*, 167.

concentrate on the play's pronouncements on women's roles. So Philip Cohen, Alan Bird, and Norbert Kohl all stress the frailty of women, as represented by Gertrude Chiltern, a woman who preaches absolute virtue while incapable of love or sacrifice herself.[12] Lord Goring's speech on women's proper role is taken as the keynote, and the play is interpreted accordingly with varying degrees of excuse or disapproval.[13]

That critics should disagree about *An Ideal Husband* is perhaps inevitable. The play is even more impenetrable and perversely ambiguous than its predecessors. Wilde's two previous social dramas centred on a distinct theme: *Lady Windermere's Fan* presented the conventional view of the fallen woman and ironically subverted it; *A Woman of No Importance* presented the conventional view of seduced and seducer and undercut it with a far more complex interpretation of the sexual power relationship. *An Ideal Husband* contains no such distinctive thesis and antithesis. Rather, the play is constructed in layer upon layer of assertion and contradiction. Characters alternately depend upon and subvert traditional stereotypes. Apparently unironic statements are rendered ambiguous by the action which accompanies them. While presenting a reassuringly familiar melodrama of intrigue and blackmail, Wilde placed his action in the centre of nineteenth-century political life, and examined the issues of private and public morality and their relation to the contemporary debate on the role of women in society.

Wilde claimed in *De Profundis* that in a week he 'wrote and completed in every detail, as it was ultimately performed, the first act of *An Ideal Husband*'.[14] This remarkably rapid and effortless composition was, according to him, then interrupted by Lord Alfred and resumed only during Douglas's absence from the country in December 1893, when, Wilde wrote: 'I collected

---

[12] C.f. Cohen, *The Moral Vision of Oscar Wilde*, 203–12; Bird, *The Plays of Oscar Wilde*, 148–55; Kohl, *Oscar Wilde*, 210–20.

[13] Peter Raby is an exception, commenting on Goring's speech: 'How much of this kind of precept Wilde approved is open to question.' *Oscar Wilde*, 97–8. Kerry Powell takes this theme furthest, interpreting the play as a conservative rejection of feminists' demand for greater male purity, and therefore as a reversal of Wilde's previous sympathy with women's developing role. *Oscar Wilde and the Theatre of the 1890s*, 85–107.

[14] To Lord Alfred Douglas (Jan.–Mar. 1897), *Letters*, 426.

again the torn and ravelled web of my imagination, got my life back into my own hands, and not merely finished the three remaining acts of *An Ideal Husband*, but conceived and almost completed two other plays of a different type, the *Florentine Tragedy* and *La Sainte Courtisane*.'[15] The numerous manuscript versions of *An Ideal Husband* belie Wilde's self-created myth of careless but inspired composition. In fact, he expended immense time and energy in taking each act through up to nine different versions to reach the final published edition of 1899. The ordering of these manuscript drafts is extremely complex and somewhat muddled, as they do not follow in strict chronological order; Wilde sometimes returned to earlier drafts in preparing his work for the printer, bypassing intermediate recensions, so that some corrections and revisions 'leap-frog' along the sequence.[16] The different drafts referred to here are in chronological order: a manuscript draft in Wilde's hand, housed in the British Library; a typescript of Act I, made from the British Library manuscript and corrected in Wilde's hand, now held in the Harvard Theatre Collection; a typescript of all four acts with Wilde's autograph revisions, held in the British Library; and a typescript of the four acts, submitted to the Lord Chamberlain's Office, but which does not represent the final performed version of the play, since it does not, for example, include the device of the bracelet whereby Mrs Cheveley is outmanœuvred.[17] Wilde prepared the play for publication while in exile in 1898–9, presumably using a typescript which postdated the Lord Chamberlain's copy and possibly one of the earlier drafts, as the published edition included some material

[15] To Lord Alfred Douglas (Jan.–Mar. 1897), *Letters*, 427.

[16] For a complete account of the composition of *An Ideal Husband* and for a stemma of all the numerous drafts, see Russell Jackson's Preface to *An Ideal Husband*, in *Two Society Comedies*, ed. Jackson and Small, 122–9.

[17] These MS drafts are as follows: (*a*) MS drafts of the four acts, including two versions of Act II, written in Wilde's hand in exercise books. First act inscribed 'Copy to be sent to St James Place by Saturday.' BL Add. MS 37946. (*b*) Typescript of Act I, with Wilde's autograph revisions, produced from BL Add. MS 37946. On title-page: '2 copies of each. 1 set for Mr Hare. Garrick Theatre. One for Oscar Wilde. 10 St James Place.' Stamped 'Mrs Marshall's Type-writing Office, 126 Strand.' Harvard Theatre Collection (uncatalogued). (*c*) Typescripts of the four acts, with corrections and stage directions added in Wilde's and other hand. First act stamped 'Mrs Marshall's Type-writing Office, 126 Strand. 10 MAR 94.' BL Add. MS 37947. (*d*) Typescript of the four acts, submitted to the Lord Chamberlain's Office. LCP, No.1. Dated 2 Jan. 1895. BL LCP Add. MS 53566A.

previously excised.[18] The first edition of the play was thus the result of considerable and painstaking effort on Wilde's part. He told his publisher, Leonard Smithers: 'Corrections are a great trouble—worse than a new play. I am quite exhausted.'[19]

Though *An Ideal Husband* did not belong to any one popular dramatic tradition, Wilde had incorporated material from a number of diverse plays: international intrigue, for example, from Sardou's *Dora* (1877); infidelity and stolen letters from Dumas's *L'Ami des femmes* (1864); and political secrets from Pinero's *The Cabinet Minister* (1890). Successive revisions removed *An Ideal Husband* further from its original material, so that the final version undermined the assumptions on which its source plays were based.

In the final published version of *An Ideal Husband*, Sir Robert Chiltern is the vehicle for Wilde's implicit criticism of nineteenth-century politics. This ambitious and unscrupulous politician, whose entire career is based upon his reputation for upright character and unshakeable honesty, is not only rewarded with a seat in the Cabinet, but backed as a possible future leader for the country. Lord Caversham declares that 'If the country doesn't go to the dogs or the Radicals, we shall have you Prime Minister, some day.'[20] The play's happy ending consists of the entry into the inner sanctum of the British government of a man who, without regrets, sold his political integrity for personal gain. No contemporary reviewer expressed outrage or disbelief at such a conclusion, though some of them observed mildly that Wilde's statesman seemed well rewarded for his lack of principle.[21] The very fact that the audience accepted the play's ending so easily demonstrates Wilde's success in portraying British politics as a scene of compromise and hypocrisy, where Sir Robert will be perfectly at home.

---

[18] *An Ideal Husband, by the Author of 'Lady Windermere's Fan'* (London: Leonard Smithers & Co., 1899), dedicated 'To Frank Harris. A slight tribute to his power and distinction as an artist, his chivalry and nobility as a friend.' Cited below as *IH*; references are to act and page number. For details of lost drafts between the Lord Chamberlain's copy and the 1st edn., see Russell Jackson's preface to *Two Society Comedies*, ed. Jackson and Small, 122–9.

[19] To Leonard Smithers (postmark 18 Mar. 1899), *More Letters*, 180. For correspondence over MSS and proofs see ibid. 181, and *Letters*, 669, 787–9, 794–5.

[20] *IH* IV. 211.

[21] *Athenæum* (12 Jan. 1895), 57; *Speaker*, 11 (12 Jan. 1895), 44.

The ironic view of contemporary politics implicit in this ending was more directly expressed in earlier drafts of the play. In the final version Mrs Cheveley undercuts Sir Robert's exclamation that, 'A political life is a noble career!', by replying 'Sometimes. And sometimes it is a clever game, Sir Robert.'[22] In the first manuscript draft of the play she further degrades the statesman's standing:

MRS CHEVELEY. But one must amuse oneself somehow. And I like the gambling element in politics.
SIR ROBERT. You would sooner play with people than with cards.[23]

Sir Robert accepts instantly Mrs Cheveley's cynical description of the political game.

Sir Robert Chiltern's guilty secret implicates the rest of society. He cannot feel remorse, for he knows his crime is sanctioned by common usage. As he explains to Goring: 'I felt that I had fought the century with its own weapons and won.'[24] In the first manuscript draft, Sir Robert's sin is symptomatic of his society. Mrs Cheveley relates how she discovered a veritable treasure-trove of corruption in the dead Baron's escritoire:

> The secret history of the nineteenth century was in it. Letters from great ladies offering their favours for money. Letters from great men offering their support for money. Letters from kings who had lost their thrones. Letters from demagogues who wanted to be kings. And a letter from you on the top of which, in that small delicate hand of his that you must remember, the Baron had written 'the origin of Sir Robert Chiltern'—and on the back of it the sum £50,000.[25]

Wilde's method of revision was to edit out more direct, and therefore cruder, social criticisms, replacing them with a more subtle satire of character. Lord Caversham and Lady Markby, for example, are transformed from stock comic characters into satirical portraits of the old order. In early drafts, Lord Caversham is just a bumbling comic prop, who has to be restrained from lavishing his not entirely paternal affections on his son's new fiancée. His dialogue consists almost exclusively of catchphrases, chorusing endlessly on draughts, family idiocy, and his

---

[22] *IH* I. 15.
[23] BL Add. MS 37946: I. 16. References are to act and page number.
[24] *IH* II. 75.   [25] BL Add. MS 37946: I. 46.

son's heartlessness. Revisions show Wilde building up a more subtly humorous character through whom he could demonstrate his observation of social and class snobbery. In the first draft Lady Markby openly declares the values of her society, as she traces her host's ancestry:

> Of course Sir Robert is well born, on one side, at any rate—his mother was Lady Adeliza Gilling, but there was not a penny of money in the family. I remember Lady Adeliza always went about in a plain silk dress, which is a great confession of failure, and it is said that she used to pay her visits in omnibuses, though perhaps that is only a malicious scandal.[26]

This obvious display of snobbery is delivered in a considerably more subtle and covert form in later drafts through Lord Caversham's comments on social mobility: 'Never go anywhere now. Sick of London Society. Shouldn't mind being introduced to my own tailor; he always votes on the right side. But object strongly to being sent down to dinner with my wife's milliner. Never could stand Lady Caversham's bonnets.'[27]

A similar process takes place with Wilde's editing of the play's comments on marriage. A number of Lord Caversham's broader comments on matrimony are removed, including his declaration to his son that: 'It was not that feeling [pleasure] that guided me in my marriages. It was duty, Sir, a sense of duty to my name and race. Had I consulted my own happiness, Sir, you would never have existed.'[28] This satire is transferred to Lady Markby, whose less self-conscious and lighter comments are revised in progressive drafts and concentrated together in Act II. Lady Markby's final speeches move from the detrimental effects of female learning on the old ideal of matrimony, to the tragedy of marrying a country curate and the danger of dining with your husband. She combines the absurdly incongruous values of Lady Berwick and Lady Bracknell with the endearing vagueness of Lady Hunstanton.

This subtle process of introducing satire through character rather than through more overt statements is also seen at work

---

[26] Ibid. 51.
[27] *IH* I. 5. Elaborated through progressive revisions from its original form in BL Add. MS 37946, I. 8: 'Hate London Society. The thing has gone to the dogs. A lot of demned nobodies talking about nothing.'
[28] BL Add. MS 37946: III. 228.

in Sir Robert Chiltern. Through successive drafts, Wilde cam-
ouflaged his social criticisms, while simultaneously widening
and strengthening their implications. In the earlier drafts of the
play Sir Robert is a considerably more unscrupulous and self-
interested character. It was Lord Caversham, and not the un-
seen Lord Radley, who employed him and whose confidence he
betrayed, a fact which makes his treachery seem deeper and
more personal.[29] He agrees to Mrs Cheveley's demands with
undignified rapidity.[30] The details of his impoverished and
undignified past elicit the audience's sympathy, but they also
present Sir Robert as himself a proponent of nineteenth-century
materialism and snobbery. Everybody has their price, Mrs
Cheveley declares: 'The drawback is that most people are so
dreadfully expensive.'[31] Sir Robert's price is raised from £50,000
in the first draft, to £85,000, and finally £110,000.[32]

It is not just that a higher value is placed on his integrity,
however, for by the final version Sir Robert has been transformed from a product of the nineteenth century into a critic
of it. Not only does he use the century's own weapons against
itself, he challenges its entire moral ethos:

> Weak? Oh, I am sick of hearing that phrase. Sick of using it of
> others. Weak! Do you really think, Arthur, that it is weakness that
> yields to temptation? I tell you that there are terrible temptations
> that it requires strength, strength and courage to yield to. To stake
> all one's life on a single moment, to risk everything on one throw,
> whether the stake be power or pleasure, I care not—there is no
> weakness in that. There is a horrible, a terrible courage. I had that
> courage.[33]

Shaw, in his review, picked out this speech for praise as striking 'the modern note'.[34] In the final version Sir Robert develops
from a man who is simply concerned with gaining the place in
society to which his birth entitles him into a man who is driven
by a personal creed of self-realization and success. So Baron
Arnheim's philosophy is expanded and explained by Sir Robert:

[29] BL Add. MS 37946: I. 38.   [30] Ibid. 49.   [31] *IH* I. 38.
[32] BL Add. MS 37946: I. 46; *IH* I. 74.
[33] *IH* II. 73–4. This speech is not present in BL Add. MS 37946; it appears in
a shorter version in BL Add. MS 37947, 28–9, where it is expanded to its final
version.
[34] *Saturday Review*, 79 (12 Jan. 1895), 45.

'[P]ower, power over other men, power over the world, was the one thing worth having, the one supreme pleasure worth knowing, the one joy one never tired of, and that in our century only the rich possessed it.'[35] The effect of these revisions is to make Sir Robert a rebel. His crime still implicates society in the combination of materialism and snobbery that drove him to the deed. Yet, by separating Sir Robert from the ethics of his century, Wilde makes his statesman not inferior to the system he betrays but superior to it. Sir Robert is no longer a product of his century; he is a critic of it, a critic who exploits its faults and uses them against it. Sir Robert follows the strictures of 'The Soul of Man', in which Wilde proclaimed:

Disobedience, in the eyes of anyone who has read history, is man's original virtue. It is through disobedience that progress has been made, through disobedience and through rebellion . . . No: a poor man who is ungrateful, unthrifty, discontented and rebellious, is probably a real personality, and has much in him. He is at any rate a healthy protest.[36]

Sir Robert may not be poor by socialist standards, but by his own assessment he is, and his reaction is to rebel against the system which made him so. Sir Robert is transformed from an uninteresting modern criminal who simply steals for money into a true individualist, who sins in remaining true to his own ethos. This is a completely different matter, for, as Wilde writes of the true personality, 'He may commit a sin against society, and yet realise through that sin his true perfection.'[37]

All the characters in *An Ideal Husband* undergo similar changes during Wilde's revisions, developing from recognizable theatrical types into more original Wildean creations. Mrs Cheveley starts as a stage-adventuress, very much in the mode of the original Mrs Erlynne. Goring comments of her that 'She is a bad lot. And as clever as they make them.'[38] Far removed from the exotic work of art of the final version, she is clearly disreputable rather than wittily *risquée*. When the Vicomte de Nanjac remarks of the first Mrs Cheveley that she is received everywhere, Goring pointedly replies, 'So I would suppose, at

---

[35] *IH* II. 72. This speech is not present in BL Add. MS 37946.
[36] 'The Soul of Man', 294–5.   [37] Ibid. 300.
[38] BL Add. MS 37946: II. 139, citing the second version of Act II in this MS.

Berlin.'[39] The tantalizing uncertainty of Mrs Cheveley's relationship with Baron Arnheim is made more explicitly sexual in
earlier drafts, mainly through Mrs Cheveley's own richly fla-
voured comments. Her denials themselves emphasize the possibility: Sir Robert says she is called the Baron's Egeria, to
which she replies, 'I assure you it is only for five o'clock tea
that he comes to my political cave.'[40] There is even a darker
hint that, like Becky Sharp in Thackeray's *Vanity Fair* (1848),
she has personally dispatched her wealthy benefactor, for Sir
Robert pointedly comments on the suddenness of the Baron's
death.[41]

Only in later drafts does Wilde endow Mrs Cheveley with
the style, poise, and depth of character that distinguish the final
version. Thus, in the published version of Act II, when Lady
Chiltern proclaims that all guilty people, without exception,
should be shunned, her visitor momentarily halts hostilities, mur-
muring, 'Then I am very sorry for you, Gertrude, very sorry for
you.'[42] Lord Goring can threaten the first Mrs Cheveley with a
loss of reputation which will bar her not only from London
society, but even from the laxer circles of Viennese society.[43]
Later drafts, by contrast, present Mrs Cheveley as a woman
who, like Mrs Erlynne, is too clever to be troubled by society's
opinions, a woman impervious to scandal, as Lord Goring
comments: 'Oh, I should fancy Mrs Cheveley is one of those
very modern women of our time who find a new scandal as
becoming as a new bonnet, and air them both in the Park every
afternoon at five-thirty.'[44]

The limits to Mrs Cheveley's transformation, the fact that
she remains a scheming adventuress, however clever and self-
assured, serves a deliberate purpose in the play's structure.
Mrs Cheveley's morality runs parallel to Sir Robert's. As Mrs
Cheveley herself observes to Gertrude Chiltern: 'It is because

[39] BL Add. MS 37946: I. 24.

[40] Ibid. 17. Egeria, a nymph credited with helping Numa to formulate laws for
early Rome. Reputedly this was more than a business association—cf. Juvenal,
Satire 3.12, where he refers to 'the place where Numa used to meet his nocturnal
lover, Egeria'.

[41] BL Add. MS 37946: I. 19.   [42] *IH* II. 112.

[43] BL Add. MS 37946: III. 190. This threat is cut in BL Add. MS 37947, Act
III.

[44] *IH* II. 80.

your husband is himself fraudulent and dishonest that we pair so well together.'[45] When Mrs Cheveley reminds Sir Robert of his corrupt past, she deliberately turns his own words back on him, presenting the supposedly upright statesman as her mirror-image: 'It was a swindle, Sir Robert. Let us call things by their proper names', she corrects him, echoing his own words spoken to her only a few minutes before.[46] In earlier versions of the play, before Wilde introduced the bracelet as a more effective stage device, Mrs Cheveley's 'dying speech and confession' was burnt along with Sir Robert's incriminating letter.[47] The parallel between the two letters was further underlined, when Mrs Cheveley and Lord Goring perused the guilty evidence:

LORD GORING. You seem rather amused. You find that document such pleasant reading?
MRS CHEVELEY. Do you find your friend's letter so very edifying?[48]

In the final version, a distinction is here introduced between the statesman and the adventuress: Mrs Cheveley is condemned not for breaking a law, but for her malice. The early version of Sir Robert is a perfect double for Mrs Cheveley, both coldly self-assured and self-seeking. The later Sir Robert differs from his blackmailer in the fatal flaw that prevents him selling himself a second time: his love for his wife. It is the tale of her short and unromantic engagement and her desire to destroy the Chilterns' marriage which separate Mrs Cheveley from her victim. Sir Robert is no more scrupulous than she is, but he is saved because he has a heart.

Just as Mrs Cheveley is transformed from a conventional stage-villainess into a quick-witted and unscrupulously self-sufficient woman, so Mabel Chiltern is transformed from a simpering *ingénue* into a pert but strong-minded young woman. In the final version of the play Mabel Chiltern is more than a match for her fiancé. Irreverent, witty, and self-possessed she outmanœuvres Lord Goring, and affectionately retains the upper hand:

---

[45] Ibid. 114.   [46] Ibid. I. 40.
[47] Four-act typescript, submitted to the Lord Chamberlain's Office, BL LCP Add. MS 53566A: III. 68; references are to act and page number.
[48] Ibid. 72–3.

LORD GORING. Of course I'm not nearly good enough for you, Mabel.
MABEL. I am so glad, darling. I was afraid you were.
LORD GORING. And I'm . . . I'm a little over thirty.
MABEL. Dear, you look weeks younger than that.[49]

The first Mabel Chiltern, by contrast, is a little girl who must be protected from all dangerous knowledge. In the first version of Act IV she plays the role of ironic innocent: while Lady Chiltern berates herself for having fallen into Lord Goring's trap and compromised herself in a moment of weakness, Mabel delivers a long diatribe against Lord Goring, his unscrupulous behaviour, and his bad habit of experimenting with people. The older woman is racked with guilt, fearing that Mabel knows all, but the younger woman is simply prattling aimlessly, blissfully unaware of the heavy irony of her speech.[50]

The first Mabel is a child to her brother and sister-in-law and little more than a child to her fiancé. She is repeatedly sent out of the room, as an infant who must be protected from adult knowledge, like the ironically innocent young Bérangère in Sardou's *Odette*. Indeed, the first Mabel is a combination of two familiar female types contained in Sardou's play: Bérangère and Juliette, the ignorant, protected maiden and the child-bride. Juliette is married to Philippe, a reformed roué who reminisces over how he first fell in love with his wife when she was still a schoolgirl.[51] So, in the first draft of the play, Lord Goring joins a long line of theatrical father-figure suitors as he confesses to Mabel's brother: 'I have loved her ever since that bleak winters day when she came home from school.'[52]

Not only is the first Mabel treated with patronizing affection by her fellow characters, but she herself lacks all the strengths of her later incarnation. The early Mabel's one poor show of

[49] *IH* IV. 185.

[50] BL Add. MS 37946: IV. 242–8. In a later draft (BL LCP Add. MS 53566A), Lady Chiltern's guilt has been edited out, but Mabel's patter remains, devoid of any dramatic purpose without the original, obviously ironic, effect. This is an unusual example of Wilde working on an isolated area of the play, without considering the overall effect of the draft at each stage.

[51] Victorien Sardou, *Odette* (1881). Such marriages are a familiar part of popular 19th-c. drama, cf. e.g. the marriages of Olivier de Jalin and the young Marcelle in Dumas's *Le Demi-Monde* (1855), and of Leslie Brudenell and Dunstan Renshaw in Pinero's *The Profligate* (1889).

[52] BL Add. MS 37946: IV. 268.

independence is to read *The Times* despite Lord Goring's disapproval.[53] Her distrust of genius and husbandly perfection is
based not on her later healthy scepticism about ideals, but on
a sense of her own inferiority: 'I wonder what it feels like,
reading a leading article on one's husband's virtues. I don't
think I should like it. It would make me feel very small. I'd
much sooner read an account of my own frocks in some horrid
society paper.'[54] Her pertness and frivolity result from her simplistic and childish view of life.

The Mabel Chiltern of the final version uses flippancy and
impertinence just as Goring does, as a dandy's pose, a frivolous
cover for serious values. She stands conventional behaviour
and morality on its head—literally so when she performs in a
tableau in aid of the Undeserving. Old-fashioned though she is
in her charms, in her independence of thought, her humorous
worsting of her suitor, and her espousal of an individual set of
values, Mabel is, as Lady Markby remarks, 'remarkably modern'.[55] Like little cousin Cecily after her, the final Mabel Chiltern
conceals a strong will and determined purpose beneath a dis-
armingly light exterior.

As Mabel Chiltern gains independence of mind and genuine
charm of character, so her sister-in-law develops from an alternately icy and hysterical woman into a dignified, poised, and
principled protagonist, capable of acting as well as reacting. In
earlier drafts, Gertrude Chiltern is harsh, cold, and vehement.
'Morality is simply the attitude we adopt towards people whom
we personally dislike', says Mrs Cheveley, and this is certainly
true of the first Lady Chiltern.[56] Her dislike of Mrs Cheveley
seems less a matter of principle than a private vendetta. In the
first manuscript version she tells Sir Robert how she once found
Mrs Cheveley guilty of stealing jewels; Gertrude told only one
person of Mrs Cheveley's guilt—Lord Goring, to whom Mrs
Cheveley was at the time engaged.[57] For all her moral posturing she is less than admirable. When Sir Robert accuses Goring
of having an affair with Mrs Cheveley, Gertrude Chiltern seems
ready to allow Goring to sacrifice his engagement rather than
confess her own weakness. Coming forward at the very last

---

[53] Ibid. 245–6.   [54] Ibid. 246–7.   [55] *IH* II. 99.
[56] Ibid. 112.   [57] BL Add. MS 37946: I. 58–9.

moment possible, her confession is made without dignity; she pitifully begs her husband to believe her innocence.[58]

The vital difference between the first Lady Chiltern and her final incarnation, however, is that the first Lady Chiltern errs, whereas the final one is truly worthy, morally superior to her husband both in theory and in practice. The first Lady Chiltern, on learning of her husband's perfidy, reacts by throwing herself into the arms of Lord Goring, an action he has foreseen and, indeed, encouraged in order to teach her a lesson in human frailty and charity. As Mrs Cheveley comments in amusement, while reading Gertrude's letter: 'As her husband has turned out not to be a saint, she has evidently determined to become a sinner. How like a woman!'[59]

The entire psychology of this episode is similar to that of Alexandre Dumas's *L'Ami des femmes*, from which Wilde borrowed the device of the ambiguous letter.[60] In Dumas's play, the beautiful Jane de Simerose has been separated from her husband for several years, and the marriage has never been consummated because the inexperienced young Jane was revolted by her husband's advances. He found comfort in the arms of another, and Jane left him, consumed with jealousy. The virgin wife is now being courted by de Montègre with whom she conducts a purely platonic relationship. At this point de Ryons, the 'ami des femmes' of the title, who makes the study of women his hobby, intervenes to save Jane from a scandal resulting from her new relationship. He successfully smuggles de Montègre from Jane's house, avoiding public discovery and her ruin. In order to persuade the suitor to leave, de Ryons delivers to him a letter from Jane: 'Venez demain. Je ne demande qu'à vous croire. JANE.' [Come tomorrow. I only ask to believe in you. JANE]. The thwarted suitor then accuses Jane of infidelity, and she, enraged, bids him never cross her threshold again. Angry, impulsive, and itching to revenge this insult, she offers herself to de Ryons. De Ryons politely turns down her offer, replying that she does not love him, and is acting foolishly in the heat of the moment.

Jane then reveals to the fascinated de Ryons that she is, in

---

[58] BL Add. MS 37946: IV. 276–7.   [59] Ibid. III. 217.
[60] Dumas *fils*, *L'Ami des femmes*, *Théâtre Complet*, iv (Paris: Calmann Lévy, 1890), 1st perf. Paris, Théâtre du Gymnase-Dramatique, 5 Mar. 1864.

fact, still in love with her husband, who is eager to renew their marriage. The only obstacle to this reunion is the ardent suitor, de Montègre, who has jealously threatened to kill her husband. Jane's letter remains a dangerous weapon in de Montègre's hands. De Ryons finds a solution: Jane will be reunited with her husband, and de Montègre will have the revenge he desires. De Ryons convinces the spurned suitor that Jane is in love with a mythical third man, and that she fears above all being forced to return to her husband. De Montègre seeks his revenge: he sends Jane's note to her husband, who immediately comes to her, believing the letter to be addressed to him. The couple are reunited, and de Montègre retires, convinced that he has thwarted Jane's pursuit of another man.

This is clearly the source of Lady Chiltern's ambiguous letter, addressed to one man and maliciously delivered to her husband, who in turn accepts it as a message of love. In the first manuscript version of *An Ideal Husband*, Lady Chiltern writes her letter for exactly the same reasons as Jane de Simerose—pique and a misguided desire for revenge.

Dumas's heroine is a feeble-minded combination of two female stereotypes—the virgin and the vamp, the innocent prude and the passionate, scheming woman. *L'Ami des femmes* is a five-act critique of women, with a long preface devoted to proving that women are devious, immoral, and sexually uncontrolled, incapable either of rational thought or principled action. At best, according to Dumas, woman is an empty vessel to be filled by man's creations:

> Le cerveau de la femme est un vase et son ventre est un moule. L'un et l'autre ne donnent une forme qu'à ce que l'Homme y dépose . . . Voilà par où elle est purement passive et instrumentaire; voilà pourquoi, au nom de la nature, il la tient en soumission.[61]

> [Woman's brain is a vase and her belly is a mould. Each of them simply gives a form to what Man puts there. . . . This is why she is purely passive and instrumental; this is why, by nature's law, he holds her in submission.]

She is incapable of real creation or originality. Like a child, either adorably vulnerable or woefully malicious, she is constantly in need of male guidance.

---

[61] Ibid., preface, 46.

The first Lady Chiltern differs little from Dumas's women. She poses as a saint, and yet her morality is no more than skin-deep; she explains to Lord Goring the reason she changed her mind: 'In a moment of folly I wrote you a foolish letter. It was Violet who by telling me what she thought I am, what I know I should be, prevented me from coming to your house at night.'[62] Her morality is simply a matter of keeping up appearances. She is a very different woman from the final Lady Chiltern, a woman who combines considerable dignity of bearing with a genuine, deeply felt moral code. The final Lady Chiltern is indeed pure and stainless. Unlike Lady Windermere, she does not learn to forgive through discovering her own fallibility; she forgives her guilty husband even though she is guiltless herself. Where the first Lady Chiltern is selfish and hysterical, crying out to Lord Goring that he should have killed Mrs Cheveley rather than let her leave with her incriminating letter, the last Lady Chiltern is more dignified and reasonable in her enmity. The final Lady Chiltern not only takes her husband back, but sacrifices her own principles to his unprincipled ambition, simply to keep his love.[63] She is a woman such as Dumas could never envisage.

The first manuscript version of *An Ideal Husband* thus echoes Dumas's *L'Ami des femmes*, not just in its use of the ambiguous letter but in its analysis of the female character. Wilde's editing deliberately distanced his play from that of Dumas, presenting woman not simply as man's equal but even, on occasions, his superior. Thus, in the manuscript version of Act IV, Sir Robert's praise of the female sex is heavily ironic since the wife he addresses has been flirting with adultery:

---

[62] BL Add. MS 37946: IV. 250. Mabel Chiltern is called Violet in parts of the first MS.

[63] Modern critics have tended to judge Lady Chiltern in terms surely more appropriate to her earlier incarnation. So Alan Bird comments: 'Her inability to forgive Mrs Cheveley's schoolgirl misdemeanours finds no counterpart in her attitude to her husband. So much for the morality of Lady Chiltern. A selfless word of pity or compassionate understanding never passes her lips ... In her character there is little feeling for others: self-esteem and self-pity and self-righteousness are leading traits.' *The Plays of Oscar Wilde*, 149–53. Cf. also Cohen, *The Moral Vision of Oscar Wilde*, 204–8; Kohl, *Oscar Wilde*, 210–21. For all the accusations of heartlessness levelled against her, Lady Chiltern's speech to her husband at the end of Act II expresses not abstract moral condemnation, but horror at his having betrayed her trust by lying to her for so long. Her love has already overpowered her puritan values by the beginning of Act III, when she has decided to stay with her husband and resolve their problems herself.

SIR ROBERT. O why is it that you women are so much finer than we are. When I look into your eyes I see truth there.

[Leave a ¼ page here. Note to type-writer.]

LADY CHILTERN. Oh, don't say those things to me, Robert. Don't ever say those things to me.

SIR ROBERT. What else should I say to the woman I worship?

LADY CHILTERN. We are not made for worship.[64]

No such irony touches the final version in which Lady Chiltern is truly worthy of her husband's unqualified worship.

In the final version of *An Ideal Husband* Sir Robert delivers a speech on his wife's perfection, which has very different ironic undertones from its predecessor. Sir Robert replies to his wife's fears: 'What! Had I fallen so low in your eyes that you thought that even for a moment I could have doubted your goodness? Gertrude, Gertrude, you are to me the white image of all good things, and sin can never touch you.'[65] The irony is not that Lady Chiltern is less perfect than he imagines, but that he himself describes her as such. Sir Robert here is making an idol of his wife, an action he attributed exclusively to women in his earlier denunciation of Gertrude Chiltern's idealistic morality:

> Why can't you women love us faults and all? Why do you place us on monstrous pedestals? We have all feet of clay, women as well as men; but when we men love women, we love them knowing their weaknesses, their follies, their imperfections, love them all the more, it may be, for that reason . . . A man's love is like that. It is wider, larger, more human than a woman's. Women think that they are making ideals of men. What they are making of us are false idols merely.[66]

Sir Robert's own sentiments hardly accord with this description of open-eyed and realistic male love. Indeed, Lord Goring even warns Lady Chiltern that by enforcing her principles on her husband she may lose his affections, asking her, 'Do you want to kill his love for you?'[67] The professedly unqualified love of the great man is dependent not only on his wife's perfection, but also on her pliability.

---

[64] BL Add. MS 37946: IV. 262–3. Wilde left a number of gaps in this MS to be filled in at a later date.
[65] *IH* IV. 210.   [66] Ibid. II. 117.   [67] Ibid. IV. 203.

'An Ideal Husband?' exclaims Mrs Allonby incredulously, in *A Woman of No Importance*, 'There couldn't be such a thing. The institution is wrong.'[68] The women of *An Ideal Husband* would not argue with her. Sir Robert's definition of feminine love as idol-worship based on uncompromising absolutes is contradicted by the evidence of the play. Lady Chiltern sacrifices her own deep-seated principles for the sake of her husband, maintaining her love for a man who has not only misled her for years, but was ready to sell himself a second time in order to save his own skin. She loves her husband with a clear-sighted understanding of his faults. Nor is she unique in this. In the opening scene, the two female dandies, Mrs Marchmont and Lady Basildon, ironically undercut the title of the play. An ideal husband, they imply, is anything but desirable; like Mrs Allonby, they find male virtue tediously unalluring. As Mrs Marchmont laments: 'My Reginald is hopelessly faultless. He is really unendurably so at times! There is not the smallest element of excitement in knowing him.'[69] Mabel Chiltern speaks for all the women in the play when she rejects the prospect of an 'ideal husband'; male perfection is not to be dreamt of by these realistic women, for 'It sounds like something in the next world.'[70]

The play criticizes ideals, both personal and political. Gertrude Chiltern's love and Robert Chiltern's career are both open to attack by Mrs Cheveley because both are based on false absolutes and illusions. Sir Robert could not survive a scandal because his career is based on a reputation for absolute integrity and unshakeable principles. It is this assumption of superiority which appeals to the old order, as embodied by Lord Caversham, and which Wilde satirizes by making Sir Robert its mascot. The rhetoric of political idealism is mocked as Lord Caversham reads out *The Times*'s article on Robert Chiltern: 'Unblemished career . . . Well-known integrity of character . . . Represents what is best in English public life . . . Noble contrast to the lax morality so common among foreign politicians.'[71]

An Ideal Husband criticizes the late-Victorian demand for absolute purity in its political leaders—a public assumption of higher morality which meant that the politically ambitious must in private resort to hypocrisy and subterfuge in order to

[68] *WNI* II. 52.   [69] *IH* I. 26.   [70] Ibid. IV. 212.   [71] Ibid. 175.

succeed. Wilde's satirical intent is here very close to Ibsen's in *The Pillars of Society* (1877).[72] Consul Bernick is also a highly respected public figure, struggling to conceal the dubious roots of his rise to fame. Both men disguise the unprincipled selfishness of their actions with the rhetoric of disinterested political necessity. Both men are saved by the intervention of a woman: Lady Chiltern in the case of Sir Robert, Lona Hessel in the case of Bernick. Neither Ibsen nor Wilde is simply concerned with unmasking the guilty protagonist, however, for the cause of their heroes' downfall is essentially the political system in which they operate, where politicians are expected to display virtues beyond the grasp of ordinary mortals, and are ruthlessly condemned for the least failing. Wilde's satire is harsher than Ibsen's. Consul Bernick is finally forced to admit his guilt, performing a public act of confession and absolution; but Sir Robert Chiltern continues his political career under false pretences. Lona Hessel lets the air of truth into Ibsen's Norwegian town, so that the townspeople are forced to accept the fallible humanity of their leaders. In Wilde's England, hypocrisy is perpetuated as Sir Robert succeeds precisely because of his reputation for unshakeable integrity.

It is Mrs Cheveley who criticizes the system which has trapped Sir Robert, laying the blame on Wilde's favourite target for criticism, puritanism:

> Remember to what point your Puritanism in England has brought you. In old days nobody pretended to be a bit better than his neighbours. In fact, to be a bit better than one's neighbour was considered excessively vulgar and middle-class. Nowadays with our modern mania for morality, every one has to pose as a paragon of purity, incorruptibility, and all the other seven deadly virtues—and what is the result? You all go over like ninepins—one after the other. Not a year passes in England without somebody disappearing. Scandals used to lend charm, or at least interest, to a man— now they crush him.[73]

---

[72] *The Pillars of Society* (1877), trans. William Archer (London: Camelot, 1888). Perf. as *Quicksands*, in Archer's trans., at the Gaiety Theatre, 15 Dec. 1880, and 17 July 1889 at the Opéra Comique, with Wilde's friend Elizabeth Robins as Martha Bernick. See Powell, *Oscar Wilde and the Theatre of the 1890s*, ch. 5, for the convincing argument that *An Ideal Husband* was a deliberate bid to write a play that would rank beside those of Ibsen.

[73] *IH* I. 41.

This speech is very similar in argument to Lord Illingworth's lecture to his son in *A Woman of No Importance*, a speech which Tree persuaded him to cut because it was too long.[74] Mrs Cheveley continues to threaten Sir Robert by describing the glee with which the press would seize upon his scandal. 'The Soul of Man under Socialism' is filled with a similar distaste for popular journalism, but in *An Ideal Husband* Wilde makes a more sophisticated link between the pretence of a higher morality and the scandal which perpetuates this myth. So, in the first manuscript draft, Mrs Cheveley makes the connection explicitly:

> If it were known that . . . that was the origin of your wealth and career, you would be hounded out of public life, and all the people who had done the same sort of thing themselves, or something much worse, would of course be the loudest against you. When a victim is offered up to public respectability it counts as a general white-washing all round, and every thief has the opportunity of dilating on the enormous importance of honesty.[75]

In order to maintain the late-Victorian tradition of high morals and strict principles, Wilde suggests, individuals were constantly sacrificed to the mob's need for absolution; the corrupt are ritually sacrificed as proof that the rest of society is clean.

Wilde's observations on the role of scandal in nineteenth-century politics, and the threat that journalism and public hypocrisy posed to renowned figures, were not simply theoretical but of great contemporary relevance. Parts of *An Ideal*

---

[74] An even closer link between the two speeches is provided by a marginal note in BL Add. MS 37947: I. 81, where, opposite Mrs Cheveley's speech on the public press, is written: 'Tartuffe and Caliban hounding you down together.' Lord Illingworth remarks of England: 'Caliban for nine months of the year, it is Tartuffe for the other three' (BL Add. MS 37945: III. 138). These two together suggest strongly felt beliefs on Wilde's part, which were, however, too direct to be left uncut.

[75] BL Add. MS 37946: I. 48–9. If evidence is necessary as to the modernity and relevance of Wilde's political commentary, Mrs Cheveley's political argument is the same as that put forward by the maniac to the journalist Feletti in Dario Fo's *Accidental Death of an Anarchist* (1970) adapted by Gavin Edwards from a trans. by Gillian Hanna (London: Methuen, 1987): 'It's just another chance for the pristine beauticians of the Communist Party to point out another wart on the body politic and pose themselves as the party of honesty. But the STATE, Miss Feletti, the State remains, still presenting corruption as the exception to the rule, when the system the State was designed to protect is corruption itself. Corruption *is* the rule.' (II. i. 63).

Husband read like prophecy: Wilde the homosexual was sacrificed to prove the healthy heterosexuality of his society.[76] Indeed, Richard Ellmann, in his biography of Wilde, reports that the writer's prosecution was inevitable from the moment the names of Rosebery and Gladstone were introduced into the trials through the reading out of Lord Queensberry's letters. As Ellmann notes:

According to Marjoribanks, who must have got it from Carson, the introduction of the names of Rosebery and Gladstone, which at once appeared in the continental press, made it inevitable that Wilde should be tried when the Queensberry case was over, in case it looked as if these men had favoured him out of a need to protect themselves.[77]

The link between social hypocrisy and the power of the press was to be of tragic relevance to Wilde.

Yet *An Ideal Husband* was also of much more immediate political relevance. As a staunch supporter of Irish Home Rule, Wilde would have been well aware of the role played by hypocrisy and scandal in the downfall of Charles Stuart Parnell. Parnell was sacrificed by both Gladstone and his own Irish party, who, though long aware of the politician's involvement with Kitty O'Shea, chose to abandon their figurehead rather than risk involving their cause with the scandal surrounding Parnell.[78] A less well known figure, however, offers a history which parallels even more closely that of Sir Robert Chiltern, so closely that he probably provided the model for Wilde's statesman. Sir Charles Dilke, like Sir Robert Chiltern, was in 1886 one of the most promising men in politics, one for whom many prophesied a premiership. Mentioned as co-respondent in a divorce suit, he was dropped from Gladstone's Liberal government and driven into the wilderness, in spite of the fact that the judge at the divorce trial (on 12 February 1886) had

---

[76] Correcting proofs of the play for publication Wilde commented: 'It reads rather well, and some of its passages seem prophetic of tragedy to come' (to Reginald Turner, (postmark 20 Mar.) 1899, *Letters*, 787).

[77] *Oscar Wilde*, 423.

[78] W. B. Yeats linked Wilde and Parnell as examples of exactly this aspect of British society. Charles Ricketts reports that 'Yeats spoke with great intelligence of the British public during its quite senseless bursts of revengeful hypocrisy and morality such as it displayed in the Parnell case, the Wilde case, the Whitaker Wright case, etc., etc.'. *Self Portrait*, 195.

dismissed the case against him, observing that 'there is no evidence worthy of the name against him'.[79] Wilde gave Sir Robert exactly the position that Dilke had held from 1880 to 1882, under-secretary for foreign affairs. In a letter to Mrs Alfred Hunt in 1881, Wilde had criticized Dilke for compromising his former radicalism: 'I have a long-standing engagement to dine with Sir Charles Dilke, a lion who has clipped his radical claws and only roars through the medium of a quarterly review now—a harmless way of roaring.'[80] According to Wilfred Hugh Chesson, Wilde still spoke of Sir Charles Dilke in 1898, remarking that his only fault was excessive knowledge, for 'Dilke's accuracy is almost a vice'.[81] By presenting in the form of Sir Robert Chiltern the profile of a renowned and promising statesman ruined by public scandal, Wilde added piquancy and pertinence to his attack on the hypocrisy of his society. *An Ideal Husband* implies that society should accept the natural human failings of its leading figures, and so bring an end to hypocrisy, blackmail, and the tragic ruin of gifted men, men like Charles Stuart Parnell, Sir Charles Dilke, and Wilde himself.

An Ideal Husband treats another topic of vital and widespread importance to nineteenth-century society—the role of women. As demonstrated above, the overall effect of Wilde's editing of the numerous manuscripts which constitute the genesis of *An Ideal Husband* was to strengthen the position of women within the play. The play's first draft is peopled with the conventional female stereotypes of theatrical cliché; the final draft contains genuinely original types drawn from life rather than from dramatic tradition.

How far Wilde's presentation of his female characters differed from that of more traditional playwrights is shown by comparing *An Ideal Husband* with contemporary plays on similar subjects. A number of critics noted the resemblance between Wilde's play and Sardou's *Dora*, better known in England in the form of Scott and Stephenson's *Diplomacy*.[82] Wilde referred to

[79] Ensor, *England, 1870–1914*, 169–70.
[80] To Mrs Alfred Hunt (17 Feb. 1881), *Letters*, 75.
[81] Wilde quoted by Chesson, in Wilfred Hugh Chesson, 'A Reminiscence of 1898', published as an appendix to *More Letters*, 204.
[82] *Illustrated London News*, 106 (12 Jan. 1895), 35; *Sketch*, 8 (9 Jan. 1895), 496; *Gentlewoman*, 10 (12 Jan. 1895), 45.

Diplomacy as 'a rather ordinary travesty' of the original play, though it in fact differs little from *Dora*, being a rather pedestrian translation of Sardou's drama.[83] He displayed little respect for the highly popular work, remarking: 'The old talk of having seen Macready: that must be a very painful memory. The middle-aged boast that they can recall *Diplomacy*: hardly a pleasant reminiscence.'[84]

Mrs Cheveley occupies the same role in Wilde's play as the Countess Zicka does in *Dora*: both are adventuresses using underhand methods for personal gain. In the original version of Mrs Cheveley's confrontation with Lord Goring, Wilde is clearly indebted to Sardou for the foiling of his adventuress: Countess Zicka and the early Mrs Cheveley both surrender when they are threatened with a letter containing details of their dubious past (though in Zicka's case the letter is a bluff and is, in fact, blank). There are, however, considerable differences between the two women. Both have as mentor a corrupt baron—named Stein in *Diplomacy*, Arnheim in *An Ideal Husband*—yet, while Zicka is a prostitute rescued from the gutter by her baron and subsequently employed as his minion, Mrs Cheveley is clearly an independent operator, who found in Arnheim an associate, not a master. Wilde's revisions distance Mrs Cheveley even further from Zicka, for Wilde's adventuress becomes impervious to all threats of scandal and mocks the system which crushes Zicka.

The pragmatic realism of Wilde's female characters also distances them from the more conventional principles of Sardou's women. An ideal husband, for Wilde's women, is a phenomenon whose very existence may be doubted and who, even if obtainable, is hardly desirable. Lady Chiltern learns to replace harsh absolutes with generous and compassionate compromise, understanding, in Sir Robert's words, that,

> It is not the perfect, but the imperfect, who have need of love. It
> is when we are wounded by our own hands, or by the hands of

[83] *Sketch*, 8 (9 Jan. 1895), 495. Sardou, *Dora* or *L'Espionne*, *Théâtre Complet*, ii, (Paris: Albin Michel, 1934), 1st perf. 22 Jan. 1877, Théâtre du Vaudeville. Wilde was clearly not concerned to hide his debt to Sardou, as this allusion to *Dora* was made during an interview on the opening of *An Ideal Husband*. Scott and Stevenson, *Diplomacy*, BL LCP, Add. MS 53198D (Jan. 1878). 1st perf. Prince of Wales's Theatre, London, Jan. 1878.

[84] 'Mr Oscar Wilde on Mr Oscar Wilde', published in *St James's Gazette* (18 Jan. 1895); repr. in *More Letters*, 192.

others, that love should come to cure us—else what use is love at all? All sins, except a sin against itself, Love should forgive. All lives, save loveless lives, true Love should pardon.[85]

In Sardou's play, the innocent and newly married Dora is accused by her husband, André, of being a spy, thanks to incriminating clues carefully laid by the jealous Zicka. Dora declares her innocence; André does not believe her and shuns her. Dora appeals to his love for her—how can he believe his *wife* to be a spy? André affirms that he can believe nothing else, and spurns her once more. Dora throws herself in his arms, and the young husband is overcome: he loves her in spite of her guilt and will fly with her to safety. Dora is outraged and repulsed:

> J'aime mieux votre mépris qui s'égare, au moins il est honnête . . . lui! Mais l'amour qui me croit coupable et qui survit et qui dure? Allons, c'est ignoble! Il n'est bon qu'à nous avilir l'un par l'autre . . . Ah! tout entière à l'amour qui m'élevait jusqu'à lui! mais à la passion brutale et stupide qui me ravale jusqu'à elle . . . jamais![86]

Sardou's heroine rejects any love except the perfect worship of a human idol. Wilde's heroine learns to reject all limitations to her love, offering genuine compassion and understanding rather than self-glorifying hero-worship.

Yet Wilde's treatment of women in *An Ideal Husband* contrasts not only with plays like Dumas's *L'Ami des femmes*, written three decades earlier, but also with the works of popular contemporary playwrights like Arthur Wing Pinero. A number of Pinero's plays deal with the 'Woman Question'. In *The Weaker Sex* (the term is used without irony) Pinero satirizes the campaign for women's rights.[87] Lady Vivash has espoused the cause of female rights in an attempt to forget an unhappy love affair. Mrs Boyle-Chewton, the leader of the Union of Independent Women, abandons all interest in her campaign as soon as she thinks a man is interested in marrying her, and her daughter Rhoda simply wishes to be allowed to study pretty

---

[85] *IH* II. 117.

[86] *Dora*, III. xiii. *Diplomacy* rather mundanely renders this as, 'Don't speak to me of your love; it horrifies me—it frightens me! . . . I prefer your disdain; for that at least is honest; but a love that believing me guilty can continue to exist is worthless, and would only destroy us both.' *Diplomacy*, Act III.

[87] Pinero, *The Weaker Sex* (1884) (London: Heinemann, 1894), 1st perf. Theatre Royal, Manchester, Sept. 1888.

clothes and men, like any normal girl, rather than principles and politics. So, by the end of the play, Mrs Boyle-Chewton is led to exclaim: 'There is something wrong with us women! With all our struggles for equality, we are so weak, so incomplete.'[88] The involvement or active influence of such creatures in any form of politics would clearly be disastrous. In *The Amazons* (1893) Pinero again depicts woman as inevitably inferior to man.[89] The play is an answer to the 'nature or nurture' question—whether woman's inferior relation to man is inevitable, or just the result of different education and treatment. The three daughters of Lady Castlejordan have all been treated as sons from their birth, due to their father's obsessive desire for male offspring. Yet, in spite of their rigorous mental and physical education, they are still prone to fainting-fits, feeble-mindedness, and an overpowering desire to find a husband.

Lady Chiltern declares that she and her husband are ardent supporters of higher education for women.[90] The main argument against it was the proposition that women were physically too weak to cope with a demanding course of study. It was, the critics claimed, beyond the frail constitution of a woman to maintain her health while unduly taxing her brain.[91] In *The Times* (1891), Pinero sides whole-heartedly with the conservative opposition to female education, when Miss Cazalet introduces her ailing niece, Lucy:

[88] Ibid. III. 106.

[89] Pinero, *The Amazons* (London: Heinemann 1895), 1st perf. Court Theatre, London, 7 Mar. 1893.

[90] *IH* II. 103. Wilde himself frequently declared his support for women's higher education in his early journalism: see e.g. comments on Miss Ramsay winning a Cambridge award in 'Literary and other Notes', *WW* (Dec. 1887), 85, and a review of *How to be Happy though Married: Being a Handbook to Marriage, by a Graduate in the University of Matrimony*, where Wilde states: 'Women have always had an emotional sympathy with those they love; Girton and Newnham have rendered intellectual sympathy possible.' 'A Handbook to Marriage', *Pall Mall Gazette*, 42 (18 Nov. 1885), 6.

[91] Cf. Emily Pfeiffer, *Women and Work: An Essay Treating on the Relation to Health and Physical Development, of the Higher Education of Girls, and the Intellectual or more Systematised Effort of Women* (London: Trubner, 1888), in which the arguments criticizing female education are summarized, challenged, and dismissed. Wilde commented in a review of this book: 'Mrs Pfeiffer's excellent essays sum up the situation very completely, and show the rational and scientific basis of the movement more clearly and logically than any other treatise I have as yet seen.' 'Literary and Other Notes', *WW* (Jan. 1888), 135.

MISS CAZALET. Poor Lucy has broken down woefully at Newnham. Her feminine intellect has drawn the line at Latin prose, and left her rubbing menthol into her brows from morning till night.
BERYL [*to Lucy*]. And have you a bad head this afternoon?
LUCY. Oh, yes.
BERYL. When did it come on?
LUCY. The year before last.[92]

In *The Cabinet Minister* Pinero offers a similarly conservative view of female abilities, while also providing Wilde with plot material for *An Ideal Husband*.[93] Sir Julian Twombley, the minister of the title, has been foolish enough to marry a simple farmer's daughter. The new Lady Twombley has acquired such extravagant tastes that, unknown to her husband, she has run up crippling debts. Her social-climbing milliner, Mrs Gaylustre, has persuaded her to borrow money from her brother, Mr Joseph Lebanon. Brother and sister then proceed to blackmail the feeble-minded lady, forcing her to introduce them to polite society, and then demanding that she leak to them the government's decision on the Rajputana Canal. Lady Twombley shows them a paper she has found on her husband's desk, and Lebanon returns her bills in exchange. Sir Julian then enters and reassures his wife that she has not betrayed a government secret: he overheard her conversation, then wrote out a note saying that the government had granted concessions for the canal, whereas they had actually been refused. Lady Twombley then makes up for her former extravagance by using her new inside knowledge of the government's intentions to make a considerable killing on the stockmarket. Mrs Gaylustre and her brother are suitably humiliated and routed. While the whole affair of the canal, shares, and blackmail by an unscrupulous adventuress is plundered by Wilde for his own purposes, the moral roles of the characters in Pinero's play are effectively reversed by the less conventional playwright. In *An Ideal Husband* it is the

[92] *The Times* (London: Heinemann, 1891), I. 29, 1st perf. Terry's, 24 Oct. 1891. The play is as socially as it is sexually conservative. Where Sir Robert's speech on the incompatibility of being poor and ambitious is an implicit criticism of a non-meritocratic society, Pinero's ambitious but bourgeois statesman is taught the error of his ways, concluding that 'there ought to be a law to stop men like me "getting on" beyond a certain point' (IV. 190).
[93] Pinero, *The Cabinet Minister* (London: Heinemann, 1892). Written early in 1889, and produced at the Royal Court Theatre, 23 Apr. 1890.

husband not the wife who is being blackmailed; it is the wife
not the husband who saves the day. Lady Chiltern is not only
considerably more intelligent than Lady Twombley, she also
provides moral guidance for her husband—hardly a possibility
for the weak-witted Kitty Twombley.

   An Ideal Husband also shares a surprising number of themes
with a play performed only months later, R. C. Carton's *The
Home Secretary*.[94] The hero is Duncan Trendel, an MP who
has become estranged from his wife because he has failed to
live up to her expectations. She saw him as a political crusader
who would struggle to right society's wrongs, but he has instead revealed himself to be a political careerist, more concerned
with parliamentary strategy than with radical reform. Disillusioned, Rhoda Trendel has found solace in the company of
Morris Lecaille, a man whom the audience knows to be an
anarchist in disguise. Rhoda has already berated her husband
for his failure to capture this same anarchist. Carton's radical
sympathies are displayed in his favourable portrait of the anarchist and the numerous speeches he delivers against British
society and politics. Lecaille recommends that the anarchist
hide where he is least noticeable: 'He is reckless—dangerous—
unscrupulous and dishonest, his methods are indefensible and
disastrous to the welfare of the public...I should search for
him carefully—among the politicians.'[95] Carton casts an equally
critical eye on modern marriage, showing a mercenary grand-
mother marrying off her young charge to a rich and ancient
suitor. The granddaughter is even implicitly criticized for her
weakness of spirit in not standing up to her guardian. Carton
recommends rebellion to the young.

   Yet the final implications of *The Home Secretary* fall short
of Wilde's seemingly more conventional play. Rhoda, like
Gertrude Chiltern, confesses to having idolized her husband:
'When you first gave me your name, I hung round it my gar-
land of wild flowers. They had no root, but you see I still trail
them after me in the dust, in those days I seemed to see the
coming of a new Tribune of the people, the pedestal was high.'[96]
Both women learn to love rather than idolize their husbands,

---

[94] R. C. Carton, *The Home Secretary* (May 1895), 1st perf. Criterion, 5 Nov.
1895 (BL LCP No. 119, Add. MS 53573).
[95] Ibid. II. 52.   [96] Ibid. IV. 110.

but Rhoda is also taught how misguided and simplistic her political opinions have been. Where Lady Chiltern has genuine moral principles and helps her husband to recognize the true nature of his actions, Rhoda Trendel is simply naïve. Rhoda's enthusiasm for radical measures leads her to associate unknowingly with a dangerous anarchist, while she fails to recognize the true qualities of her husband. Sir Robert Chiltern is genuinely corrupt and unscrupulous and his inclusion in government is an implicit criticism of that establishment. Duncan Trendel, on the other hand, is shown to be a truly worthy and upright politician, whose softer methods of compromise achieve the best results. So Carton's play is ultimately more conventional than Wilde's, for it upholds the honour of the establishment, while once again showing the husband to be the wiser partner than the wife.

The contemporary play which most closely mirrors the radical concerns of *An Ideal Husband* was, perhaps, *Une Journée parlementaire* by Maurice Barrès, in which a government deputy, Thuringe, who once betrayed his position for money, fears exposure and the loss of his wife's love.[97] Thuringe attempts to buy his way out of trouble by exposing the similar corruption of two of his fellow deputies, but to no avail. He is left with no alternative but to save his honour by shooting himself, while his equally dishonest colleagues continue in government. Though Wilde was well acquainted with Barrès, there is no evidence that he borrowed from the French writer; the radical political criticism contained in the first manuscripts of *An Ideal Husband* was completed well before *Une Journée parlementaire* opened in Paris.

Like Wilde's play, *Une Journée parlementaire* reveals the endemic corruption of government, and implicates the press as maintaining the façade which protects this hypocritical system. So, in Barrès's play, while Thuringe is alternately condemned and exalted by the public, a political cartoonist turns in bewilderment to a journalist:

LE CARICATURISTE. Thuringe est donc honnête homme?
LE JOURNALISTE. Ce n'est pas la question. Sous un même dessin, ne

---

[97] Barrès, *Une Journée parlementaire: Comédie de mœurs en trois actes* (Paris: Charpentier et Fasquelle, 1894), 1st perf. Théâtre Libre, Jan. 1894.

vous arrive-t-il pas d'essayer successivement plusieurs légendes? Eh
bien! Thuringe, c'est toujours le même bonhomme, mais on n'est
pas encore fixé sur la légende à lui donner.[98]

[CARTOONIST. So Thuringe is an honest man, then?
JOURNALIST. It not a question of that. Don't you sometimes try out
several captions under the same drawing? Well! Thuringe is always
the same chap, but one hasn't yet decided which caption to give
him.]

The power of the press to make and break reputations was
absolute on both sides of the Channel.

Despite the similarly radical criticisms contained in both plays,
they met with very different fates. Where *An Ideal Husband*
was dismissed as a concoction of hackneyed theatrical devices,
Barrès's own political career ensured that *Une Journée parlementaire* was treated sufficiently seriously to worry even Antoine,
the director of the Théâtre Libre, who was himself involved in
anarchist politics. Antoine noted in his diary: 'We repeat Barrès.
His comedy is a violent pamphlet against the present régime,
which makes me ill at ease, for it is linked to political schemings
of which I strongly disapprove.'[99]

When interviewed about the opening of *An Ideal Husband* and
its critical reception, Wilde complained that the critics had mis-
judged his play, having missed

'Its entire psychology—the difference in the way in which a man loves
a woman from that in which a woman loves a man, the passion that
women have for making ideals (which is their weakness) and the
weakness of a man who dare not show his imperfections to the thing
he loves. The end of Act I, the end of Act II, and the scene in the last
act, where Lord Goring points out the higher importance of a man's
life over a woman's—to take three prominent instances—seem to
have been quite missed by most of the critics. They failed to see their

[98] Ibid. II. iv. 45. Barrès, a close acquaintance of Wilde's, wrote his theatrical
exposé of political corruption after his own electoral defeat. For friendship with
Wilde, see e.g. Jacques-Émile Blanche, *Portraits of a Lifetime*, repr. in E. H. Mikhail,
Oscar Wilde: Interviews and Recollections, 2 vols. (London: Macmillan, 1979), ii.
351–3.
[99] Antoine, *Mes souvenirs sur le Théâtre Libre*, 301, 15 Jan. 1894, quoted in
Sonn, *Anarchism and Cultural Politics in Fin de Siècle France*, 76.

meaning; they really thought it was a play about a bracelet. We must educate our critics—we must really educate them,' said Mr Wilde, half to himself.[100]

Wilde deliberately extended the play's scope so that the issues at stake did not solely concern the specific situation of Gertrude Chiltern and her husband, but were relevant to the more general nineteenth-century debate on the proper role and position of women. The speeches cited by Wilde in this interview all refer to issues of central importance to the controversy over woman's sphere: the essential difference between the sexes; whether there should be different ethical codes for men and women; whether woman's sphere was exclusively that of private life, man's of public life; whether women exercised a particularly beneficial influence on the opposite sex, and what was necessary to safeguard this influence.

The speech of most vital importance, as Wilde pointed out, is Goring's final speech to Lady Chiltern, in which he persuades her to prevent Sir Robert from abandoning his political career:

> Women are not meant to judge us, but to forgive us when we need forgiveness. Pardon, not punishment, is their mission . . . A man's life is of more value than a woman's. It has larger issues, wider scope, greater ambitions. A woman's life revolves in curves of emotions. It is upon lines of intellect that a man's life progresses. Don't make any terrible mistake, Lady Chiltern. A woman who can keep a man's love, and love him in return, has done all the world wants of women, or should want of them.[101]

In view of Wilde's sympathy with the struggle of intelligent women to gain an equal footing in society, his editorship of the *Woman's World*, his portrayal of women in his previous plays, and, above all, his presentation of women in this play in particular, the conservatism of this speech comes as a considerable surprise. The message of charity and forgiveness is familiar from all Wilde's other work, but the implied limitation of woman's role in society contrasts strongly with the direction of his other writings.[102]

[100] *Sketch*, 8 (12 Jan. 1895), 495.   [101] *IH* IV. 203–4.
[102] It may fairly be said that this speech stands in relation to Wilde's other writings as Kate's final speech in *The Taming of the Shrew* ('A woman moved is like a fountain troubled . . .' V. ii. 143) does to Shakespeare's: both seem to

The simplest answer to this apparent contradiction would be to distance Wilde from the words of his character, to argue that Goring's speech is in no way an expression of Wilde's own opinions. The final version of *An Ideal Husband*, however, seems to offer little encouragement to an ironic approach to Goring, Wilde's most perfect dandy to date.[103] But a tracing of Goring's development reveals him to be less omniscient than he at first appears. In the first manuscript version there is scarcely a hint of his dandyesque wit. Though still delivering many of the same epigrams, and priding himself on his incomprehensibility, the first Lord Goring is at heart an entirely conventional man, whose saving grace is sufficient idleness to ensure that he leads the life of a dilettante rather than falling into the vulgar error of usefulness. His witticisms are a light disguise for his thoroughly traditional morality:

SIR ROBERT. You have enabled me to tell you the truth. That is something. The truth has always stifled me.
LORD GORING. Ah! I get rid of it as soon as possible. Bad habit! makes one very unpopular. But it keeps one in good condition.[104]

Goring's flippant wit ends with a boy-scout motto. He deliberately tempts Lady Chiltern into sin, and, when she falls, delivers a speech whose simplistic division of women into two types is reminiscent of the inexperienced Lady Windermere: 'It is curious what stupid things good women do! It is part of their charm. Bad women as they are [. . .] never do foolish things. It is part of their charm.'[105]

Playing the elderly and conventional suitor, he treats Mabel like a child, sending her out of the room and protecting her from any harmful knowledge of the world. In asking Sir Robert for Mabel's hand in marriage, before approaching Mabel herself, he sounds positively pompous:

contradict the strong position allotted to women in other plays, and both are unusual in their conservative didacticism.

[103] A number of modern critics have viewed Lord Goring as so perfect a character as to approximate to a self-portrait by the author, and Goring's views have therefore frequently been taken to be Wilde's own: see e.g. E. H. Mikhail, 'Self-Revelation in *An Ideal Husband*', *Modern Drama*, 11/2 (Sept. 1968), 180–6; Shewan, *Oscar Wilde*, 177–86.
[104] BL Add. MS 37946: II. 141–3.
[105] Ibid. III. 233. Word in brackets is very difficult to decipher in manuscript.

There is a difference between our ages I admit. But not more than I think is better for married life. I have money as you know. I hate talking about it, but it is right that these things should be stated on an occasion of this kind. She will have a settlement suitable to the rank she will occupy.[106]

In progressive drafts Lord Goring is transformed from this older, more conventional and serious, character into the perfectly poised dandy of the final version. His age is gradually reduced, from 38 in the first manuscript, to 36 in the Lord Chamberlain's version, ending up as a sprightly 34, admitting to 31½ with a really good buttonhole. Yet, while Goring slowly metamorphoses into the far more likeable dandy, his role as wise and witty commentator is undermined by constant challenges from his manservant, his father, and his fiancée: Mabel grows out of his shadow from a schoolgirl into a witty and self-assured woman; Lord Caversham develops from a ridiculous comic caricature into a man who may be puzzled by his son but is never bewildered by him; his valet, Phipps, develops from an ordinary servant, soliloquizing on his preference for bachelor establishments, into the sphinx-like character of the final version.[107]

The stage directions which pronounce Lord Goring to be 'the first well-dressed philosopher in the history of thought', and introduce Goring's speech on woman's duty with the stage direction, '*showing the philosopher that underlies the dandy*', seem to preclude all possibility of treating this speech as anything but Wilde's own opinion.[108] Yet these stage directions were only added to the very final draft of *An Ideal Husband* when he was preparing it for publication in 1898–9. This grooming of the dandy may thus have been an attempt by Wilde, destitute and shunned, to present the impeccable dandy as an infallible figure, an idealized version of himself before the fall. Also, in the intervening years after his trial, Wilde found

[106] BL Add. MS 37946: IV. 268.

[107] Phipps's 'Yes, my lord's, and cryptic comments on the loss of relations, make him the effective master of this scene, like Shaw's omniscient waiter in *You Never Can Tell* (1898) Bodley Head Collected Plays, i (London, 1970), or Straker, the cockney chauffeur who out-talks his master in *Man and Superman: A Comedy and a Philosophy* (London: Constable, 1903).

[108] *IH* I. 18 and IV. 203.

himself financially dependent on the forgiveness of his wife. The validation which the stage direction gives to Lord Goring's speech could be the result of bitter personal experience breeding the wish for a perfect and unconditionally charitable wife. The development of Goring's character and the care that Wilde takes in preventing him from reigning as an unchallenged wit in the play, however, suggest that he is not necessarily to be taken as Wilde's own representative, nor is his word gospel.

Lord Goring's speech is very close to a section of Ruskin's 'Of Queens' Gardens', in which Ruskin analysed the difference between the sexes and defined woman's particular sphere:

The man's power is active, progressive, defensive. He is eminently the doer, the creator, the discoverer, the defender. His intellect is for speculation and invention; his energy is for adventure, for war, and for conquest wherever war is just, wherever conquest necessary. But the woman's power is for rule, not for battle,—and her intellect is not for invention or creation, but for sweet ordering, arrangement, and decision. She sees the qualities of things, their claims, and their places. Her great function is Praise: she enters into no contest, but infallibly judges the crown of contest. By her office, and place, she is protected from all danger and temptation. The man, in his rough work in the open world, must encounter all peril and trial:—to him, therefore, must be the failure, the offence, the inevitable error: often he must be wounded, or subdued; often misled, and always hardened. But he guards the woman from all this; within his house, as ruled by her, unless she herself has sought it, need enter no danger, no temptation, no cause of error or offence.[109]

The similarity between the two speeches is obvious. In 'Of Queens' Gardens', Ruskin was arguing for an enlargement of woman's sphere beyond the narrow concerns of household and family. While confining women to an inactive, supportive role, he argued that women must use their superior sympathy and sensitivity to control men's more aggressive instincts. Thus women are ultimately held responsible for all the ills of society: 'There is not a war in the world, no, nor an injustice, but you women are answerable for it; not in that you have provoked, but in that you have not hindered . . . There is no suffering, no injustice, no misery in the earth, but the guilt of it lies

[109] John Ruskin, 'Of Queens' Gardens', in his *Sesame and Lilies* (London: Allen, 1892), 135–6 (1st pub. 1865).

with you.'[110] Yet, while supporting improved (though not higher) education for women and encouraging them to concern themselves with larger social problems, Ruskin still upheld the nineteenth-century ideal of man's protective devotion to his innocent, angel wife.

It is, therefore, not enough to associate Lord Goring's speech with Ruskin's lecture, and thereby argue that the views presented are not conservative. Ruskin's views, though unconventional, still fell far short of Wilde's more radical sentiments. Ruskin's emphasis on woman's role as, for all its importance, one of limited action, whose significance lay primarily in the support it offered to the more active male, ran counter to all Wilde's strictures on the free and selfish development of the individual. Ruskin's emphasis on women ruling through influence, also contradicts Wilde's consistent suspicion of all forms of influence, or any impediment to the individual's own personality and conscience.[111] Ruskin defined the wife's role thus: 'She must be enduringly, incorruptibly good; instinctively, infallibly wise—wise, not for self-development, but for self-renunciation.'[112] *Lady Windermere's Fan* presented an almost direct counter-argument to this.

Lord Goring's speech on the different qualities of men and women is in fact undercut by details within the play itself: his analysis of women is contradicted by that of his friend, Sir Robert Chiltern; and his attempt to confine women's activity to a purely private, emotional sphere becomes ironic when placed in the context of the play's previous action. So, for example, Lord Goring's warning to Lady Chiltern that she risks losing her husband's love if she persuades him to abandon his political career contrasts with Sir Robert's declaration that men forgive all women's faults, because their love is boundless and based on an understanding of real life and its limitations.[113] Lord Goring's warning, by contrast, implies that a man's love is dependent on his wife's capacity for infinite forgiveness, and her willingness to allow her husband to pursue any goal he chooses.[114]

---

[110] *Sesame and Lilies*, 171–2.
[111] Cf. the denunciation of influence and authority and celebration of difference and free self-development in 'The Soul of Man', 292–319.
[112] *Sesame and Lilies*, 138–9.   [113] *IH* II. 116–18.   [114] Ibid. IV. 203.

The contradictions multiply as Goring goes on to define the essence of man's more valuable life: 'larger issues, wider scope, greater ambitions'.[115] The word 'ambitions' cannot pass without an echo of irony, when throughout the play 'ambition' has been the keyword connected with Sir Robert Chiltern's secret corruption. When he confesses his shameful secret to his friend, 'ambition' recurs like a baneful chorus: 'Every man of ambition has to fight the century with its own weapons. . . . You have never been poor, and never known what ambition is. . . . my ambition and my desire for power were at that time boundless.'[116] Greater ambitions, in the context of *An Ideal Husband*, mean unscrupulousness, self-interest, and a driving obsession which temporarily unbalances the individual's judgement.

Lord Goring continues his lecture to Lady Chiltern by dividing the spheres of intellect and emotion: emotion is the province of woman, intellect of man. Yet emotion, to Wilde, was hardly secondary to intellect. The most valuable quality in Wilde's characters is not intelligence—Lord Darlington, Lord Illingworth, Mrs Allonby, and Mrs Cheveley all possess more than their fair share—but charity, the capacity to understand and accept, to avoid judgement, and instead to tolerate and forgive. If women are the sole guardians of emotion in this sense, then their lives are not less, but more, valuable than men's.

This division between emotion and intellect is further undercut, however, by its similarity to the first stage description of Sir Robert: '*The firmly-chiselled mouth and chin contrast strikingly with the romantic expression in the deep-set eyes. The variance is suggestive of an almost complete separation of passion and intellect, as though thought and emotion were each isolated in its own sphere through some violence of willpower.*'[117] Sir Robert is taught to connect intellect and emotion, his public and private lives, by Gertrude Chiltern. It is through his love for his wife that the statesman is brought to reconsider his past actions, to live by the rules he preaches publicly, and to reject a second chance to sell his integrity to further his career. Indeed, both partners are educated by their emotions, learning to abandon their previous codes of behaviour. An exchange in Act I reveals the incompatibility of their moral codes:

[115] Ibid. 204.   [116] Ibid. II. 69, 72, and 73.   [117] Ibid. I. 9.

SIR ROBERT. Besides, Gertrude, public and private life are different things. They have different laws, and move on different lines.
LADY CHILTERN. They should both represent man at his highest. I see no difference between them.[118]

Gertrude Chiltern learns to abandon her uncompromising demand for perfection, and her husband learns that public and private life are not different spheres, but that the same combination of intellect and emotion is needed for both.

This implicit criticism of the separation of public and private life which ascribes one set of values to women, another to men, is strongly reminiscent of a review Wilde wrote in 1889 of David Ritchie's *Darwinism and Politics*:

Mr Herbert Spencer, in his *Sociology*, expresses his fear that women, if admitted now to political life, might do mischief by introducing the ethics of the family into the State. 'Under the ethics of the family the greatest benefits must be given where the merits are smallest; under the Ethics of the State the benefits must be proportioned to the merits.' In answer to this, Mr Ritchie asks whether in any society we have ever seen people so get benefits in proportion to their merits, and protests against Mr Spencer's separation of the ethics of the family from those of the State. If something is right in a family, it is difficult to see why it is therefore, without any further reason, wrong in the State. If the participation of women in politics means that as a good family educates all its members so must a good State, what better issue could there be? The family ideal of the State may be difficult of attainment, but as an ideal it is better than the policeman theory. It would mean the moralisation of politics. The cultivation of separate sorts of virtues and separate ideals of duty in men and women has led to the whole social fabric being weaker and unhealthier than it need be.[119]

An Ideal Husband illustrates this argument against the division of House and home, woman's and man's sphere. Sir Robert

---

[118] *IH* I. 55.
[119] 'Some Literary Notes', *WW* (May 1889), 390. This review is in fact a close précis of pp. 85–92 of David Ritchie's *Darwinism and Politics* (London: Sonnenschein, 1889) a fact which does not, however, undermine its status as Wilde's own opinions. No matter how lazy he became, Wilde never allowed a book he disagreed with to pass without fierce criticism—see e.g. his crushing review, 'Mr Froude's Blue Book' published a month earlier in *Pall Mall Gazette*, 49 (13 Apr. 1889), 3, in which he took great exception to Froude's views on Ireland.

Chiltern learns the danger of treating politics as an isolated province to which the normal rules of life do not apply, and, under the watchful eye of his wife, he will no longer be free to put personal interest and ambition before the public good. Lady Chiltern learns to reject her absolute idealism and rarefied morality, finally allowing her chastened husband his seat in the Cabinet despite his feet of clay.

Conservative moralists portrayed women as the guardians of uncompromising morality, true and absolute purity—a role which was dependent on their sheltered position in the home, protected from the corrupting influences of competition, compromise, and the more sordid necessities of life.[120] More radical supporters of women's rights argued that it was precisely woman's superior moral status which made her political influence so necessary. Reformers advocated women's active participation in public affairs in order that their moral, caring, and emotional qualities—the qualities of the home—might infuse the impersonal male machine of state. So Josephine Butler wrote in an introduction to *Woman's Work and Culture*:

The tendency at present is to centralization of rule, to vast combinations, large institutions, and uniformity of system . . . For the correction of the extreme tendencies of this reaction, I believe that nothing whatever will avail but the large infusion of Home elements into Workhouses, Hospitals, Schools, Orphanages, Lunatic Asylums, Reformatories, and even Prisons: and in order to this there must be a setting free of feminine powers and influence from the constraint of bad education, and narrow aims, and listless homes where they are at present too often a superfluity.[121]

[120] See. e.g. Sarah Ellis, *The Wives of England, their Relative Duties, Domestic Influence, and Social Obligations* (London: Fisher, Son & Co., 1843); John Bright, 'Speech on the Women's Disabilities Removal Bill 26 April 1876', W. E. Gladstone, 'Female Suffrage: A Letter to Samuel Smith', and Mrs Humphrey Ward *et al.*, 'An Appeal Against Female Suffrage' (June 1889), all repr. in Jane Lewis (ed.), *Before the Vote was Won: Arguments for and Against Women's Suffrage* (London: Routledge & Kegan Paul, 1987). Sara Lewis, *Woman's Mission* (1st pub. London, 1839), repr. in Elizabeth K. Helsinger, Robin Sheets, and William Veeder (eds.). *The Woman Question: Society and Literature in Britain and America, 1837–1883, Defining Voices* (Manchester: Manchester University Press, 1983).

[121] 'Introduction, by the Editor', in Josephine E. Butler (ed.), *Woman's Work and Culture: A Series of Essays* (London, 1869), p. xxxvii; see also Julia Wedgwood, 'Female Suffrage, Considered Chiefly with Regard to its Indirect Results', ibid. 247–89; Millicent Garrett Fawcett, 'Home and Politics', repr. in Jane Lewis, (ed.), *Before the Vote Was Won*, 418–24.

Lady Chiltern's influence is already at work in precisely this political fusion of House and home: a member of the Women's Liberal Association, she discusses 'Factory Acts, Female Inspectors, the Eight Hours Bill, the Parliamentary Franchise . . .'.[122] Sir Robert at first seeks to exclude his wife from public affairs, brushing aside her interest with the declaration that 'politics is a very complex business'.[123] While House and home are thus separate, Lady Chiltern remains a naïve idealist, whose influence on her husband's politics is purely destructive, encouraging him to corrupt himself further rather than reveal to her the murkier facts of life. Once Lady Chiltern has lost her domestic innocence and been initiated into the shabby secrets of political reality, she can allow her reformed husband his place in public. The Chilterns' marriage is saved only when public and private, male and female values are united. Lord Goring's speech advocating separate spheres and values for men and women lies at the end of a play which effectively argues for the rejection of precisely such divisions.

That Lady Chiltern's lesson in wifely support does not preclude the continuation of her political activity is demonstrated by the parallel case of Lady Dilke. On hearing of Sir Charles Dilke's involvement in a divorce case, the then Emilia Pattison responded by telegraphing an announcement of their, previously secret, engagement to *The Times*. Once married to the disgraced politician, she not only supported him in his attempts to regain his place in government, but also continued her involvement with the Women's Trade Union League and her campaigning against sweated labour.[124]

An Ideal Husband is thus as ambiguous and complex a play as its predecessors. Beneath the surface melodrama of society intrigue, political blackmail, and conventional definitions of sexual

---

[122] *IH* II. 84. It was in precisely such reforming social legislation that Wilde became overtly involved after his imprisonment, writing letters to the newspapers on the treatment of children and the insane and supporting the Prison Reform Bill—see Conclusion.

[123] *IH* I. 56.

[124] Roy Jenkins, *Sir Charles Dilke: A Victorian Tragedy* (London: Collins, 1958). Wilde was not only well acquainted with Sir Charles Dilke, he also requested a copy of Lady Dilke's book, *Renaissance of Art in France* (1879) while in Reading Gaol (*Letters*, 522).

roles lies a more subtly contradictory play of social and political satire. *An Ideal Husband* is not a play of answers. Like its predecessor it highlights the flaws in any absolute definition or social generalization. Just as *A Woman of No Importance* revealed the more complex reality which underlay the conventional cliché of wronged woman and brutal seducer, so *An Ideal Husband* reveals the complexities beneath the traditional clichés of ideal and idolizing woman and ambitious, protective man.

The only unambiguous message in the play is that of love. *An Ideal Husband* presents two of Wilde's most carefully created couples. The zany courtship of Lord Goring and Mabel Chiltern develops out of the flat and conventional proposal of the earlier manuscript versions. The marriage of Sir Robert and Lady Chiltern starts out similarly flat and unappealing, but warmth and passion are added to their union. In later drafts, Sir Robert no longer compliments his wife on her flower-arranging but on her beauty, and Lady Chiltern ends the play by promising her husband that it is not pity that she feels for him, but 'Love, and only love'.[125] Wilde preaches a message of personal and political charity to an uncharitable age, hiding his more serious intent under a mask of wit and sentiment. The play, like its author, is deliberately deceptive. As Wilde wrote in a letter enclosing a copy of an early manuscript of *An Ideal Husband*, 'In so vulgar an age as this we all need masks.'[126]

---

[125] BL Add. MS 37946: I. 58—alteration made in BL Add. MS 37947: Act I. BL Add. MS 37946: IV. 307, final exchange (*IH* IV. 213), added in BL Add. MS 37947: IV. 96.

[126] To Philip Houghton (?late Feb. 1894), *Letters*, 353.

6

The Importance of Being Earnest

> I made art a philosophy, and philosophy an art: I altered
> the minds of men and the colours of things: there was
> nothing I said or did that did not make people wonder: I
> took the drama, the most objective form known to art,
> and made it as personal a mode of expression as the lyric
> or the sonnet.[1]

OF all Wilde's plays *The Importance of Being Earnest* is the
most frivolous, most capricious, and most uniquely Wildean. It
is a farce, perfectly crafted and constantly amusing. Its action
has been removed from reality to the comic world where the improbable always happens, and where even the manservant and
the governess are unfailing epigrammatists. The dialogue is so
perfectly orchestrated, so delightfully void of rational argument,
as to be the dramatic equivalent of music; as W. H. Auden
observed: *Earnest* is 'perhaps the only purely verbal opera in
English.'[2]

Wilde's farce offered impeccable credentials to its contemporary audience for, like its successful predecessor *Lady Windermere's Fan*, it was produced by George Alexander at the St
James's Theatre. Under Alexander's management, the St James's
had become one of the most fashionable theatres in the West
End, its dramatic fare treading the careful line between the
correct and the risky.[3] As one theatre historian has summed
up Alexander's policy: 'It was the drama of the genteel—the
Apotheosis of the Butterfly. In a commercial age, he adhered

---

[1] To Lord Alfred Douglas (Jan.–Mar. 1897), *Letters*, 466.
[2] 'An Improbable Life', review of *The Collected Letters of Oscar Wilde*, ed.
Hart-Davis, repr. in Ellmann (ed.) *Oscar Wilde: A Collection of Critical Essays*,
136.
[3] Superficially *risqué* but essentially safe plays performed under Alexander's management included Haddon Chambers's *The Idler* (26 Feb. 1891), Pinero's *The
Second Mrs Tanqueray* (27 May 1893), and H. A. Jones's *The Masqueraders* (28
Apr. 1894). For a full list of Alexander's productions see Mason, *Sir George
Alexander and the St James's Theatre.*

strictly to commercial plays; the box office receipts were his justification and his reward.'[4] *The Importance of Being Earnest* seemed perfect for such a theatre, an irridescent fantasy, described by the author himself as 'written by a butterfly for butterflies.'[5]

Yet the play was as deceptive as its predecessors; its nonsensical frivolity was the camouflage for Wilde's most subversive and satirical work. In 'The Soul of Man under Socialism' Wilde had noted farce's potential for concealing revolutionary art from the eye of the censor: 'burlesque and farcical comedy, the two most popular forms, are distinct forms of art. Delightful work may be produced under burlesque and farcical conditions, and in work of this kind the artist in England is allowed very great freedom.'[6] Wilde exploited this freedom to create a double-edged comedy, a bright bubble of nonsense which mocked every principle, law, and custom, of the society he lived in. *Earnest* was 'A trivial comedy for serious people.'[7] The play has its philosophy, as Wilde explained: 'That we should treat all the trivial things of life very seriously, and all the serious things of life with sincere and studied triviality.'[8] This philosophy was not simply one of comic flippancy; it was also the method of the satirist and the revolutionary. The play is as subtly deceptive as its predecessors, for the light-hearted exterior conceals a more sinister purpose. It challenged society's values, reversed its conclusions, eschewed its responsibilities, and introduced the comic note of anarchy. In *The Importance of Being Earnest* Wilde had found a perfect dramatic form for his own uneasy relation to society. The play has an 'ethical scheme', as he explained in a letter to the artist Philip Houghton:

To the world I seem, by intention on my part, a dilettante and dandy merely—it is not wise to show one's heart to the world—and as seriousness of manner is the disguise of the fool, folly in its exquisite

[4] Pearson, *Modern Men and Mummers*, 81.
[5] To Arthur L. Humphreys (*c*.12 Feb. 1895), *Letters*, 382.
[6] 'The Soul of Man', 305.
[7] *The Importance of Being Earnest: A Trivial Comedy for Serious People* (London: Leonard Smithers, 1899), dedicated to Robert Ross.
[8] 'Mr Oscar Wilde on Mr Oscar Wilde: An Interview', *St James's Gazette* (18 Jan. 1895), 5. Hart-Davis believes that this interview was written in collaboration between Robbie Ross and Wilde (*More Letters*, 128).

modes of triviality and indifference and lack of care is the robe of the wise man. In so vulgar an age as this we all need masks.[9]

The Importance of Being Earnest was to all appearances a conventional nineteenth-century farce. As with Wilde's previous plays, most of the basic ingredients of the plot were familiar from innumerable other farces: misplaced parents, forbidden engagements, false identities, overbearing mothers, and the copious consumption of food were all clichés of the comic stage. Yet Wilde used his material to highly unconventional ends, for the world of *Earnest* is an anarchic one.

All farce contains an element of anarchy. Pinero's farces are a perfect example of controlled comic chaos, where a figure of authority—schoolmistress, magistrate, or dean—disrupts the proper order by pursuing improper pastimes—singing comic operas, drinking after hours, or betting on horses.[10] The disruption spreads as respectable persons are forced to lie, steal, and assume false identities to cover up their indiscretions. Yet, ultimately, law, order, and the *status quo* are re-established. The disorder is short-lived and the only after-effects are that the errant figures of authority have been led to a more sympathetic understanding of human error.[11] The spirit of anarchy is constantly opposed by the ruling spirit of civilized society, and civilized society eventually achieves an impressive victory. In Wilde's farce, however, there is no division between chaos and order, fact and fiction. It is not a civilized society temporarily disrupted, but a perfect anarchic state in which the characters live, luxuriating in its benevolent lack of rules, morals, and principles.

Contemporary reviewers greeted *The Importance of Being Earnest* as comedy unadulterated by sense: 'midsummer madness', as the *Daily Graphic* declared.[12] Some described it as quintessential farce, perfect dramatic nonsense.[13] Others jibbed at

[9] To Philip Houghton (?late Feb. 1894), *Letters*, 353.
[10] Pinero, *The Schoolmistress* (London: Heinemann, 1894), 1st perf. Royal Court, London, 27 Mar. 1886; *The Magistrate* (London: Heinemann, 1892), 1st perf. Royal Court, London, 21 Mar. 1885; *Dandy Dick* (London: Heinemann, 1893), 1st perf. Royal Court, London, 27 Jan. 1887.
[11] The exception to this rule is *The Schoolmistress*, where the teacher–heroine chooses the comic opera as the more lucrative career by which to support her aristocratic husband.
[12] *Daily Graphic* (15 Feb. 1895), 7.
[13] *Black and White*, 9 (23 Feb. 1895), 240; *Daily Graphic* (15 Feb. 1895), 7; the *World* (20 Feb. 1895), 24–5; *Illustrated London News*, 106 (23 Feb. 1895), 227.

the apparent ease with which Wilde's comedy had been written, protesting as they laughed that his wit was not diamond but paste, and variously describing it as 'spurious', 'sham', and 'tinsel'.[14] The commonest observation, however, was that Wilde was treading in the footsteps of W. S. Gilbert.[15] Wilde, like Gilbert, they believed, was offering a light-hearted fantasy which poked fun at society without ever seriously questioning the tenets of its belief. Bernard Shaw condemned the play for precisely this lack of depth, observing: 'It amused me, of course; but unless comedy touches me as well as amuses me, it leaves me with a sense of having wasted my evening. I go to the theatre to be moved to laughter, not to be tickled or bustled into it.'[16] He impatiently brushed aside suggestions that *The Importance of Being Earnest* could not have been written without the example of his own comedy of the previous year, *Arms and the Man*.[17]

A. B. Walkley, however, while describing *Earnest* as farce with 'no discordant note of seriousness', unconsciously hinted at the greater potential power of the play by grouping it with *The Wasps* and *Le Médecin malgré lui* as farcical works which still qualified as great literature.[18] It was left to William Archer, critic of the *World*, to recognize the deliberately elusive quality of Wilde's play. Remarking on the difficulty of writing anything about a play which amounted to a *rondo capriccioso*, he noted that *Earnest* rejected all conventional values and thereby eluded conventional evaluation:

It is like a mirage-oasis in the desert, grateful and comforting to the weary eye—but when you come up close to it, behold! it is intangible, it eludes your grasp. What can a poor critic do with a play that raises no principle, whether of art or morals, creates its own canons and

---

[14] *The Graphic*, 51 (23 Feb. 1895), 214; *Theatre*, 25 (1 Mar. 1895) 170; *Athenæum*, 105 (23 Feb. 1895), 260.

[15] *Athenæum*, 105 (23 Feb. 1895), 260; *Daily Graphic* (15 Feb. 1895), 7; *Black and White*, 9 (23 Feb. 1895), 240; *Punch*, 108 (23 Feb. 1895), 85; *Saturday Review*, 79 (23 Feb. 1895), 249; the *World* (20 Feb. 1895), 24–5. The plays of Gilbert's to which particular reference was made were *The Palace of Truth* (1870) and *Engaged* (1877).

[16] *Saturday Review*, 79 (23 Feb. 1895), 250.

[17] But years later the comparison was still being made. The playwright, St John Hankin, for example, grouped together *Arms and the Man*, *The Philanderer*, and *The Importance of Being Earnest* as 'psychological farce, the farce of ideas'. *The Dramatic Works of St John Hankin*, iii (London, 1912), 187, repr. in Ellmann (ed.), *Oscar Wilde: A Collection of Critical Essays*, 61–72.

[18] *Speaker*, 4 (23 Feb. 1895), 212.

conventions, and is nothing but an absolutely wilful expression of an irrepressibly witty personality?[19]

While trying to sell the play to a West End theatre, Wilde was at pains to present *Earnest* as pure farce, a play written to please the public and fill his pocket. Offering it to George Alexander, he warned that the play might be too slight, and to Charles Mason he reported that, 'it is quite nonsensical and has no serious interest', but 'will I hope bring me in a lot of red gold'.[20] Yet, years later, when preparing the play for publication, Wilde emphasized a very different aspect of the play: *Earnest* was not as harmless as he had first pretended, but something more *risqué* and harder for the public to stomach. An exile with a criminal record, he was not optimistic as to the reception of his newly published play. English society was hardly likely to regard him with their previous indulgence, for

while the public liked to hear of my pain—curiosity and the autobiographical form being elements of interest—I am not sure that they will welcome me again in airy mood and spirit, mocking at morals, and defiance of social rules.[21]

This airy farce had become dangerous contraband to be smuggled in under the public's nose; writing to Reggie Turner he marvelled at his former audacity: 'It was extraordinary reading the play over. How I used to toy with that tiger Life!'[22] Even when the play first opened, Wilde clearly saw it as something more powerful than a frivolous piece of entertainment. As Ada Leverson recalled: 'When a friend said that the farce should be like a piece of mosaic, he answered, "No; it must go like a pistol shot." '[23]

Modern critics have been quicker to see beneath *Earnest*'s scintillating surface to Wilde's more serious concerns. Some identify only a personal frame of reference for the play, arguing that in it Wilde parodied and reduced to nonsense the themes

---

[19] The *World* (20 Feb. 1895), 24–5.
[20] To George Alexander (Aug. 1894), *Letters*, 359; to Charles Spurrier Mason (Aug. 1894), *Letters*, 364.
[21] To Frank Harris (18 Feb. 1899), *Letters*, 780.
[22] To Reginald Turner (postmark 3 Feb. 1899), *Letters*, 778.
[23] Leverson, *Letters to the Sphinx*, 31.

he had treated more soberly in his previous works.[24] Most critics, however, allow *Earnest* a wider scope, noting how Wilde's comedy reduced the central tenets of Victorian society to farce.[25] *Earnest* is allowed a place apart from Wilde's other dramas, free from the melodrama or inconsistency which marred its predecessors. Yet *The Importance of Being Earnest* had much in common with Wilde's earlier plays; like them, it simultaneously mimicked and subverted the conventions of a popular theatrical genre, and, like them, it hid a more radical play beneath a smoothly reassuring surface.

As with all his previous plays, Wilde took *The Importance of Being Earnest* through a number of drafts to reach its final, apparently effortlessly witty, form.[26] The first version of the play was immensely long, filling four exercise books with farcical accidents, broad puns, and a number of familiar comic devices. This manuscript was tightened and reshaped in successive drafts,

---

[24] See e.g. Christopher Nassaar who describes the play as 'absolutely devoid of sober content' and 'basically a self-parody' (*Into the Demon Universe*, 130 and 131), and Philip Cohen, who comments of *Earnest*, 'His literary transformations of these personal elements exemplify his intent to trivialize the serious, and thus to escape his anxieties' (*The Moral Vision of Oscar Wilde*, 219).

[25] Rodney Shewan notes that *Earnest* 'succeeded completely in penetrating the fortress of established morality' (*Oscar Wilde: Art and Egotism*, 187); Alan Bird says it 'made fun of everything the English held—and hold—sacred, not least money, baptism, birth, religion, food and property' (*The Plays of Oscar Wilde*, 182). Christopher Craft demonstrates how *Earnest*'s punning subtext derides the stock devices of heterosexual narrative in 'Alias Bunbury: Desire and Termination in *The Importance of Being Earnest*', *Representations*, 31 (summer 1990), 19–46. Gagnier, while noting Wilde's satirical intent, argues that the play's absurd action allows the audience to escape the charges levelled against it: 'While the social criticism and the farcical action effectively cancel each other out, the audience receives reinforcement from its own dominant and fetishized image on stage' (*Idylls of the Marketplace*, 111).

[26] Drafts referred to are as follows: (*a*) Aut. MS (Aug. 1894), handwritten in four exercise books. Acts I and II are in the Arents Collection, New York Public Library (this MS contains only intermittent page-numbering in Wilde's hand), cited below as Aut. MS NY; Acts III and IV: BL Add. MS 37948 (page-numbering, as in all BL MSS, is the library's own). (*b*) Typescript of Acts I, III, and IV, with Wilde's autograph corrections. Arents Collection, Act I stamped 'Mrs Marshall's Type Writing Office. 126 Strand. 1 Nov 1894'. Cited below as Arents typescript NY. (*c*) Typescript of four-act version (dated 31 Oct. 1894). Burnside–Frohman Collection, New York. (*d*) Licensing copy, BL Add. MS 53567 (17). Entitled 'Lady Lancing. A Serious Comedy for Trivial People'. (*e*) Typescript typed by Winifred Dolan, revised by Wilde to provide copy for 1899. Arents Collection. (*f*) *The Importance of Being Earnest* (see n. 7 above; cited below as *IBE*; references are to act and page number). For a full stemma see the introduction to *The Importance of Being Earnest*, ed. Jackson.

and Wilde even continued to revise the play long after it had been performed, devoting much time to editing and proof-reading in order to perfect the final published version of 1899. This elaborate process of revision reveals the remarkable care that Wilde took with the play. Through each successive draft he gradually transformed it from a highly plotted, frequently absurd, but essentially harmless and familiar comedy into an insidiously subversive, satirical, and undeniably unique drama, a psychological farce. The existence of earlier versions of *Earnest* is more generally acknowledged than is the case with his earlier plays, primarily because it is known that Wilde complied with a request from George Alexander to cut the play from four acts to three. Much material had in fact already been excised before this apparently radical change, and the only major excision which resulted on this occasion was that of Algy's arrest for 'Ernest''s dining debts. Wilde characteristically concealed the meticulous attention he had already devoted to the play, complaining to Alexander that, 'This scene you feel is superfluous cost me terrible exhausting labour and heart-rending nerve-wracking strain. You may not believe me, but I assure you that it must have taken me fully five minutes to write!'[27]

Though one inevitably longs for a play as delightful as *Earnest* to be twice its length, Wilde's revisions tightened, sharpened, and improved his play. Conventional comic turns, unfunny witticisms, and genuine nonsense were cut: for example, a long speech by Jack on the superior merits of a handbag as opposed to a perambulator as a method of transporting babies was cut, as was a tussle between Jack and Algy over the sherry decanter, and a spurious 'echo', actually produced by Algy and Cecily whispering behind a screen while hiding from Lady Bracknell.[28] Some of the lines cut are distinctly Gilbertian in their humour, as in the case of Jack's pompously insincere delight at Algy and Cecily's engagement: '*Dear* Aunt Augusta, that marriage has been the *dream* of my life for the last ten minutes!'[29] Compressing the dialogue, Wilde transformed standard nonsense into the

[27] Quoted in Hyde, *Oscar Wilde*, 222.
[28] Aut. MS NY: Act I; page numbers, where given, are Wilde's own intermittent numbering. Aut. MS BL Add. MS 37948: IV. 139 and 109–14.
[29] Aut. MS BL Add. MS 37948: IV. 184.

more systematic and disconcerting illogicality which characterizes *Earnest*'s dialogue. The first autograph version contains
the following speech from Lady Bracknell on the presumed fate
of the baby entrusted to Miss Prism:

> It was I suppose left at the offices of one of those publishers who
> do not return rejected contributions unless accompanied by stamps.
> With your usual carelessness Prism I suppose you never dreamed of
> putting stamps with the baby. That unfortunate child is probably
> at the present moment lying in the waste-paper basket of some
> large commercial house.[30]

The main joke here—Lady Bracknell's assumption that the baby
has been magically frozen in time—is compressed in the final
version into the ambiguously ridiculous demand, 'Prism! Where
is that baby?'[31]

The main effect of Wilde's revisions, however, was to sharpen
the satirical thrust of the play; as the dialogue is honed so is
its impact. Thus Lady Bracknell, the embodiment of society,
develops through successive drafts from the familiar overbearing duchess into a quirkier and more disturbing character. The
draconian older woman was, and still is, a stock character in
farce; she is the nanny from whom the errant children try to
hide their misdemeanours, the unsympathetic but essential figure of authority. So, in Lestoq and Robson's farce *The Foundling* (1894), the henpecked Major Cotton seeks to hide his
assignations with the actress Maybud, while Mrs Cotton
prefigures Lady Bracknell by rejecting her daughter's suitor on
the grounds of his lack of parents, declaring: 'I will never allow
a daughter of mine to marry a man who has no genealogy—
I want blood.'[32] Indeed, thwarting love-matches was one of the

---

[30] Ibid. 167.

[31] *IBE* III. 143. Having edited out the joke against publishers, Wilde contented
himself with calling Algy's manservant Lane after one of his own publishers, John
Lane.

[32] W. Lestoq and E . M. Robson, *The Foundling* (1894), Licence No. 232 (Terry's
Theatre, 11 Aug. 1894) BL LCP Add. MS 53555. I am indebted to Kerry Powell's
Oscar Wilde and the Theatre of the 1890s for drawing attention to this play.
Professor Powell presents a thesis that *Earnest* was reshaped from a Sheridan-like
comedy into its final farcical form thanks to Wilde's attending a performance of
The Foundling (pp. 108–23). The dating of the play's composition is just plausible.
Peter Raby's discovery of Wilde's first scenario for the play has since shown the
earliest outline to include essentials such as the fictional brother (called George),

primary duties of nineteenth-century theatrical matriarchs. In Tom Robertson's *Society* (1865) the formidable Lady Ptarmigant obstructs her ward's marriage to the penniless Sidney Daryl, backing instead the wealthier, if low-born, Chodd Junior.[33] In *Caste* (1867) another of Robertson's fearsome women, the Marquise de St Maur, refuses to acknowledge her son's wife because of her lowly lineage.[34] Lady Ptarmigant and the Marquise of St Maur are representatives of the old order, theirs is the voice of society. Robertson presents them as mercenary, snobbish, domineering, and stubborn, but he also gives them warm hearts beneath their unsympathetic exteriors, and, more importantly, their views are not wholly condemned. Lady Ptarmigant is shown to be right in forbidding a penniless match, and the drunken wastrel, Eccles, confirms all the Marquise's doubts about the lower orders.

The first version of Lady Bracknell, named 'Lady Brancaster', had much in common with these women. Unlike her unapproachable final version, Lady Brancaster is very much the mother. Her authority appears less arbitrary and outrageous: Algy and Gwendolen bicker peevishly and Lady Brancaster admonishes them: 'Now, children, don't quarrel.'[35] She is clearly much closer to Algy than in the final version, enquiring sympathetically after his state of debt.[36] At the same time, Lady Brancaster's faults are far more obvious, making her a two-dimensional, but not necessarily unsympathetic, caricature of society's failings. Her love of money is unambiguous, and her control of her husband becomes a running joke in the play, a recurring theme which turns her into the classic domineering wife. The Duchess of Berwick in *Lady Windermere's Fan*

double engagements, etc. which Professor Powell attributes to the influence of *The Foundling*. The guardian's lack of parents and the mislaying of the baby, however, are not yet present. This discovery thus alters but does not confound the basis of Powell's theory. For a copy of the scenario, see Ian Small, *Oscar Wilde Revalued: An Essay on New Materials and Methods of Research* (Greensboro, NC: ELT Press, 1993), 65–8.

[33] *Society*, in *The Principal Dramatic Works of Thomas William Robertson*, ii (London: Samuel French, 1889), 1st produced, Prince of Wales Theatre, Liverpool, 8 May 1865.

[34] *Caste*, in *The Principal Dramatic Works of Thomas William Robertson*, i (London: Samuel French, 1889), 1st produced, Prince of Wales's Royal Theatre, London, 6 Apr. 1867.

[35] Aut MS NY: Act I.   [36] Ibid.

highlighted the subtle hypocrisies of the respectable Victorian marriage, when she advised Lady Windermere to turn a blind eye to her husband's infidelity and to hurry him off to Homburg where she might rejuvenate their marriage—a remedy which the Duchess herself had frequently sought, though she also suffered the penalty of being 'obliged to drink the most unpleasant mineral waters, merely to get Berwick out of town'.[37] There is no such ambiguity involved in Lady Brancaster's marital relationship; mineral waters are simply one more ordeal for the conventionally henpecked Lord Brancaster. As Lady Brancaster warns Gwendolen:

> Tomorrow I will make arrangements for taking you abroad. I am going to order your father to Carlsbad; and a course of those saline waters would I think have a chastening effect on your foolish attempts at independence. In your father's case, at any rate, I have never found them fail. And your conduct today reminds me somewhat of his own behaviour in the early days of our happy married life.[38]

Often Wilde's revisions appear to be primarily concerned with the comic impact of the dialogue. So, for example, Lady Brancaster's indignant reply to Jack stands in the first manuscript version as follows: 'Me, sir! What *has* it to do with me? You do not, I sincerely trust, suppose for an instant that I would tolerate as a son-in-law a gentleman who by his own admission is closely connected with unclaimed luggage.'[39] In the final version of the play, Lady Bracknell exclaims instead: 'Me, sir! What has it to do with me? You can hardly imagine that I and Lord Bracknell would dream of allowing our only daughter—a girl brought up with the utmost care—to marry into a cloak-room and form an alliance with a parcel?'[40] The shift from the commonsensical first version to the surreal and illogical final version is not simply a comic one, however. Lady Bracknell's methods are far more subtle than her predecessor's. The absurd convolutions of Lady Bracknell's speech hide the brute force behind it; Lady Bracknell, unlike Lady Brancaster, conceals her will beneath a polite veneer of maternal, wifely,

---

[37] *LWF* I. 19.   [38] Aut. MS BL Add. MS 37948: IV. 112.
[39] Aut MS NY: Act I, 1st notebook.   [40] *IBE* I. 39.

180 The Importance of Being Earnest

and social duty, while, without addressing Jack directly, she reduces her daughter's suitor to a social impossibility.

Lady Bracknell's interviewing of Jack, the centre-piece of Wilde's satire of fashionable social values, was painstakingly honed and sharpened. Slight jabs at social snobbery—such as the suggestion that Jack change his surname to Worthing-Worthing—were excised, while the real satire cut deeper.[41] Lady Bracknell's opposition to modern education, on the grounds that it causes social unrest and endangers the supremacy of the upper classes, was added to a late typescript, while the final specific location of the ensuing acts of violence 'in Grosvenor Square' was only added by Wilde to the last proof version.[42] Thus, the implication that nothing could be worse than distasteful riots in a fashionable district of London is added to Lady Bracknell's opposition to widespread education. Wilde obviously took great care to tread the narrow line of acceptability. Earlier drafts contain a jibe at the expense of revolutionary politics when Lady Bracknell enquires if Jack has any radical sympathies, and he replies: 'Oh! I don't want to put the asses against the classes if that is what you mean, Lady Brancaster.'[43] In a later typescript Jack adds, 'the difficulty is to find out on which side the asses are'.[44] This was going too far in the opposite direction, and the entire exchange was later cut.[45] The final version simply dismisses all claims to progressiveness on the part of Liberal Unionists, who rejected Home Rule for Ireland, when Lady Bracknell declares that 'they count as Tories' and grants them the dubious pleasure of dining with her.[46]

Every single exchange in this interview ridicules some tenet of the fashionable social creed, be it the superiority of old landed wealth over the *nouveaux riches*—dismissed by Lady Bracknell, because land 'gives one position, and prevents one from keeping it up'—or the importance of genealogy.[47] The great matriarch only has to refer to a principle to reduce it to nonsense. As she declares in the dignified tones of a social oracle:

[41] Aut MS NY: Act I, 1st notebook.
[42] Typescript owned by George Alexander, Harvard Theatre Collection, Act I, and page proofs for 1899 edn, Act I, quoted in *The Importance of Being Earnest*, ed. Jackson, 27.
[43] Aut. MS NY: Act I, 1st notebook.   [44] Arents typescript, NY: I. 20.
[45] Discarded in licensing copy, BL Add. MS 53567 (17): Act I.
[46] *IBE* I. 35.   [47] Ibid. 34.

To be born, or at any rate bred in a handbag, whether it had handles or not, seems to me to display a contempt for the ordinary decencies of family life that reminds one of the worst excesses of the French Revolution. And I presume you know what that unfortunate movement led to?[48]

Lady Bracknell's enormous logical leap (emphasized by the fact that no one can be quite sure what it *did* lead to) effectively ridicules the conservative argument that class distinctions of birth and breeding are necessary to prevent a social revolution.

For all its apparent absurdity, there is a distinctly logical pattern to Lady Bracknell's interrogation of Jack. Her questions and her reactions to Jack's answers are mostly the opposite of what one would expect. Jack sheepishly admits that he smokes—Lady Bracknell is delighted he has some occupation. Jack admits to knowing nothing—Lady Bracknell cherishes the delicate bloom of male ignorance.[49] The rationale behind all this is that Lady Bracknell regards men as essentially useless and ornamental creatures—a view more traditionally applied to the female sex. Significantly, the first manuscript draft contains another version of this defence of ignorance, but more conventionally applied to women; Lady Brancaster thanks Algy for arranging the musical programme, and adds: 'One can't be too careful nowadays. There are so many girls in society, and they know so much more than they should. I regret anything that tampers with the ignorance of a young girl. Ignorance is like a delicate exotic fruit. Touch it and the bloom is gone.'[50] Under Lady Bracknell's matriarchal rule it is male ignorance which must be preserved.

Wilde's revisions produced more radical and unconventional roles for *Earnest*'s female characters, transforming them through

---

[48] Ibid. I. 38. Lady Bracknell's huge logical leap in fact echoed the moral panic at the beginning of the century. So a correspondent to the *Public Ledger* (17 Jan. 1816), pleased by the imprisonment of a vendor of indecent prints, commented: 'That the French Revolution, with all its consequent horrors, was preceded by a total revolution of decency and morality, the virtuous qualities of mind being sapped and undermined by the baneful exhibition of pictures, representing vice in the most alluring and varied forms, to a depraved mind, is a truth that unfortunately will not admit a doubt.' (p. 3). Quoted in Eric Trudgill, *Madonnas and Magdalens: The Origins and Development of Victorian Sexual Attitudes* (London: Heinemann, 1976), 30.

[49] *IBE* I. 33.   [50] Aut. MS NY: Act I, 1st notebook.

successive drafts into stronger and more original individuals. The poised, independently minded Gwendolen starts life as a caricature bluestocking. Her pursuit of learning is either ridiculed as irrelevant, or reduced to a display of female vanity. So, in a childish squabble, Algy mocks Gwendolen's learning, while she defends herself in distinctly ambiguous terms:

ALGY. I don't care to talk about music to Gwendolen any longer. She has grown far too intellectual during the three months. She seems to think that music does not contain enough useful information.
GWENDOLEN. Algy! how dare you be so impertinent? And you don't know anything about the University Extension Scheme at all: I never return from any one of their lectures without having been extensively admired.[51]

Unlike the rather terrifyingly self-possessed young woman of the final version, the first Gwendolen is often reduced to comic caricature. She delivers absolute statements and contradicts them in her next breath. Not only female learning but female intuition is mocked, as Gwendolen proudly declares at the end of the play: 'Ernest! my own Ernest! I felt from the first that you could have had no other name. Even all man's useless information, wonderful though it is, is nothing compared to the instinct of a good woman.'[52] The first Gwendolen is a less dignified figure, but she is also a more disagreeable one. In the final version Jack's concern that Gwendolen might become like her mother in about 150 years is comic because the daughter's stylish command and quiet determination are clear echoes of her mother's domineering ways.[53] In the first manuscript version this subtle hint is more broadly stated, as Algy assures Jack he will have no authority over his future wife, because 'Gwendolen has one of those soft yielding natures that always have their own way.'[54] Algy defines the hypocritical power of the female, and Gwendolen is reduced to a bullying gorgon like her mother.

In the final version, Gwendolen is the sophisticated, fashionable woman of the town, while Cecily is the natural, unspoilt country girl. Much of the humour derived from Cecily's character springs from the contrast between her supposed maiden simplicity and her actual intelligence, self-possession, and knowing

[51] Aut. MS NY: Act I, 1st notebook.
[52] Aut. MS BL Add. MS 37948: IV. 191.   [53] *IBE* I. 40.
[54] Aut MS NY: I. 16.

acuteness. Wilde was not the first dramatist to exploit the stereotype of the innocent country maid to comic effect. In *The Palace of Truth* (1870), W. S. Gilbert presents a maiden, Azema, whose country innocence is a thin disguise for her sexually predatory intentions.[55] Azema, 'whose manner is characterised by extreme modesty and timidity', is forced by the spell on the palace unconsciously to betray her true motives. On meeting Prince Philamir, she explains her own hypocrisy:

PHILAMIR. I beg your pardon, but the furniture
  Has caught your dress.
AZEMA. [*rearranging her dress hastily*]
            Oh, I arranged it so,
That you might see how truly beautiful
My foot and ankle are. [*As if much shocked at the exposé.*][56]

Gilbert's Azema is simply one stock character pretending to be another stock character: she is the devious, sexually experienced woman assuming the guise of the pure and modest maiden. Wilde's Cecily offers a far more subtle combination of these character-types, a combination which ultimately undermines the stereotypes themselves.

While being more in thrall to Miss Prism and her guardian and less quietly in control of Algy, the early Cecily is also a more manipulative and worldly character. Unscrupulously mercenary like so many of W. S. Gilbert's women, she sweetly informs Algy that: 'The next morning I bought this little ring in your name; and put it down to an account I have opened for you at a very artistic jewellers who has such a nice shop in our little country town.'[57] She is knowing to the point of being cynical, commenting that the dullness of society is due to it having far more culture than conversation.[58] As with the heartless Mrs Cheveley, her engagement to Ernest was broken off because he suspected her of flirting with a lord; in Cecily's case, however, the suspicion was unfounded, as she explains: 'Of course it wasn't true at all. And even if it had been, Lord Kelso is unmarried. And it was not likely that I should have taken any

---

[55] *The Palace of Truth*, repr. in *Plays by W. S. Gilbert*, ed. George Rowell (Cambridge: Cambridge University Press, 1982), 1st produced Theatre Royal, Haymarket, London, 19 Nov. 1870.
[56] Ibid. II. 50.   [57] Aut. MS BL Add. MS 37948: III. 38–9.
[58] Aut. MS NY: Act II.

interest in an unmarried man. It is so easy to take an unmarried man at an unfair advantage.'[59] In some ways the early Cecily is more openly carnal than her successor. The first Cecily approves of Jack refusing Algy an invitation to dinner because: 'Two luncheons would not be really good for your brother Ernest. He might lose his figure.'[60] Yet she is also more traditionally passive, waiting for Algy to make all the first moves and simply responding with enthusiasm to his advances. The first Cecily is a country innocent along the lines of Wycherley's Margery Pinchwife, who longs to exchange her enforced rural inexperience for more sophisticated and corrupt knowledge.[61] So when Miss Prism leaves Cecily in Algy's company, urging her to pursue her studies, Cecily eagerly replies: 'By the time that you return I feel sure that I shall know very much more than I do at present.'[62]

The final Cecily is remarkable in that she combines the sheltered upbringing of the typical country innocent with the self-possession and intelligent poise of the experienced woman-about-town. Without being cynical or worldly, she has sufficient self-assurance to make her intentions and desires quite clear; when Algy declares that he loves her 'wildly, passionately, devotedly, hopelessly', Cecily calmly replies: 'Hopelessly doesn't seem to make much sense, does it?'[63]

It is this honesty and forthrightness which distinguish Cecily from similar theatrical models. The heroine of W. S. Gilbert's short play, *Sweethearts* (1874), for example, has much in common with Cecily.[64] Gilbert's Jenny Northcott is an apparently self-possessed young woman, who frequently succeeds in disconcerting her enthusiastic suitor, Harry Spreadbrow. There are a number of similarities between the two plays, for both couples meet in a garden and both young men ask for a flower as a token from their beloved—Jenny responds by offering Spreadbrow a geranium in a pot, but finally gives him a piece of mignonette, while he gives her a rose.[65] Jenny's self-possession,

[59] Aut. MS BL Add. MS 37948: III. 42.   [60] Aut. MS NY: II. 70.
[61] William Wycherley, *The Country Wife*, 1st perf. probably 12 Jan. 1675.
[62] Aut. MS BL Add. MS 37948: III. 21.   [63] *IBE* II. 86.
[64] Gilbert, *Sweethearts*, repr. in *Plays by W. S. Gilbert*, ed. Rowell, 1st produced Prince of Wales's Theatre, London, 7 Nov. 1874.
[65] Ibid. I. 80.

however, is all a sham. She is playing the game of the flirt, but misplays it and lets her suitor leave without bringing him to a proposal; when she realizes that Spreadbrow has left for India and is not coming back to submit himself to more of her teasing, she bursts into bitter tears of despair. It is precisely this coquetry which separates the two heroines and brings about Jenny's downfall. Gilbert's heroine is made to suffer for her manipulative ways. The second act witnesses her humiliation: thirty years later Spreadbrow returns from India to find Jenny an old maid, still reproaching herself for her lost love. Spreadbrow not only fails to recognize his former love, but has forgotten every detail of their courtship. Jenny can produce the rose he once gave her, carefully pressed in the leaves of her book, whereas Spreadbrow tells her that he proposed to a governess only a week after leaving her. Jenny having thus been suitably humbled, Harry takes pity on her, and their courtship is renewed, with the man now in the dominant position and the woman at his mercy.

Nothing could be further from Algy and Cecily's courtship, where every attempt at patronizing superiority on Algy's part is gently deflated by his beloved. Right from the start Cecily is quietly in control, so when Algy greets her as his 'little cousin Cecily', she disconcertingly replies, 'You are under some strange mistake. I am not little. In fact, I believe that I am more than usually tall for my age.'[66] The relationship between Wilde's lovers is summed up by the early Cecily's response to the romantic gibberish Algy recites for her diary: 'The fact is that men should never try to dictate to women. They never know how to do it, and when they do do it, they always say something particularly foolish.'[67]

[66] *IBE* II. 62.

[67] *The Complete Works of Oscar Wilde*, with an introduction by Vyvyan Holland (London: Collins, 1988): *The Importance of Being Earnest* (four-act version), III. 358. This four-act reconstruction, supposedly representing the state of the play before Alexander requested that it be reduced to three acts, is based on a typescript sent by Robert Ross, or someone acting for him, to the German translator, Hermann Freiherr von Teschenberg. His translation, entitled *Ernst Sein!*, was published in Leipzig in 1903. Vyvyan Holland offers a translation of this four-act version as 'the play as written by Oscar Wilde' (introduction, 13). There are signs that Ross or the translator may have incorporated elements of the 1899 edn. into the early four-act typescript.

The unusual contrasts of Cecily's character owe much to another precocious innocent, the heroine of Alfred de Musset's play, *Il ne faut jurer de rien*.[68] De Musset's play was performed as a matinée by the Comédie-Française as part of their London tour on 18 June 1879, and the similarities between this play and *The Importance of Being Earnest* mark it out as another drama plundered by Wilde to his own ends.[69] *Il ne faut jurer de rien* centres on a young man-about-town, Valentin, whose insouciant wit and liking for luxury on credit are shared by Algernon Moncrieff. Like Algy, Valentin assumes a false identity to win his entry to a young woman's home, but his motives are murkier than Algy's, for Valentin seeks to seduce Cécile in order to prove that she is not worthy to become his wife. He is, however, outmanœuvred by this country innocent and, contrary to his first intentions, ends up proposing to her.

The difference between the two plays lies primarily in the presentation of Cécile. Like Cecily, Cécile is outspoken in her emotions and straightforward in her actions. She comes to a midnight rendezvous at Valentin's request, then outwits him by saying she had seen through his pretence immediately, and recognized him as the man she once danced with and fell in love with. Challenged as to why she came to the rendezvous, she replies, 'Pourqoui ne serais-je pas venue, puisque je sais que vous m'épouserez?'[70] Valentin's response is ambivalent:

> Ou j'ai près de moi le plus rusé démon que l'enfer ait jamais produit, ou la voix qui me parle est celle d'un ange, et m'ouvre le chemin des cieux.[71]

> [Either I have next to me the craftiest demon that hell has ever produced, or the voice speaking to me is that of an angel, and offers me a way to heaven.]

---

[68] De Musset, *Il ne faut jurer de rien*, *Théâtre Complet* (Paris: Éditions Gallimard, 1990), 1st pub. in *Revue des Deux Mondes* (1 July 1836), 1st perf. Comédie-Française, 22 June 1848.

[69] Got, *La Comédie Française à Londres (1871–1879)*, 135–8. Charles B. Paul and Robert D. Pepper conclude in their article, 'The Importance of Reading Alfred: Oscar Wilde's Debt to Alfred de Musset', *Bulletin of the New York Public Library*, 75 (1971), 506–41, that 'Almost the entire play, in plan and detail, is (we think) an adaptation, cleverly disguised, of *Il ne faut jurer de rien*' (p. 513). However, they base their argument primarily on structural similarities, ignoring the significant differences between the two plays and disregarding the influence of other contemporary farces on Wilde's play.

[70] *Il ne faut jurer de rien*, III. v. 50.   [71] Ibid. 52.

Valentin settles for the second option, and the couple are happily betrothed by the end of the play. Yet the explanation of Cécile's actions remains uncertain: she may be either angel or devil, extraordinarily devious or quite incredibly naïve and innocent. De Musset preserves the dichotomy between the two stereotypes of womanhood, the mystery of the play being to which category Cécile belongs. Wilde, by contrast, subverts the stereotypes that de Musset promotes. Cecily Cardew is neither angel nor devil but a young woman who proves that female innocence need not necessarily mean ignorance; she combines astuteness with honesty, and simplicity with intelligence.

It is Cecily's frankly displayed sexual eagerness which separates her most clearly from the conventionally innocent heroine. Not only does she do more than offer Algy encouragement, being herself the active partner in their courtship, she even rejects the role of eternally faithful maiden who waits patiently to be united with her beloved. She cannot countenance the possibility of enduring seventeen years of 'passionate celibacy' (nothing compared to Jenny Northcott's thirty) to secure Algy.[72] Her views on this matter are shared by Gwendolen, who assures Jack that nothing can alter her eternal devotion to him, although her mother 'may prevent us from becoming man and wife, and I may marry someone else, and marry often'.[73] This combination of actual female virtue with healthy appetites and urges was extremely unconventional. In *Man and Superman* (1903) Shaw deliberately challenged public prejudice by presenting a perfectly respectable but sexually voracious woman in the form of Ann Whitefield, but this play was judged too strong for the public and had to wait three years to be performed only twice. In the published version Shaw also included an 'Epistle Dedicatory' in which he defended the behaviour of his heroine:

Among the friends to whom I have read this play in manuscript are some of our own sex who are shocked at the 'unscrupulousness', meaning the utter disregard of masculine fastidiousness, with which the woman pursues her purpose. It does not occur to them that if women were as fastidious as men, morally or physically, there would be an end of the race.[74]

[72] *IBE* III. 138–9.   [73] Ibid. I. 47.
[74] Shaw, *Man and Superman*, Epistle Dedicatory to A. B. Walkley, 1903 (pp. xvii–xviii), 1st perf. (without Act III) by the Stage Society, Royal Court Theatre, London, for two perfs., 21 May 1905.

Wilde's women suffer from no such fastidiousness.

Not only are Cecily and Gwendolen unconventionally will-ing to take the initiative in their courtships, they are also more than a match for their men. Cécile takes the lead with Valentin, just as Cecily does with Algy, but her freedom of speech and action only make her all the more vulnerable to the young rake's dubious intentions. Fortunately Valentin is disarmed by Cécile's trusting naïvety, but right up to the end of the play there remains the possibility that he will take advantage of her. Valentin sees himself as Lovelace, determined to triumph over Cécile's virtue and thereby revenge himself on her family; the tension of the final scene springs from the fact that this blindly trusting young girl is completely at his mercy. Similarly, Gilbert's *Sweethearts* shows that when the woman is the dominant part-ner she is insincere and manipulative, but when the man is in control he is kind, chivalrous, and sensible; *Sweethearts* implies that the woman must be humbled before either man or woman can be happy together.

In the first draft of *The Importance of Being Earnest* Cecily and Gwendolen are far from being on equal terms with their men. Indeed, many of the jokes in the first manuscripts are at the expense of women and their aspirations to equality. Just as Gwendolen's bluestocking pursuits are mocked by Algy in the first manuscript version, so Cecily's education is, unintention-ally, ridiculed by Jack. His very seriousness on the subject of female education renders it laughable. So Miss Prism relays his exaggerated ideals:

> Indeed, he remarked to me privately in the hall when you had gone upstairs for your hat, that he had always been of the opinion that true femininity could not be attained without a thorough knowl-edge of the foreign languages, mathematics, and the ascertained principles of Political Economy.[75]

The first Cecily does not share her guardian's reverence for female learning; while laughing at male vanity, she gives a low estimate of the capacity of women to acquire significant knowl-edge: 'Men have always despised women for their ignorance. And nothing so impresses a man as when he finds out that a woman knows half as much as he does. He thinks so much

[75] Aut. MS NY: II. 4.

more of the other half.'[76] Women are not only inferior as regards knowledge, they are also a literary embarrassment. Cecily condemns three-volume novels as not simply unreliable, but as a weakness on the part of one sex and below the notice of the other, for they are books that, 'every woman writes nowadays, and that no cultivated man ever reads'.[77]

In the first manuscript draft, Jack and Algy regard the opposite sex not with the humorous awe which characterizes later drafts, but with an air of cynical superiority. When Algy counts through the few relatives he does not hate, they all, apart from Gwendolen, suffer from a succession of female failings, for he likes 'Mary Farquhar, when she isn't chattering about her husband; and Gladys, when she isn't chattering about someone else's husband: and dear old uncle Geoffrey, who isn't half a bad sort in his silly way, considering what a thoroughly typical woman Aunt Augusta is.'[78] What hope is there for the female sex if the awful Lady Brancaster is a 'typical woman'?

In successive drafts Wilde readjusts this balance between the sexes, until the two wield equal power and draw equal sympathy. If, in the final version, Cecily and Gwendolen take the initiative, it is to encourage Algy and Jack to pursue a course they already desire to follow. The young men are neither henpecked nor patronizingly superior; when Algy attempts any such pose, Cecily rapidly deflates it. Male domination is mocked as thoroughly as female education was in the first draft. In a statement, perhaps too obvious to escape Wilde's blue pencil, Miss Prism warns her pupil that: 'The fact is, you have fallen lately, Cecily, into a bad habit of thinking for yourself. You should give it up. It is not quite womanly.... Men don't like it.'[79] The disapproval of the ludicrously old-fashioned and curiously opinioned governess is quite enough to endorse the ideal of female independence. Indeed, the very idea that men dislike women thinking for themselves confirms the threat it poses to their fragile claim to supremacy.

Wilde's revisions also edited out the note of cynicism which marked the earlier versions, and introduced instead the carefree optimism and charm which characterize the final version. So,

[76] Ibid. 7.   [77] Ibid. 10.   [78] Ibid. Act I.
[79] *The Importance of Being Earnest* (four-act version), in *The Complete Works of Oscar Wilde*, III. 356.

in the first manuscript version, Cecily expresses the opinion that 'marriage, as an institution, was quite impossible unless the husband gave up to the wife in every single thing'.[80] Cecily's resolution to assume a Lady Brancaster-like control over her husband links her closely to W. S. Gilbert's devious female leads. In *Engaged* (1877) the mercenary and manipulative Minnie Symperson disguises a cool business head under the simpering manners of the *ingénue*:

> Papa dear, I have thought the matter over very carefully in my little baby-noddle, and I have come to the conclusion—don't laugh at me, dear papa—that it is my duty, my *duty*—to fall in with Cheviot's views in everything *before* marriage, and Cheviot's duty to fall into my views in everything after marriage. I think that is only fair, don't you?[81]

The characters of *Engaged* are lovers in no more than name, for marriage is simply a form of stock market where you wheel and deal to secure the largest share of available money for yourself. Their rapturous professions of love are simply the hypocritical language of greed. Earlier versions of *The Importance of Being Earnest* came closer to this, though Wilde's characters never sank to quite the same levels of hypocrisy. So, in early versions, Wilde's lovers are tainted by mercenary motives. The emphasis on Algy's debts suggests that he may share some of his aunt's interest in Cecily's fortune. Cecily and Gwendolen are driven by genuine desire for their respective Ernests, but even their motives are mixed, as their interrogation of Jack reveals:

CECILY. We would naturally like to learn something about Ernest's personal appearance.
GWENDOLEN. Any information regarding Ernest's income would be eagerly welcomed.[82]

The first *Earnest* has much in common with the cynical world of *Engaged*. The earlier incarnations of the lovers regard marriage with world-weary cynicism, not as the fulfilment of their romantic dreams but as the mundane conclusion of a far more

[80] Aut. MS BL Add. MS 37948: III. 43.
[81] Gilbert, *Engaged* repr. in *Plays by W. S. Gilbert*, ed. Rowell, II. 152; 1st produced, Theatre Royal, Haymarket, London, 3 Oct. 1877.
[82] Aut. MS BL Add. MS 37948: III. 83.

pleasant flirtation. In the final version Algy observes: 'It is very romantic to be in love. But there is nothing romantic about a definite proposal.'[83] Algy's emphasis on uncertainty as the essence of romance is the last witty remnant of his and Jack's earlier disparaging views on marriage. So, in the first version, Jack does not wish to be a good husband as that sounds 'so tedious and second-rate'.[84] Algy observes rather more fairly that: 'If a chap makes a good husband there must have been something rather peculiar about him when he was a bachelor. To be a good husband requires considerable practice.'[85] He does, however, set the final seal on the married state by replying to Jack's enthusiastic eulogy over Gwendolen with the sceptical theory that 'all women are far too good for the men they marry. That is why men tire of their wives so quickly.'[86] Nor is this critical attitude to marital bliss confined to the men; Gwendolen, too, informs Jack that, fortunately, she does not trust him, because 'If I could do *that*, I fear I would find you tedious.'[87]

This view of marriage as monotonous, second-rate, but financially necessary is very much in line with the dark comedy of *Engaged*. The final version of *The Importance of Being Earnest*, however, paints a very different picture. It is Lady Bracknell alone who regards marriage firstly as a financial and social transaction, and secondly as a battle for domination. The young lovers have a considerably more optimistic view of the matter; their professions of love are sincere, and they persevere in the face of much opposition. Their relationships are, of course, influenced by the comic traditions of love at first sight, but the unusual outspokenness of the women and the comic determination of the men separate them from the automatic responses of convention. This separation between the lovers' and Lady Bracknell's views on marriage is important to the satirical thrust of the play. When Lady Bracknell's snobbery and mercenary greed stand in the way of genuine attachments they appear not merely ridiculous but pernicious. In just the same way, Gwendolen's obvious self-possession and strength of mind make her mother's insistence on ruling her life not just

---

[83] *IBE* I. 6.   [84] Aut. MS NY: Act I, 2nd notebook.   [85] Ibid.
[86] Ibid.   [87] Aut. MS BL Add. MS 37948: IV. 171.

humorous but unjust. Lady Bracknell's declaration that, 'An engagement should come on a young girl as a surprise, pleasant or unpleasant, as the case may be' again underlines the division between her unnatural and old-fashioned approach to marriage and the happier, irrepressible energies of the younger generation.[88]

In a review of *The Importance of Being Earnest* entitled 'The Unimportance of Being Oscar', the American theatre critic Mary McCarthy characterized the play as 'a ferocious idyll', where:

Depravity is the hero and the only character, the people on the stage embodying various stages of it . . . Humanitarian considerations are out of place here; they belong to the middle class. Insensibility is the comic 'vice' of the characters; it is also their charm and badge of prestige. Selfishness and servility are the moral alternatives presented.[89]

Curiously, this is a far closer description of the first version of *Earnest* than of its final form. In the autograph manuscript Lady Brancaster is at one with the rest of the characters, for all are equally insensitive, grasping, and ruthless in the pursuit of their desires. Once again, there is little to separate the laws of society, as embodied in Lady Brancaster, from its inhabitants. All are satirized together and thus the satire lacks edge, becoming not a pointed attack on certain social mores and customs but a far more harmless comedy of manners.

In the final version, Algy and Jack's extremely healthy appetites and their constant tussles over all available food are a comic, nursery echo of their original mercenariness. It is easy to sympathize with the greed of the final characters, for it is a symptom of their childish energy, unrestrained by propriety, morality, or Lady Bracknell. The greed of the first version is more exaggeratedly comic—Cecily provides Algy with a second luncheon of six lobsters, and reports that, under doctor's orders, Jack can drink nothing but '74 champagne, because 'Even the cheaper clarets are, he tells us, strictly forbidden to him.'[90] Yet there is also a far more mercenary and callous aspect to their greed. Algy's debt goes beyond a pose: his opening exchanges with Lane are concerned with the creditors whom he

[88] *IBE* I. 31.
[89] *Mary McCarthy's Theatre Chronicles 1937–62* (New York: Noonday, 1963), 107–8.
[90] Aut. MS NY: Act II.

has kept waiting all day and finally evaded. His debts are part of the equipment of a nonchalant man-about-town, but he seems less than charming when he utters the wish that 'some ass would leave me a large fortune'.[91] The entire Gribsby episode, which was only finally cut when Wilde reduced the play from four acts to three at Alexander's request, sets Jack on a par with Algy when it comes to heedless consumption. Having spent the impossible sum of £762. 14s. 2d. on dinners at the Savoy alone, Jack is quite willing to see Algy arrested for his debts. Little sympathy can be spared for Algy, however, who tries to force Gribsby to walk to the station by insisting that he has no right to the cab which was obtained for his own convenience.[92]

The characters of the earlier version are, thus, not simply childish but cruelly so. The laughter here is cynical and unsympathetic, and it undermines any truly subversive aims of the play, for these characters are children in need of a controlling hand, even if it be that of the muddled and misguided Miss Prism or the awesome and arbitrary Aunt Augusta.

As the younger characters are transformed from callous infants into charmingly wilful individuals, so the role of the authoritarian, moralistic older generation is undermined. In the final version there is no call for a restraining authority, for Wilde has created an anarchic idyll. All attempts to assert authority seem ridiculous and ineffectual—as Wilde learnt from his reading of the Chinese sage, Chuang Tsu, 'there is such a thing as leaving mankind alone; there is no such thing as governing mankind'.[93] So, when Lady Bracknell appeals to the unalterable rules of polite society she renders them ridiculous. Miss Prism espouses the same Old Testament morality that Hester Worsley and Lady Windermere first advocated, but in the governess's words its stern judgements appear not so much harsh as ludicrously inapposite. 'As a man sows so shall he reap', she solemnly intones, reducing poetic justice to hilarious nonsense by applying it to Ernest's perishing of a severe chill in Paris.[94] The puritan ethic of punishment, the idea that suffering chastens

---

[91] Ibid. I. 4.

[92] Ibid. II. 53–65; *The Importance of Being Earnest* (four-act version), in *The Complete Works of Oscar Wilde*, 352.

[93] 'The Soul of Man', 301; 'A Chinese Sage', 144–6.   [94] *IBE* II. 71.

the sinner, so vigorously attacked by Wilde in 'The Soul of
Man under Socialism', is shown up as a lunatic fallacy when
Miss Prism exclaims at the news of Ernest's death: 'What a
lesson for him! I trust he will profit by it.'[95] The Victorian ideal
of art as a moral vehicle, which Wilde attacked throughout his
career from the preface to *The Picture of Dorian Gray* to his
testimonies at the trials, is neatly dispatched by the governess's
stricture that 'The good ended happily, and the bad unhappily.
That is what Fiction means.'[96] The subtle ambiguity of the
word 'fiction' here highlights the unreality of imposing artificial
laws of poetic justice on artistic creation.

Miss Prism and Dr Chasuble are the moralizing members of
the population who condemn vice, while at the same time clearly
taking vicarious pleasure in hearing about it, and whose strict
virtue is probably the result of never having had the opportunity to do otherwise. They are people who have never developed
their personalities, whose emotions must escape to find expression through hilariously mischosen metaphors, or the child-
substitute of the three-volume novel. Their lives have never
progressed beyond abstractions. So Miss Prism condemns the
poorer classes for lack of thrift in producing too many children, while Dr Chasuble conducts his life according to the
strictures of canonical practice.[97] His religion is of a theoretical
and abstract kind. He lacks even the excessive enthusiasm of
the first manuscript version, where, on hearing that Jack no
longer intends to be baptized, he remarks with regret: 'in the
case of adults compulsory christening is uncanonical'.[98]

The Importance of Being Earnest is remarkable less for any
specific satire within it than for the fact that the play itself is
the perfect realization of all Wilde's anarchist ideals; it is the
society of 'The Soul of Man under Socialism' made real. In his
political essay Wilde condemns all authority as degrading; in
Earnest he reduces all authority to an absurdity.[99] It is a utopia
where all attempts to assert authority are doomed to failure. Its

[95] 'The Soul of Man', 301–2; *IBE* II. 70.
[96] *IBE* II. 58; preface to *The Picture of Dorian Gray* (London: Ward Lock &
Co., 1891), p. vii.
[97] *IBE* II. 73–4.   [98] Aut. MS BL Add. MS 37948: IV. 160.
[99] 'The Soul of Man', 301.

characters are free to realize themselves perfectly, for there are no harsh laws to intervene. It is an idyll of wish-fulfilment, where Cecily has only to dream she is engaged to Ernest for it to come true. Jack declares he is called Ernest and, sure enough, he is. Algy pretends to be Jack's younger brother, and by the end of the afternoon, this fantasy too has materialized.[100] Nothing stands in the way of their self-creation, for reality itself is infinitely adaptable. So, when Lady Bracknell pronounces that Jack lives on the unfashionable side of Belgrave Square, the solution is simple:

LADY BRACKNELL. I thought there was something. However, that could easily be altered.
JACK. Do you mean the fashion, or the side?
LADY BRACKNELL. Both, if necessary, I presume.[101]

In this magical world, the perfect state of anarchy is realized, for the individual may pursue his own desires without obstructing those of his neighbour. In 'The Soul of Man', Wilde declared: *'Selfishness is not living as one wishes to live, it is asking others to live as one wishes to live.* And unselfishness is letting other people's lives alone, not interfering with them.'[102] So Gwendolen, Jack, Algy, and Cecily forge ahead, oblivious to anyone else's desires, and yet, in spite of Jack's determination to forbid Cecily's marriage unless he be allowed to marry Gwendolen, each achieves his or her goal without interfering with the others. Even Lady Bracknell, the one character who seeks to impose her own standards on everyone else, is transformed from a gorgon into the play's fairy godmother: contrary to her intentions, she finds herself playing the *dea ex machina* and granting the other characters' wishes.

This anarchic freedom, in which the characters are at liberty to create themselves, once again separates *Earnest* from other, more conventional, farces. The double lives led by Algernon, Jack, Cecily (through her diary), and even Miss Prism (via her abandoned three-volume novel) are another means by which they liberate themselves from the formal strictures of society.

[100] Algy does not, however, acquire the name of 'Ernest', in spite of which Cecily accepts him as a husband. This is the one (unavoidable) flaw in the otherwise perfect plotting of the play.
[101] *IBE* I. 35. [102] 'The Soul of Man', 316.

Characters have assumed false identities in almost every farce ever written. In Brandon Thomas's extremely popular *Charley's Aunt* (1892), for example, the unfortunate Lord Fancourt Babberley is forced by friends to assume the guise of Charley's aunt from Brazil, in order to provide a chaperon for their female guests.[103] The young students spend the next three acts desperately trying to sustain the pretence in the face of innumerable complications. In the last act Fancourt Babberley is released from the constrictions of his disguise and returned to his true identity. No such unmasking ends *The Importance of Being Earnest*; Cecily, Algy, and Jack become their own fantastic doubles, permanently granted the freedom which their fictions allowed them. Wilde, whose own sexuality was outlawed by the rigid and inhuman legislation of Victorian society, had created a fantasy world in which such laws had no power and double lives like his own no longer had to be kept secret.

Wilde's use of the double life may owe a certain amount to a contemporary farce entitled *Godpapa*, by Charles Brookfield and F. C. Philips.[104] There are a significant number of similarities between this play and Wilde's own: a young woman excuses her use of unladylike slang by attributing uncouth phrases to her brother Ernest, a individual who, it turns out, cannot exist, because she is an only child; a character named Bunbury, whose first name is Jack; and a host of false identities—various characters leading double lives as 'Mr Smith', 'Mr Aubrey Plantaganet' and 'Mr Launcelot'.[105] The plot of *Godpapa* is in turn reminiscent of Gilbert's *Engaged*, as it centres round a matrimonial agency and the attempts of various individuals to secure themselves as lucrative a match as possible. The characters of *Godpapa* are all motivated by the same ruthless greed and self-interest that drive the cast of *Engaged*, and, as with

---

[103] Brandon Thomas, *Charley's Aunt* (New York: Samuel French, 1962), 1st produced, Royalty Theatre, London, 21 Dec. 1892.

[104] Brookfield and Philips, *Godpapa* (1891), BL LCP Add. MS 53483M, LCP No. 248. 1st perf. Comedy Theatre, London, Oct. 1891. Once again, I am indebted to Professor Powell's *Oscar Wilde and the Theatre of the 1890s* for the rediscovery of this play.

[105] It is, however, far from certain that Wilde's 'Bunbury' has his origins here, as there were at least two other gentlemen named Bunbury (one a hypochondriac) with whom Wilde was familiar. See William Green, 'Oscar Wilde and the Bunburys', *Modern Drama*, 21/1 (Mar. 1978), 67–80.

the earlier play, the characters are in direct competition, someone inevitably losing out at the end.

In *Godpapa*, one little old lady has applied to the Mayfair
Matrimonial Service advertising herself as 'Flossie and Maud',
as she explains to the bewildered director:

> 'Flossie and Maud, two sisters. Flossie is merry, musical and laugh-
> ter loving. Maud a trifle staider perhaps—melancholy and poetical.
> One would make a loving bright little help mate to a partner with
> means. The other a sympathetic companion to one whose wealth
> has made him sad.' It's not a *really* serious taradiddle, my dear Sir
> George. For I possess both temperaments and would lavish the
> gems of either on a husband grave or gay with a suitable income.[106]

Wilde's characters exploit their double identities in exactly the
same way, giving themselves the opportunity to indulge opposite sides of their characters. So Jack lives the morally upright
life of John Worthing, JP, in the country, escaping to town to
assume the persona of Ernest Worthing, reckless spendthrift
and man-about-town. In the first manuscript version of the
play even the solicitor Gribsby boasts a double persona:

JACK. You are Gribsby, aren't you? What is Parker like?
GRIBSBY. I am both, Sir. Gribsby when I am on unpleasant business.
Parker on occasions of a less severe kind.[107]

This freedom to create more than one life for themselves is
the norm for Wilde's characters, whereas 'Flossie and Maud'
are the exception in *Godpapa*. In Philips's and Brookfield's
farce, false identities are not a means to greater liberty but a
desperate attempt to hide a past indiscretion. Much of the
play's comedy derives from increasingly complicated attempts
by the characters to hide former marriages and affairs, and
their real social status. In the end the truth is revealed, and the
fictitious characters of Smith, Launcelot, and Plantaganet
evaporate. In *The Importance of Being Earnest*, on the contrary,
the characters' fantasies are brought to life at the end of the
play; in its anarchic world characters are free to multiply themselves, like Flossie and Maud, and to live fantasy lives without
anyone else intervening to insist on the higher authority of the
truth. Algy may force Jack to tell him the truth 'pure and

simple', yet he does not explode his friend's fantasy but rather brings it to life. When Jack announces the death of his brother and then, minutes later, is forced to accept his resurrection, Dr Chasuble simply greets this as 'joyful tidings'. Wilde here deleted an original note of scepticism, for Chasuble first called them 'strange tidings'.[108] In the first version of *Earnest* the cast live in fear of being discovered and having their fantasies exploded—Jack advises Algy to do away with Bunbury, as 'Inventions of that kind are all very well in their way, but they are invariably found out in the end.'[109] In the final version, there is no such fear of unwanted revelation, for each character accepts the others' fantasies and endows them with life; even after Algy and Jack have been denied the name of Ernest, Cecily and Gwendolen still insist on their engagements to this fictitious young man.

In this anarchic world of self-creation even language is infinitely adaptable. Words no longer have any pre-established import but are the most unstable element of all. So Dr Chasuble declares proudly:

> My sermon on the meaning of the manna in the wilderness can be adapted to almost any occasion, joyful, or, as in the present case, distressing. I have preached it at harvest celebrations, christenings, confirmations, on days of humiliation and festal days. The last time I delivered it was in the Cathedral, as a charity sermon on behalf of the Society for the Prevention of Discontent among the Upper Orders.[110]

The characters impose their own meaning on the words they hear, never deflating the fantasy but creating it anew. When Algy hurriedly declares that Bunbury has been 'quite exploded', Lady Bracknell simply concludes that he was 'the victim of a revolutionary outrage', an appropriate punishment for his morbid interest in social legislation.[111] Collisions are constantly threatened but never materialize. Wilde crafted dialogue so ephemeral and gymnastic that it twists and turns out of every

---

[108] *IBE* III. 76; Aut. MS NY: II. 44.   [109] Aut. MS NY: I, 1st notebook.
[110] *IBE* II. 72. The homosexual puns contained in words like 'Ernest' and 'Bunbury' are another unstable and anarchic element in *Earnest*'s language. For an ingenious analysis of this homosexual subtext, see Craft, 'Alias Bunbury', 19–46.
[111] *IBE* III. 128–9.

apparently inevitable disaster. So Jack, dressed in mourning, is greeted by an enthusiastic Cecily:

CECILY. Who do you think is in the dining-room? Your brother!
JACK. Who?
CECILY. Your brother Ernest. He arrived about half an hour ago.
JACK. What nonsense! I haven't got a brother.
CECILY. Oh, don't say that. However badly he may have behaved to
  you in the past he is still your brother. You couldn't be so heartless
  as to disown him.[112]

This is language at its most anarchic, and every law, whether of literature, style, morality, society, or even reality, dissolves under its influence. As Gwendolen so rightly observes: 'In matters of grave importance, style, not sincerity is the vital thing.'[113] So long as the characters maintain their poise and equanimity, the facts adapt to fit their fantasies. Wilde uses style to subvert meaning: Lady Bracknell's regal illogicality undermines the social mores she intends to exalt; Miss Prism reduces to ridicule the morality she reveres. With a masterly manipulation of different literary styles, Wilde mocks the morality which traditionally lies beneath them. So, as Jack greets Miss Prism as his mother in a mixture of melodramatic, biblical, moralistic, and sentimental rhetoric, the sexual double standard and all the literature devoted to it (including Wilde's own) are transformed into farce: 'Unmarried! I do not deny that is a serious blow. But, after all, who has the right to cast a stone against one who has suffered? Cannot repentance wipe out an act of folly? Why should there be one law for men, and another law for women? Mother, I forgive you.'[114] Hester Worsley's Old Testament morality sinks into the quicksand of *Earnest*'s shifting language.

In *The Importance of Being Earnest*, Wilde created the perfect dramatic form for his philosophy. Within a deceptively familiar farcical structure, he not only smuggled in sharp satirical criticism of his society and its mores, he also gave imaginative life to his perfect anarchist state. *Earnest* is not a political tract, for politics, like morality, education, religion, justice, and every other serious matter, are reduced to absurdity by the author's wilful touch. The play is, however, a realization of Wilde's most idealistic theories of self-development. *Earnest*'s world

---

[112] Ibid. II. 76.   [113] Ibid. III. 123.   [114] Ibid. 147.

has no authority, no laws, and, most delightful of all, no consequences. The perfectly crafted comic dialogue almost imper-
ceptibly subverts all it touches, from the value of money and
social position to the creed of just punishment.

Wilde presented the most fashionable London audiences with
a farce which set forth in comic form all the subversive ideas
propounded in his anarchist essay, 'The Soul of Man under
Socialism': Lady Bracknell startles Jack by expounding Wilde's
dictum that 'Property is really a nuisance'; Miss Prism highlights the cruel illogicality of seeking to reform the sinner through
suffering; the young lovers show how right Wilde was to declare that mankind cannot be ruled.[115] The wilful, childish,
and greedy lovers of *The Importance of Being Earnest* are the
unlikely embodiments of Wilde's philosophy of perfect individualism. Concerned with nobody's wishes but their own, reducing
everything important to delightful nonsense and never taking
life seriously, they are the comic realization of Wilde's vision.
As Wilde wrote in 'The Soul of Man':

It will be a marvellous thing—the true personality of man—when we
see it. It will grow naturally and simply, flowerlike, or as a tree grows.
It will not be at discord. It will never argue or dispute. It will not
prove things. It will know everything. And yet it will not busy itself
about knowledge. . . . It will not be always meddling with others, or
asking them to be like itself. It will love them because they will be
different. And yet while it will not meddle with others, it will help all,
as a beautiful thing helps us, by being what it is. The personality of
man will be very wonderful. It will be as wonderful as the personality
of a child.

. . . For it will not worry itself about the past, nor care whether
things happened or did not happen. Nor will it admit any laws but
its own laws; nor any authority but its own authority.[116]

[115] Cf. 'The Soul of Man', 294, 301–2, and *IBE* I. 33–4, II. 70–2.
[116] 'The Soul of Man', 298.

Conclusion

> I ... wish we could meet to talk over the many prisons of
> life—prisons of stone, prisons of passion, prisons of intel-
> lect, prisons of morality, and the rest. All limitations, external
> or internal, are prison-walls, and life is a limitation.[1]

In August 1894, while working on the first draft of *The Importance of Being Earnest*, Wilde wrote to George Alexander
describing the scenario of another play he had in mind.[2] The
scenario pointed not to a comedy in the mode of *Earnest*, but
rather to a society drama along the lines of *Lady Windermere's
Fan* and *An Ideal Husband*, combining the high emotional
drama of marital conflict with the sophisticated wit of a fashionable country house party.

The play was to begin conventionally: a man of rank and
fashion marries a sweet country-bred lady, but, tiring of his
unsophisticated marriage, invites a group of *fin-de-siècle* men
and women to his country house. The husband then proceeds
to flirt with Lady X, a married woman. Lord X suspects and
the guilty couple are only saved from public exposure by the
generous intervention of the wronged wife. The wronged wife
then turns to the one friend she has, Gerald Lancing, and, as
it becomes clear that they love each other, they decide to go
away together. The errant husband then, rather repentantly,
asks Gerald to intervene on his behalf and win his wife's forgiveness. Gerald, in an act of obvious self-sacrifice, agrees to do
so. It is at this point that Wilde's scenario strikes out in a
radically new direction:

Enter wife: Gerald asks her to go back to her husband. She refuses
with scorn. He says: 'You know what it cost me to ask you to do
that. Do you not see that I am really sacrificing myself?' Etc. She
considers: 'Why should you sacrifice me? I love you. You have made
me love you. You have no right to hand my life over to anyone else.

---

[1] To R. B. Cunninghame Graham (*c*.20 Feb. 1898), thanking Graham for his
praise of *The Ballad of Reading Gaol, More Letters*, 165.
[2] To George Alexander (Aug. 1894), *Letters*, 360–2.

All this self-sacrifice is wrong, we are meant to live. That is the meaning of life.' Etc. She forces him by her appeals and her beauty and her love to take her away with him.[3]

Wilde's heroine openly propounds a philosophy which sets love above duty, society, and the vows of marriage; not only that, this heretic philosophy is then recognized and accepted by the abandoned husband himself. When the husband discovers the illicit couple three months later, he challenges the lover to a duel. The wife then confronts her husband and stoutly informs him that he will never win her back, and that of the two she wishes him to die, because she is pregnant by her lover. The husband leaves and shots are heard: he has killed himself. The curtain falls as Gerald and the wife cling to each other, 'as if with a mad desire to make love eternal'.[4]

The moral of the play was to be the triumph of love, not, as in *An Ideal Husband*, the triumph of marital love, forgiveness, and charity, but the triumph of a love without social, legal, or religious sanction, a love whose claims lay solely in the strength of its passion. As Wilde wrote to Alexander:

I want the sheer passion of love to dominate everything. No morbid self-sacrifice. No renunciation. A sheer flame of love between a man and a woman. That is what the play is to rise to—from the social chatter of Act I, through the theatrical effectiveness of Act II, up to the psychology with its great *dénouement* in Act III, till love dominates Act IV and accepts the death of the husband as in a way its proper right, leaving love its tragedy, and so making it a still greater passion.[5]

The claims of the individual were to prevail in spite of the constricting claims of society, morality, and law. In 'The Soul of Man' Wilde had rejected all restraints upon individual freedom and self-development, condemning self-sacrifice and duty, and predicting that without marriage love would become a nobler and more powerful passion:

With the abolition of private property, marriage in its present form must disappear. This is part of the programme. Individualism accepts this and makes it fine. It converts the abolition of legal restraint into a form of freedom that will help the full development of personality,

---

[3] *Letters*, 361.   [4] Ibid.   [5] Ibid. 361–2.

and make the love of man and woman more wonderful, more beautiful, more ennobling.[6]

Mrs Erlynne had previously espoused such a doctrine, asserting her individual needs over her duty as a mother, but Mrs Erlynne was a fallen woman and her unconventional views could therefore be dismissed as further evidence of her debased nature. The heroine of Wilde's synopsis, however, is a pure woman, sufficiently virtuous and unworldly for her husband to instruct her at the beginning of the play, 'not to be prudish, etc.—and not to mind if anyone flirts with her'.[7] It was this character— a wronged wife who nobly protects her rival, a worthy woman whom the audience are clearly called upon to sympathize with— that Wilde chose as the mouthpiece for his subversive creed of anarchic passion.

Wilde thus felt sufficiently sure of his reputation as a fashionable dramatist to consider writing a play which presented a direct and unmistakable challenge to orthodox morality.[8] Wronged wives might criticize their husbands or assert their own marital rights, but outright rebellion was not sanctioned. Dumas's Francillon might inform her adulterous husband that she had taken her revenge in kind, but her actual innocence was soon revealed and her contrite husband allowed to kiss her hand.[9] La Princesse Georges could only watch helplessly as her husband pursued another woman, and when his mistress proved unfaithful and he returned to his wife, he did not have to wait long for forgiveness.[10]

Up to this point, the contrast between Wilde's plays and the conventional dramas from which he borrowed had remained implicit, the radical implications of Wilde's revisions being primarily confined to the subtext. In this new scenario, the contrast was to become explicit: the last act was to begin with the eloped wife reading Frou-Frou and then discussing the play with her lover. In Meilhac and Halévy's drama a young wife unjustly suspects her husband of adultery, and is therefore prompted to

---

[6] 'The Soul of Man', 300.
[7] To George Alexander (Aug. 1894), Letters, 360.
[8] Wilde's scenario was also overtly Ibsenite in as far as the wife's rejection of her marriage vows and her duty to her husband in favour of her own personal needs parallels Nora's departure from the family home in Ibsen's A Doll's House.
[9] Francillon (1887).   [10] La Princesse Georges (1871).

elope with a lover herself. The husband follows and kills the lover in a duel, leaving the guilty wife to pine, repent, devote her life to charity, and finally to die begging forgiveness of her husband.[11] Mrs Erlynne had first challenged this convention by asserting that pleasure not repentance was to be the reward of a fallen woman, and exiting in possession of a rich husband. Wilde's later heroine was to have gone even further, rejecting the very validity of marriage, and ending the play triumphantly in the arms of her lover, with a child in prospect. Mrs Erlynne chose the freedom of individuality over the conflicting duties and rewards of parenthood; Wilde's later heroine was to enjoy the freedom of self-determination without relinquishing the comforts and companionship of a family.

Wilde never did write the play. Scarcely had *The Importance of Being Earnest* been completed and the first production opened at St James's Theatre than the Marquess of Queensberry left his fateful card at the Albemarle Club. Emerging from prison after two years' hard labour, Wilde had lost the lightness, frivolity, and ironic detachment which had always combined with the more serious import of his plays to ensure their success. As he explained to a friend in 1898:

I hope soon to begin a new play, but poverty with its degrading preoccupation with money, the loss of many friends, the deprivation of my children, by a most unjust law, by a most unjust Judge, the terrible effects of two years of silence, solitude and ill-treatment—all these have, of course, to a large extent, killed if not entirely that great joy in living that I once had.[12]

Unable to face the task of transforming his scenario into a fully fledged play, Wilde instead sold it to Frank Harris, among several others.[13]

Harris wrote the play up under the title of *Mr and Mrs Daventry*, and it opened at the Royalty Theatre, London, on

[11] *Frou-Frou* (1869).
[12] To Georgina Weldon (31 May 1898), *Letters*, 751.
[13] Besides selling rights to the scenario to Harris for a considerable sum, Wilde also sold some sort of options on the play to Mrs Brown-Potter, Horace Sedger, Ada Rehan, Louis Nethersole, and Leonard Smithers. Harris was forced to pay reparation to a number of other claimants, and deducted these from his payment to Wilde.

25 October 1900. It achieved more than 100 performances, but to at least one critic Wilde's touch was sadly lacking. Missing the delicate and subtle nature of Wilde's satire, Bernard Shaw pointed out to Harris the difference between his and Wilde's style:

you have undoubtedly amused yourself by writing some imaginary conversations on Wilde's lines . . . Here I think you should not encourage yourself, because it is not natural to you to play with an idea in Wilde's way, and make people laugh by showing *its* absurdity: your notion of gambolling is to unexpectedly fix your teeth in the calf of some sinner and hold on.[14]

Without Wilde's subtle and ambiguous touch, the forthright, radical message was liable to take over the play.[15] It is mere speculation to consider how the drama would have turned out in Wilde's hands, but Shaw at least had confidence in the skills of his fellow playwright: as he remarked of Harris's attempt: 'If Oscar had written it, it would now be a classic.'[16]

Wilde's experiences in court and in prison changed him irrevocably. Having suffered the injustice, prejudice, and brutality of authority at first hand, he was no longer able to maintain the detachment necessary to condemn them with wit, irony, and apparent frivolity. He retained his radical and reforming interests but his old methods were no longer suited to his purpose. While still in Reading Gaol, Wilde wrote on a scrap of paper to Thomas Martin, a warder who had shown him some kindness: 'I hope to write about prison life and to try and change

[14] Shaw to Frank Harris (4 Nov. 1900), *Bernard Shaw, Collected Letters, 1898–1910*, ed. Dan H. Lawrence (London; Bodley Head, 1972), 193.

[15] Reviews of Frank Harris's *Mr and Mrs Daventry* attest to the difference between his and Wilde's methods. Max Beerbohm compared Harris's play to a bull in a china shop: 'Horns to the floor, hoofs in the air, tail-a-whirl, the unkindly creature charges furiously hither and thither, and snap! crash! bang! into flying smithereens goes the crockery of dramatic laws and conventions, while the public lies quailing under the counter.' *Saturday Review*, 90 (3 Nov. 1900), 551. Another reviewer commented on Harris's 'frank indifference to ethical questions': *Athenæum*, 3810 (3 Nov. 1900), 587, and the critic of the *Daily Telegraph* remarked caustically: 'While Mr Harris was so bold in his dénouement, he should have been a little bolder. Why not call his play "The Adulterers" and hang the conventions?': *Daily Telegraph* (6 Oct. 1900), 8.

[16] Preface by George Bernard Shaw to Frank Harris, *Oscar Wilde: His Life and Confessions* (London: Constable, 1938), p. xxv.

it for others, but it is too terrible and ugly to make a work of art of. I have suffered too much in it to write plays about it.'[17] On his release from prison, Wilde did indeed find it impossible to reconcile his own intense suffering and his powerful feelings on the evils of the prison system with his previous artistic methods. He did write about prison life and try to change it, but his writing took the form of the realistic and polemical poem, *The Ballad of Reading Gaol*. He also addressed letters to the editor of the *Daily Chronicle* on the subject of prison conditions and their necessary reform.[18]

Wilde's writings on prison reform represent his only direct, active participation in practical politics. His letters to the *Daily Chronicle* were serious in tone, full of minute details of the psychological and physical life within an English prison, and concerned directly with the parliamentary processes involved in changing them. *The Ballad of Reading Gaol* was almost equally saturated with details of prison life, its degrading brutality and systematized cruelty. Recounting the hanging of a soldier for the murder of his wife and the impact of the execution on the other inmates of the gaol, the poem demonstrates how much more degrading and inhuman is the punishment meted out by society than any crime committed by the individual. Yet, for all his impassioned interest in preventing others from suffering as he had done, Wilde still had qualms about using literature as a polemical vehicle. He felt that his art could only be compromised by his politics:

The poem suffers under the difficulty of a divided aim in style. Some is realistic, some is romantic: some poetry, some propaganda. I feel it keenly, but as a whole I think the production interesting: that it is interesting from more points of view than one is artistically to be regretted.[19]

[17] To Thomas Martin (c.Apr. 1897), *Letters*, 528.
[18] To the editor of the *Daily Chronicle* (27 May 1897), *Letters*, 568–74, printed in the *Daily Chronicle*, 28 May, under the heading THE CASE OF WARDER MARTIN, SOME CRUELTIES OF PRISON LIFE; a letter to the editor of the *Daily Chronicle* (23 Mar. 1898) *Letters*, 722–8, appeared under the heading DON'T READ THIS IF YOU WANT TO BE HAPPY TODAY, on 24 Mar., when the House of Commons began the debate on the second reading of the Prison Bill. Wilde's efforts to help his fellow prisoners were not confined to words. Soon after his release, for example, despite his own straitened circumstances, Wilde paid the fines of three children convicted of snaring rabbits and so secured their release (*Letters*, 554).
[19] To Robert Ross (8 Oct. 1897), *Letters*, 654.

In this sense the ballad was, as he observed, 'a sort of denial of my own philosophy of art in many ways'.[20] In Wilde's society plays the politics had lain buried beneath the surface, a secret detectable only by the select few; deprived by years of intense suffering and humiliation of the vivacity, courage, and detachment which had allowed him to play with ideas, Wilde no longer toyed with his audience but finally sought to educate it.[21]

Despite this new tone of seriousness, there was little change to Wilde's political philosophy. *The Ballad of Reading Gaol* and the letters to the *Daily Chronicle* object to the prison system on much the same grounds as Wilde had condemned it years before, in 'The Soul of Man under Socialism'. In his essay Wilde had asserted that 'one is absolutely sickened, not by the crimes that the wicked have committed, but by the punishments that the good have inflicted; *and a community is infinitely more brutalised by the habitual employment of punishment than it is by the occasional occurrence of crime*'.[22] *The Ballad of Reading Gaol* describes the brutal and dehumanizing effects of solitary confinement, silence, monotony, and the coarse work inflicted on the prisoners. Yet it is those enforcing the punishment, not the criminals themselves, who appear most inhuman. The warders, the chaplain, the governor, and the doctor remain impassive and clinically detached when faced with the torment and suffering of the condemned soldier, while the other inmates suffer with him, admitting the common guilt which binds all humankind and according him the pity that the authorities deny.[23]

In a letter written to the *Daily Chronicle* soon after his release, Wilde objected to the isolation of children in prison on the grounds that:

[20] To Laurence Housman (22 Aug. 1897), *More Letters*, 153.
[21] Wilde believed he succeeded to some extent in this aim, taking personal credit for having secured changes in the system: 'I think that, aided by some splendid personalities like Davitt and John Burns, I have been able to deal a heavy and fatal blow at the monstrous prison-system of English justice. There is to be no more starvation, nor sleeplessness, nor endless silence, nor eternal solitude, nor brutal floggings. The system is exposed, and, so, doomed.' Letter to Georgina Weldon (31 May 1898), *Letters*, 751.
[22] 'The Soul of Man', 301.
[23] See *The Ballad of Reading Gaol, by C.3.3* (London: Leonard Smithers, 1898), 4–5, 10, 14.

A child is utterly contaminated by prison life. But the contaminating influence is not that of the prisoners. It is that of the whole prison system—of the governor, the chaplain, the warders, the lonely cell, the isolation, the revolting food, the rules of the Prison Commissioners, the mode of discipline, as it is termed, of the life . . . But the only really humanising influence in prison is the influence of the prisoners. Their cheerfulness under terrible circumstances, their sympathy for each other, their humility, their gentleness, their pleasant smiles of greeting when they meet each other, their complete acquiescence in their punishments, are all quite wonderful, and I myself learned many sound lessons from them.[24]

Similarly, 'The Soul of Man under Socialism' advocated a complete rejection of all forms of authority, arguing that power debased both those who wielded it and those on whom it was imposed.[25] Wilde attributed the cruelty of the prison system to precisely those degrading effects:

It is the result in our days of stereotyped systems of hard-and-fast rules, and of stupidity. Wherever there is centralisation there is stupidity. What is inhuman in modern life is officialism. Authority is as destructive to those who exercise it as it is to those on whom it is exercised.[26]

Wilde did, however, come to revise one significant assertion contained in 'The Soul of Man': his careless dismissal of the human instinct to sympathize with pain as 'tainted with egotism', 'curiously limiting', and marred by 'a certain element of terror for our own safety'.[27] By contrast, in *The Ballad of Reading Gaol* the inmates' sympathy with the suffering of the condemned man is the only source of emotional redemption, and it was to the absence of this capacity that Wilde attributed all the failings of the judicial system and of the English establishment as a whole: '[It] is difficult to teach the English either pity or humanity. They learn slowly . . . It is the lack of imagination in the Anglo-Saxon race that makes the race so stupidly, harshly cruel.'[28] The injustice, cruelty, and suffering, of which Wilde had always been aware, had become part of his own

---

[24] To the editor of the *Daily Chronicle* (27 May 1897), *Letters*, 571.
[25] 'The Soul of Man', 301.
[26] To the editor of the *Daily Chronicle* (27 May 1897), *Letters*, 569.
[27] 'The Soul of Man', 317.
[28] To Georgina Weldon (31 May 1898), *Letters*, 751.

personal experience, and he found himself forced to voice his opposition more openly and directly than ever before. The subtlety and ambiguity of his dramatic method were no longer suited to the urgent and practical matters which Wilde now sought to remedy.

From the conventions of the stage to the regulations of the prison system, from sexual stereotypes to the unbending rules of puritan morality, all laws and systems which sought to categorize or control humankind were targets for Wilde's attack. His plays subverted the conventions of the popular stage, challenged the strict morality they upheld, and offered instead a creed of understanding, sympathy, and forgiveness. The radical message of the plays was never didactic. He achieved in his drama the combination of diversity, tolerance, and humanity which he had admired in the work of other radical, committed artists. In 1889 he praised a collection of socialist poems, *Chants of Labour: A Song-Book of the People*, in terms which could appropriately be applied to his own dramatic achievement:

It shows that Socialism is not going to allow herself to be trammelled by any hard and fast creed or to be stereotyped into an iron formula. She welcomes many and multiform natures. She has the attraction of a wonderful personality and touches the heart of one and the brain of another, and draws this man by his hatred of injustice, and his neighbour by his faith in the future, and a third, it may be, by his love of art or by his wild worship of a lost and buried past. And all of this is well. For, to make men Socialists is nothing, but to make Socialism human is a great thing.[29]

[29] 'Poetical Socialists', review of *Chants of Labour: A Song-Book of the People*, ed. Edward Carpenter, in *Pall Mall Gazette*, 49 (15 Feb. 1889), 3.

Bibliography

MANUSCRIPTS AND AUTHORITATIVE AND
SIGNIFICANT EDITIONS OF WILDE'S PLAYS

Vera; or, The Nihilists

Autograph MS notebook, containing a fragment of the first draft of
Vera, twenty-nine fos. Beinecke Rare Books and Manuscript Lib-
rary, Yale.
Vera; or, The Nihilists. A Drama in Four Acts by Oscar Wilde (London:
Ranken & Co., 1880).
Vera; or, The Nihilists. A Drama in a Prologue and Four Acts (USA:
privately printed, 1882), with Wilde's autograph corrections. BL,
London.
Vera; or, the Nihilists, in *The Complete Writings of Oscar Wilde*, ed.
Robert Ross (London: Methuen, 1908), vol. ii.
Oscar Wilde's 'Vera; or, The Nihilist', ed. Frances Miriam Reed
(Lewiston: Edwin Mellen Press, 1989).

Lady Windermere's Fan

Autograph MS BL Add. MS 37943. Acts I–IV, first draft with correc-
tions and additions. Entitled 'Play'. The MS is written in ink and
is in many places incomplete.
Early typescript of Acts I and II, under the title, 'A Good Woman'.
With autograph corrections by Wilde, and corrections by another
(unidentified) hand. Magdalen College, Oxford, MS 300, 69 fos.
Licensing copy, BL (dated 15 Feb. 1892). Lord Chamberlain's Plays,
BL LCP Add. MS 53492H.
Lady Windermere's Fan: A Play About a Good Woman. By Oscar
Wilde (London: Elkin Mathews & John Lane, 1893).

A Woman of No Importance

Autograph MS draft entitled 'Mrs Arbuthnot'. BL Add. MS 37944.
Typescript corrected in author's hand, entitled 'Mrs Arbuthnot'. BL
Add. MS 37945.
Typescript of *A Woman of No Importance* submitted to the Lord
Chamberlain's Office. BL Add. MS 53524N.

Herbert Beerbohm Tree Collection, University of Bristol:
  HBT 18/1. Four acts entitled 'Mrs Arbuthnot', marked 'Prompt copy'. Typescript with corrections in Wilde's and others' hands.
  HBT 18 (a)/1. Prompt copy of *A Woman of No Importance*. Two sets of revisions on a typescript. Used as prompt copy for 1905 production.
  HBT 18 (a)/5. Carbon copy of typescript of *A Woman of No Importance*. A working copy of the play. Title-page marked 'As revived at His Majesty's Theatre May 22nd 1907.' Incorporates ink corrections made to HBT (a)/1.
  A Woman of No Importance. By Oscar Wilde (London: John Lane, 1894).

An Ideal Husband

MS drafts of the four acts, including two versions of Act II, written in Wilde's hand. BL Add. MS 37946.
Typescript of Act I, with Wilde's autograph revisions, produced from BL Add. MS 37946. Harvard Theatre Collection (uncatalogued).
Typescripts of the four acts, with corrections and stage directions added in Wilde's and other hand. First act stamped '10 MAR 94'. BL Add. MS 37947.
Typescript of the four acts, submitted to the Lord Chamberlain's Office. Dated 2 Jan. 1895. BL LCP Add. MS 53566A.
An Ideal Husband, by the Author of 'Lady Windermere's Fan' (London: Leonard Smithers & Co., 1899).

The Importance of Being Earnest

Autograph MS (Aug. 1894), handwritten in four exercise books. Acts I and II, Arents Collection, New York Public Library. Acts III and IV, BL Add. MS 37948.
Typescript of Acts I, III, and IV, with Wilde's autograph corrections. Arents Collection, New York Public Library. Act I stamped 1 Nov. 1894.
Typescript of four-act version (dated 31 Oct. 1894). Burnside–Frohman Collection, New York.
Licensing copy, BL Add. MS 53567 (17). Entitled 'Lady Lancing. A Serious Comedy for Trivial People'.
Typescript typed by Winifred Dolan, revised by Wilde to provide copy for 1899. Arents Collection, New York Public Library.
The Importance of Being Earnest. A Trivial Comedy for Serious People in Three Acts (London: Leonard Smithers, 1899).

OTHER PUBLISHED WORKS BY WILDE

The Ballad of Reading Gaol, by C.3.3 (London: Leonard Smithers, 1898).
'A Chinese Sage', *Speaker*, 1/6 (8 Feb. 1890), 144–6.
The Collected Works of Oscar Wilde, 1st collected edn, 14 vols., ed. Robert Ross (London: Methuen & Co., 1908).
The Complete Works of Oscar Wilde, with an introduction by Vyvyan Holland (London: Collins, 1988).
The Importance of Being Earnest, ed. Russell Jackson (London: Benn, 1980).
Lady Windermere's Fan: A Play About a Good Woman, ed. Ian Small (London: Benn, 1980).
The Picture of Dorian Gray (London: Ward Lock & Co., 1891).
Poems (London: David Bogue, 1881).
'The Soul of Man under Socialism', *Fortnightly Review*, 49/290 (Feb. 1891), 292–319.
Two Society Comedies: 'A Woman of No Importance' and 'An Ideal Husband', ed. Russell Jackson and Ian Small (London: A. & C. Black, 1983).

UNPUBLISHED PLAYS CONTAINED IN THE LORD CHAMBERLAIN'S
COLLECTION, BRITISH LIBRARY, LONDON

Listed by author, or by title where author unknown.

BROOKFIELD, CHARLES, and PHILIPS, F. C., *Godpapa* (1891), Add. MS 53483M.
CARTON, R. C., *The Home Secretary* (1895), Add. MS 53573.
CHAMBERS, HADDON, *John O'Dreams* (1894), Add. MS 53560R.
DAVENTRY, G., *The English Nihilist* (1887), Add. MS 53377B.
FARNIE, H. B., and REECE, R., *Russia* (1877), Add. MS 53193B.
GRUNDY, SYDNEY, *The Glass of Fashion* (1883), Add. MS 53291L.
HAZLEWOOD, C. H., *The Russian Bride* (1874), Add. MS 53153E.
LECLERQ, PIERRE, *Illusion* (1890), Add. MS 53453G.
LESTOQ, W., and ROBSON, E. M., *The Foundling* (1894), Add. MS 53555.
Mardo; or, the Nihilists of St Petersburg (1883), Add. MS 53298G.
OUTRAM, TRISTRAM, *The Red Lamp* (1887), Add. MS 53377B.
SARDOU, VICTORIEN, *Odette* (1894), trans. Clement Scott, Add. MS 53270.

—— *Diplomacy*, trans. and adapted Clement Scott, in collaboration with B. C. Stephenson, Add. MS 53198D.

SMITH, M. ELLIS, *Vera* (1890), Add. MS 53454.

TOWERS, E. J., *The Nihilist, or Wed Yet No Wife* (1897), Add. MS 53624B.

OTHER PUBLISHED WORKS

Articles from 19th-c. periodicals are documented fully in the footnotes, and are not listed here.

AMOR, ANNE CLARK, *Mrs Oscar Wilde* (London: Sidgwick and Jackson, 1983).

ARCHER, WILLIAM, *The Theatrical World for 1893–97* (London: Walter Scott, 1894–8).

—— and LOWE, W. H., (eds.), *Dramatic Essays: John Forster, George Henry Lewes. Reprinted from the 'Examiner' and the 'Leader'* (London: Walter Scott, 1896).

AUGIER, ÉMILE, *Le Mariage d'Olympe, Théâtre Complet d'Émile Augier*, iii (Paris: Calmann Lévy, 1897).

—— *Les Fourchambault, Théâtre Complet d'Émile Augier*, vii (Paris: Calmann Lévy, 1897).

AUERBACH, NINA, *The Woman and the Demon: The Life of a Victorian Myth* (Cambridge, Mass.; Harvard University Press, 1982).

BARLAS, JOHN E., *Oscar Wilde: A Study* (Edinburgh: Tragara, 1978).

BARRÈS, MAURICE, *Une Journée parlementaire: Comédie de mœurs en trois actes* (Paris: Charpentier et Fasquelle, 1894).

BEHRENDT, PATRICIA FLANAGAN, *Oscar Wilde: Eros and Aesthetics* (London: Macmillan, 1991).

BIRD, ALAN, *The Plays of Oscar Wilde* (London: Vision Press, 1977).

BRASOL, BORIS, *Oscar Wilde: The Man, the Artist, the Martyr* (New York: Williams & Norgate, 1938).

BUTLER, JOSEPHINE E. (ed.), *Woman's Work and Culture: A Series of Essays* (London, 1869).

CAINE, BARBARA, *Victorian Feminists* (Oxford: Oxford University Press, 1992).

CHERNYSHEVSKY, NIKOLAI, *What Is To Be Done?*, trans. Michael R. Katz (Cornell: Cornell University Press, 1989).

Chuang Tzu: Mystic, Moralist and Social Reformer, trans. from the Chinese by Herbert A. Giles (London: Bernard Quaritch, 1889).

COHEN, ED, 'Writing Gone Wilde: Homoerotic Desire in the Closet of Representation', *Publications of the Modern Language Association*, 102/5 (1987), 801–13.

—— *Talk on the Wilde Side: Toward a Genealogy of Discourse on Male Sexualities* (New York: Routledge, 1993).

COHEN, PHILIP, *The Moral Vision of Oscar Wilde* (London: Associated University Press, 1978).

COLE, G. D. H., *Socialist Thought: Marxism and Anarchism, 1850–1890* (London: Macmillan, 1954).

COLE, MARGARET, *The Story of Fabian Socialism* (London: Heinemann, 1961).

COLLINS, WILKIE, *The New Magdalen* (London: published by the author, 1873).

CRAFT, CHRISTOPHER, 'Alias Bunbury: Desire and Termination in *The Importance of Being Earnest*', *Representations*, 31 (summer 1990), 19–46.

DELLAMORA, RICHARD, 'Traversing the Feminine in Oscar Wilde's *Salomé*', in Thaïs Morgan (ed.), *Victorian Sages and Cultural Discourse: Renegotiating Gender and Power* (New Brunswick, NJ: Rutgers University Press, 1990).

DOLLIMORE, JONATHAN, 'Different Desires: Subjectivity and Transgression in Wilde and Gide', *Textual Practice*, 1/1 (1987), 48–67.

DUMAS *fils*, ALEXANDRE, *La Dame aux Camélias, Théâtre Complet de Dumas Fils*, i (Paris: Calmann Lévy, 1890).

—— *Le Demi-Monde, Théâtre Complet*, ii (Paris: Calmann Lévy, 1890).

—— *Le Fils naturel, Théâtre Complet*, iii (Paris: Calmann Lévy, 1890).

—— *L'Ami des femmes, Théâtre Complet*, iv (Paris: Calmann Lévy, 1890).

—— *La Princesse Georges, Théâtre Complet*, v (Paris: Calmann Lévy, 1890).

—— *Francillon, Théâtre Complet*, vii (Paris: Calmann Lévy, 1890).

ELIZAVETA, T. S., 'Contemporary Life and Thought in Russia', *Contemporary Review*, 31 (Feb. 1878), 620–33.

ELLIS, SARAH, *The Wives of England, their Relative Duties, Domestic Influence, and Social Obligations* (London: Fisher, Son & Co., 1843).

ELLMANN, RICHARD (ed.), *Oscar Wilde: A Collection of Critical Essays* (Englewood Cliffs, NJ: Prentice Hall, 1969).

—— *Oscar Wilde* (London: Hamish Hamilton, 1987).

ENSOR, R. C. K., *England, 1870–1914* (Oxford: Clarendon Press, 1960).

FINDLATER, RICHARD, *Banned! A Review of Theatrical Censorship in Britain* (London: MacGibbon & Kee, 1967).

FINZI, JOHN CHARLES, *Oscar Wilde and his Circle: Catalog of Manuscripts and Letters in the William Andrews Clark Memorial Library* (Berkeley and Los Angeles: University of California Press, 1957).

Fo, Dario, *Accidental Death of an Anarchist*, adapted by Gavin Edwards from a trans. by Gillian Hanna (London: Methuen, 1987).

Gagnier, Regenia, *Idylls of the Marketplace: Oscar Wilde and the Victorian Public* (Aldershot: Scolar Press, 1987).

—— (ed.), *Critical Essays on Oscar Wilde* (New York: Twayne, 1991).

Gaskell, Elizabeth, *Ruth*, 3 vols. (London: Chapman & Hall, 1853).

Gilbert, W. S., *The Palace of Truth, Sweethearts*, and *Engaged*, in *Plays by W. S. Gilbert*, ed. George Rowell (Cambridge: Cambridge University Press, 1982).

Girardin, Émile, *Le Supplice d'une femme* (Paris, 1865).

Gissing, George, *The Unclassed* (London: Lawrence & Bullen, 1895).

Godwin, William, *An Enquiry concerning Political Justice, and its Influence on General Virtue and Happiness*, 2 vols. (London, 1793).

Got, E., *La Comédie-Française à Londres (1871–1879): Journal inédit de E. Got. et F. Sarcey*, with an introduction by Georges d'Heyli (Paris: Ollendorff, 1880).

Green, William, 'Oscar Wilde and the Bunburys', *Modern Drama*, 21/1 (Mar. 1978), 67–80.

Halperin, Joan Ungersma, *Félix Fénéon: Aesthete and Anarchist in Fin-de-Siècle Paris* (New Haven, Conn.: Yale University Press, 1988).

Hankin, St John, *The Last of the De Mullins* (London: Martin Secker, 1908).

Harris, Frank, *Oscar Wilde: His Life and Confessions*, with a preface by George Bernard Shaw (London: Constable, 1938).

Hawthorne, Nathaniel, *The Scarlet Letter* (Cambridge: Riverside Press, 1879).

Helsinger, Elizabeth K., Sheets, Robin, and Veeder, William (eds.), *The Woman Question: Society and Literature in Britain and America, 1837–1883*, 3 vols. (Manchester: Manchester University Press, 1983); vol. i: *Defining Voices* (1983).

Hingley, Ronald, *Nihilists: Russian Radicals and Revolutionaries in the Reign of Alexander II, 1855–81* (London: Weidenfeld & Nicolson, 1967).

Holland, Merlin, 'Plagiarist or Pioneer?', in George Sandalescu (ed.), *Rediscovering Oscar Wilde* (Gerrards Cross: Colin Smyth, 1994).

Hyde, H. Montgomery, *Oscar Wilde* (London: Mandarin, 1976).

Ibsen, Henrik, *The Pillars of Society*, trans. William Archer (London: Camelot, 1888).

—— *A Doll's House*, trans. William Archer (London: Walter Scott, 1889).

Jackson, Russell, and Small, Ian, 'Some New Drafts of a Wilde Play', *English Literature in Transition*, 30/1 (1987), 7–15.

Jenkins, Anthony, *The Making of Modern Drama* (Cambridge: Cambridge University Press, 1991).

JENKINS, ROY, *Sir Charles Dilke: A Victorian Tragedy* (London: Collins, 1958).

JEROME, JEROME K., *Stage-Land: Curious Habits and Customs of its Inhabitants* (London: Chatto & Windus, 1889).

JOLL, JAMES, *The Anarchists* (London: Methuen, 1979).

JONES, HENRY ARTHUR, *Saints and Sinners* (London: Macmillan, 1891).

—— *Mrs Dane's Defence* (London: privately printed, 1900).

—— *The Dancing Girl* (London: Samuel French, 1907).

JUVENAL, *The Sixteen Satires*, trans. Peter Green (Harmondsworth: Penguin, 1974).

KAPLAN, JOEL H., 'A Puppet's Power: George Alexander, Clement Scott, and the Replotting of *Lady Windermere's Fan*', *Theatre Notebook*, 46/2 (1992), 59–73.

—— and STOWELL, SHEILA, *Theatre and Fashion: Oscar Wilde to the Suffragettes* (Cambridge: Cambridge University Press, 1994).

KOHL, NORBERT, *Oscar Wilde: The Works of a Conformist Rebel* (Cambridge: Cambridge University Press, 1989).

KROPOTKIN, PIERRE, 'Law and Authority, An Anarchist Essay' (London, 1886).

—— *Mutual Aid* (Harmondsworth: Pelican, 1939).

LEMAÎTRE, JULES, *Révoltée* (Paris: Calmann Lévy, 1889).

LEVERSON, ADA, *Letters to the Sphinx from Oscar Wilde and Reminiscences of the Author* (London: Duckworth, 1930).

LEWIS, JANE (ed.), *Before the Vote was Won: Arguments For and Against Women's Suffrage* (London: Routledge & Kegan Paul, 1987).

MCCARTHY, MARY, *Theatre Chronicles, 1937–62* (New York: Noonday, 1963).

MARSHALL, PETER, *Demanding the Impossible: A History of Anarchism* (London: Fontana Press, 1992).

MASON, A. E. W., *Sir George Alexander and the St James's Theatre* (London: Macmillan, 1935).

MASON, STUART, *A Bibliography of Oscar Wilde*, with a note by Robert Ross (London: T. Werner Laurie, 1914).

MEILHAC, HENRI, and HALÉVY, LUDOVIC, *Frou-Frou, Théâtre de Meilhac et Halévy Complet*, i (Paris: Calmann Lévy, 1899).

MEISEL, MARTIN, *Shaw and the Nineteenth-Century Theatre* (Princeton, Mass.: Princeton University Press, 1963).

MIKHAIL, E. H., 'Self-Revelation in *An Ideal Husband*', *Modern Drama*, 11/2 (Sept. 1968), 180–6.

—— *Oscar Wilde: An Annotated Bibliography of Criticism* (London: Macmillan, 1978).

—— *Oscar Wilde: Interviews and Recollections*, 2 vols. (London: Macmillan, 1979).

MILL, JOHN STUART, *On Liberty* (London: John W. Parker & Son, 1859).

MILLER, KEITH, *Oscar Wilde* (New York: Ungar, 1982).

MORRIS, WILLIAM, *News from Nowhere, or, An Epoch of Rest, being some chapters from A Utopian Romance* (London: Reeves & Turner, 1891).

MUSSET, ALFRED DE , *Il ne faut jurer de rien, Théâtre Complet* (Paris: Éditions Gallimard, 1990).

NASSAAR, CHRISTOPHER, *Into the Demon Universe: A Literary Exploration of Oscar Wilde* (New Haven, Conn.: Yale University Press, 1974).

NOWELL-SMITH, SIMON, *The House of Cassell, 1848–1958* (London: Cassell, 1958).

OFFEN, KAREN, 'Defining Feminism: A Comparative Historical Approach', *Signs*, 14 (1988), 119–57.

OLIVER, HERMIA, *The International Anarchist Movement in Late Victorian London* (London: Croom Helm, 1983).

PALMER, JOHN, *The Censor and the Theatres* (London: T. Fisher Unwin, 1912).

PAUL, CHARLES B., and PEPPER, ROBERT, 'The Importance of Reading Alfred: Oscar Wilde's Debt to Alfred de Musset', *Bulletin of the New York Public Library*, 75 (1971), 506–41.

PEARSON, HESKETH, *Modern Men and Mummers* (London: George Allen & Unwin, 1921).

—— *The Life of Oscar Wilde* (London: Methuen, 1946).

—— *Beerbohm Tree: His Life and Laughter* (London: Methuen, 1956).

PETERS, CATHERINE, *The King of Inventors: A Life of Wilkie Collins* (London: Secker & Warburg, 1991).

PFEIFFER, EMILY, *Women and Work: An Essay Treating on the Relation to Health and Physical Development, of the Higher Education of Girls, and the Intellectual or more Systematised Effort of Women* (London: Trubner, 1888).

PINERO, ARTHUR WING, *The Profligate* (London: Heinemann, 1891).

—— *The Times* (London: Heinemann, 1891).

—— *The Magistrate* (London: Heinemann, 1892).

—— *The Cabinet Minister* (London: Heinemann, 1892).

—— *Dandy Dick* (London: Heinemann, 1893).

—— *The Weaker Sex* (London: Heinemann, 1894).

—— *The Schoolmistress* (London: Heinemann, 1894).

—— *The Second Mrs Tanqueray* (London: Heinemann, 1895).

—— *The Amazons* (London: Heinemann, 1895).

POWELL, KERRY, *Oscar Wilde and the Theatre of the 1890s* (Cambridge: Cambridge University Press, 1990).

PROUDHON, JOSEPH-PIERRE, *What is Property? An Inquiry into the Principle of Right and Government*, trans. Benjamin Tucker (Princeton, Mass.: Benjamin R. Tucker, 1876).

—— *Selected Writings*, ed. Stewart Edwards, trans. Elizabeth Fraser (London: Macmillan, 1969).

QUAIL, JOHN, *The Slow-Burning Fuse: The Lost History of the British Anarchists* (London: Granada, 1978).

RABY, PETER, *Oscar Wilde* (Cambridge: Cambridge University Press, 1988).

READE, CHARLES, *A Terrible Temptation* (London: Chatto & Windus, 1871).

RICKETTS, CHARLES, *Self Portrait, Taken from the Letters and Journals of Charles Ricketts, RA*, collected and compiled by T. Sturge Moore, ed. Cecil Lewis (London: Peter Davies, 1939).

RITCHIE, DAVID, *Darwinism and Politics* (London: Sonnenschein, 1889).

ROBERTSON, GRAHAM, *Time Was* (London: Hamish Hamilton, 1931).

ROBERTSON, T. W., *Principal Dramatic Works*, 2 vols. (London: Samuel French, 1889).

RUSKIN, JOHN, *Sesame and Lilies* (London: Allen, 1892).

SAN JUAN, EPIFANIO, *The Art of Oscar Wilde* (Princeton, NJ: Princeton University Press, 1967).

SARDOU, VICTORIEN, *Fédora, Théâtre Complet*, i (Paris: Albin Michel, 1934).

—— *Dora* or *L'Espionne, Théâtre Complet*, ii (Paris: Albin Michel, 1934).

—— *Odette, Théâtre Complet*, vi (Paris: Albin Michel, 1935).

SHAW, GEORGE BERNARD, *The Quintessence of Ibsenism* (London: Walter Scott, 1891).

—— *The Quintessence of Ibsenism: Now Completed to the Death of Ibsen*, rev. edn. (London: Constable, 1913).

—— *You Never Can Tell* (1898), *Collected Plays*, i (London: Bodley Head, 1970).

—— *Man and Superman: A Comedy and a Philosophy* (London: Constable, 1903).

—— *The Apple Cart* (1928), *Collected Plays*, vi (London: Bodley Head, 1973).

—— *Letters to Granville Barker*, ed. C. B. Purdom (New York: Phoenix House, 1956).

—— *Collected Letters*, ed. Dan H. Lawrence, 3 vols. (London: Bodley Head, 1965–85).

SHERARD, ROBERT HARBOROUGH, *The Life of Oscar Wilde* (London: T. Werner Laurie, 1906).

SHEWAN, RODNEY, *Oscar Wilde: Art and Egotism* (London: Macmillan, 1977).

SHILLITO, JOSEPH, *Womanhood: Its Duties, Temptations and Privileges* (London: Henry S. King & Co., 1877).

SMALL, IAN, *Conditions for Criticism: Authority, Knowledge and Literature in the Late Nineteenth Century* (Oxford: Clarendon Press, 1991).

—— *Oscar Wilde Revalued: An Essay on New Materials and Methods of Research* (Greensboro, NC: ELT Press, 1993).

SONN, RICHARD, *Anarchism and Cultural Politics in Fin de Siècle France* (Lincoln, Nebr.: Univ. of Nebraska Press, 1989).

STEPHENS, JOHN RUSSELL, *The Censorship of English Drama, 1824–1901* (Cambridge: Cambridge University Press, 1980).

—— *The Profession of the Playwright: British Theatre, 1800–1900* (Cambridge: Cambridge University Press, 1992).

STIRNER, MAX, *The Ego and His Own* (1845), trans. Steven Byington (London: Rebel Press, 1982).

STOKES, JOHN, *Resistible Theatres: Enterprise and Experiment in the Late Nineteenth Century* (London: Paul Elek, 1972).

SULLIVAN, KEVIN, *Oscar Wilde* (New York: Columbia University Press, 1972).

THOMAS, BRANDON, *Charley's Aunt* (New York: Samuel French, 1962).

THOMAS, DONALD, *A Long Time Burning: A History of Literary Censorship in England* (London: Routledge & Kegan Paul, 1969).

THOMPSON, E. P., *William Morris: Romantic to Revolutionary* (New York: Pantheon, 1976).

TRUDGILL, ERIC, *Madonnas and Magdalens: The Origins and Development of Victorian Sexual Attitudes* (London: Heinemann, 1976).

ULAM, ADAM, *Russia's Failed Revolutions: From the Decembrists to the Dissidents* (London: Weidenfeld & Nicolson, 1981).

WILDE, Lady, *Notes on Men, Women and Books* (London: Ward & Downey, 1891).

WOODCOCK, GEORGE, *The Paradox of Oscar Wilde* (London: Boardman, 1949).

—— 'Anarchism or Chaos?' (London: Freedom, 1944).

—— 'Anarchism and Morality' (London: Freedom, 1945).

—— 'What is Anarchism?' (London: Freedom, 1945).

WORTH, KATHARINE, *Oscar Wilde* (London: Macmillan, 1983).

Index